VITAL REENCHANTMENTS

BEFORE YOU START TO READ THIS BOOK, take this moment to think about making a donation to punctum books, an independent non-profit press,

@ https://punctumbooks.com/support/

If you're reading the e-book, you can click on the image below to go directly to our donations site. Any amount, no matter the size, is appreciated and will help us to keep our ship of fools afloat. Contributions from dedicated readers will also help us to keep our commons open and to cultivate new work that can't find a welcoming port elsewhere. Our adventure is not possible without your support.

Vive la Open Access.

Fig. 1. Hieronymus Bosch, *Ship of Fools* (1490–1500)

First published in 2019 by punctum books, Earth, Milky Way.
https://punctumbooks.com

ISBN-13: 978-1-950192-07-6 (print)
ISBN-13: 978-1-950192-08-3 (ePDF)

LCCN: 2018968577
Library of Congress Cataloging Data is available from the Library of Congress

Editorial team: Casey Coffee and Eileen A. Joy
Book design: Vincent W.J. van Gerven Oei
Cover image: Valerie Hammond, *Traces 8*, pigment, color pencil, graphite, wax,
glass beads and thread on Japanese paper, 16 × 17" (2010). Courtesy of the artist
and Littlejohn Contemporary.

HIC SVNT MONSTRA

Lauren Greyson

VITAL REENCHANTMENTS

*Biophilia, Gaia, Cosmos,
and the Affectively Ecological*

Ⓟ

Contents

Acknowledgments

I owe so much of the vitality of this work to others. punctum books took a chance on this book and embraced it for what is. I am enormously grateful for their support. The Graduate Center for the Study of Culture at Justus Liebig University not only originally made this project possible, but also introduced me to brilliant colleagues who wisely suggested I not fight the urge to write about Carl Sagan. I am particularly thankful to Sebastian Brand and Elizabeth Kovach, both great conjugators of ideas, for their comments and conversation over the years. To my first and second advisors, Ingo Berensmeyer and Hanjo Berressem, I am also deeply grateful — they have been exceptional readers and the most productive of critics.

Finally, to Philipp, my reenchanteur — your infinite charms are behind the best bits in these pages. A thank you does not even begin to do your contribution justice.

1

Popular Science as Hot Philosophy

Not all charms fly at the touch of cold philosophy.[1] This work examines so-called "cold philosophy," or science, that does precisely the opposite — rather than mercilessly emptying out and unweaving, it operates as a philosophy that animates. Taking up a selection of popular works by scientists who have engaged in attempts to rail against the idea of disenchantment (*Entzauberung*) first introduced by Max Weber, it investigates the concepts and strategies of scientific reenchantment. It demonstrates how the "poet-in-scientists"[2] operating during the late 1970s and '80s direct our attention to the marvelous unfolding of life in the world and the cosmos. Both in terms of the subjects they take up and the ethics they espouse, these figures attempt to turn science to life in an age in which the counter-culture in particular had made the institution of science synonymous with technologies of destruction and alienation. What is so unique about them is that they reenchant without pandering to what Dawkins will later term "cosmic sentimentality"[3] — Carl Sagan may have

1   John Keats, "Lamia," Project Gutenberg, http://www.gutenberg.org/ files/2490/2490 h/2490 h.htm, ll. 229 32.
2   Edward O. Wilson, *Biophilia* (Cambridge: Harvard University Press, 1984), 85.
3   Richard Dawkins, *Unweaving the Rainbow: Science, Delusion, and the Appetite for Wonder* (New York: Mariner Books, 1998), ix. It is in this book

said "We are made of starstuff,"[4] but he would never insist, as Joni Mitchell did in 1969, that "we've got to get ourselves back to the garden."[5] Instead, they insist on a third way that does not rely on the idea of an ecological Eden — a vigorously vital materialism in which the affective trumps the sentimental. Although not without its precedents,[6] this vital materialism has found unique expression in the set of works I will discuss. Its reverberation in ecological circles (and well beyond), moreover, merit the works' reevaluation. Far from existing merely as books that popularize science, these works reanimate a world that was, in any case, never really dead.

More concretely, this book looks at what I call "affective wonder," understood as the experience of and attunement to novel affects, within a selection of works by E.O. Wilson, James Lovelock, and Carl Sagan. Although the works it focuses upon, namely *Biophilia* (1984), *Gaia* (1979),[7] and *Cosmos* (1980), were all published within five years of one another during what one might reasonably still call the dawn of the environmental movement, the concepts they flesh out have continued to circulate since their publication and live on in ecological and popular thought today; they elaborate what I will call affective ecologies. I will also insist that their historical emergence was no accident: They respond to an ever-deepening sense of environmental crisis, certainly, but along with it they respond to perhaps more than marginally related narratives of the large-scale disenchantment brought on by modernity or science. More often than not, they respond to a mixture of the two.

that Dawkins accuses Carl Sagan of "cosmic sentimentality," but Chapter 5 takes up this debate in more detail.

4   Carl Sagan, *Cosmos* (New York: Random House, 1980), 190.
5   Joni Mitchell, "Woodstock," *Ladies of the Canyon*, CD, MCA, 1970.
6   Jane Bennett, *The Enchantment of Modern Life* (Princeton: Princeton University Press, 2001) explores many of these, looking at authors as diverse as Paracelsus, Kant, Thoreau, and Latour in light of an "enchanted materialism."
7   James Lovelock, *Gaia* (Oxford: Oxford University Press, 1979).

Their mode of reenchanting may thus be understood as vital in three senses: first, in their celebration of the bountiful and precarious life on Earth[8]; secondly, in the manner in which they reverberate with and prefigure the scientifically informed "vital materialism" appearing in the twenty-first century; and thirdly, in their orientation towards the most basic ecological concerns — the protection and maintenance of life and living systems. As Jane Bennett writes, "To be enchanted is, in the moment of its activation, to assent wholeheartedly to life — not to this or that particular condition or aspect of it but to the experience of living itself."[9] In reaching out to science in order to reenchant, these authors also insist on its life-affirming qualities and the potential it has to serve as an ally in ecological struggles.

This orientation toward and affirmation of life is neither new nor anomalous, although this work does make the claim that this set of popular science writers embrace and direct us to life in unique and unprecedented ways. There is a rich history of scientifically-informed vitalism and cultural production surrounding it. Indeed, the literary scholar Robert Mitchell has gone so far as to locate three vitalist waves, the first coinciding with the Romantic period at the end of the eighteenth and beginning of the nineteenth century: "a transnational European affair, as British, French, and German physicians, surgeons, philosophers, and literary authors struggled to understand the relationship of a "principle of life" that seemed to animate and con-

---

8   This, as will become more clear in the following chapters, is life understood not merely as organisms we immediately recognize as creaturely. Indeed, there is no precise definition of life to be found in these pages; the closest we might come is in Lovelock's assertion, appearing in Chapter 4 of *Gaia,* that it is "something edible, lovable, or lethal." As Lynn Margulis and Dorion Sagan astutely observe, "Life, although material, is inextricable from the behavior of the living. Defying definition — a word that means 'to fix or mark the limits of' — living cells move and expand incessantly. They overgrow their boundaries; one becomes two become many" (*What Is Life?* Berkeley and Los Angeles: University of California Press [1995], 4). Life, even in the works here that orient themselves towards the natural sciences, is understood more in relation to what it does than what it is.

9   Bennett, *Enchantment,* 159–60.

nect living beings to the concrete matter of which these bodies were composed."[10] The second, according to Mitchell, occurred at the turn of the following century and might be associated with neo-vitalists such as Hans Driesch, as well as "life philosophers" such as Nietzsche, Scheler, and Bergson.[11] The final wave, which began towards the end of the twentieth century, he refers to as "the vital turn." This period is characterized by increasing numbers of philosophers, literary scholars, and cultural critics growing dissatisfied with "the exclusive emphasis of poststructuralist thought on representations and signs" and attempting to grapple in different ways with the "ontological dimensions of vitality that exceed, or stand as the conditions of possibility of, semiotics and representation."[12] In this context, Mitchell mentions Giorgio Agamben's "bare life" and Butler's "precarious life," but one could as easily understand the movement in cultural studies towards ecological questions, first in the form of ecocritical efforts, and now in the development and explosive growth of the ecological humanities, as belonging to this vital turn. This book, as well as the works it investigates and the majority of the theory that it draws upon, is anchored in this third wave but is constantly haunted, particularly in its reliance on Jakob von Uexküll's thought, by the two that came before it.

With this long and varied vitalist history in mind, Wilson, Lovelock, and Sagan are, predictably, not the only figures that stand for a kind of "scientific reenchantment,"[13] but they do of-

---

10 Robert Mitchell, *Experimental Life: Vitalism in Romantic Science and Literature* (Baltimore: John Hopkins University Press, 2013), 2.

11 Ibid.

12 Ibid., 1–2.

13 We might also add Stephen Hawking, Richard Dawkins, and Stephen Jay Gould to the list of celebrity scientist writers of popular science operating in the 1980s. Although these authors certainly rely on some of the tactics associated with affective wonder that I will outline later, they are less concerned with linking experience, whether their own or that of the reader, to their claims, nor are they especially attentive to more broadly ecological concerns. Thus, while a more exhaustive study might include them, I have chosen to attend here to texts that more explicitly concern themselves with the earth and, on very fundamental levels, what humans do on its surface.

fer their own particular flavor of it. Not only do they discuss wonder and its analogs (awe, amazement, marvel), but as author figures they are wonder machines, perpetually describing fits of it and pointing the reader to the sources that might occasion it. Time after time, moreover, these poet-in-scientists undermine the separation between subject and object traditionally characterizing the scientific gaze and, in a great many narratives, modern disenchantment. The "felt reality of relation"[14] eclipses attempts to understand and communicate the world in supposedly objective terms. The works explored here are also united by their pleas for and explorations of new modes of attentiveness, ones that consistently challenge both the boundaries of the human *Umwelt*[15] in absolute terms and the notion that we can draw any clear distinction between our own bodies and the matter that surrounds them. Although billed as popular science, they do more to offer an "ecology of affect" than to flesh out, in any detail, the assumed workings of our immediate biological surroundings, the larger Earth system, or, for that matter, the universe. Far from laying out a coherent ecological program, these works serve, rather, as fragmentary guides to "being at home in the universe."[16] That they often evoke mystical or quasi-religious experience is not merely an exception to their self-proclaimed secular-scientism, but integral to the kind of enchanted science they offer.

14 Brian Massumi, *Parables for the Virtual: Movement, Affect, Sensation* (Durham: Duke University Press, 2002), 16.
15 Defined here as the subjective surroundings of an organism; the term is discussed at length in 2.3.2.
16 As such, they might also be described as embodying a peculiarly American kind of spirituality. See William Clebsch, *American Religious Thought* (Chicago: University of Chicago Press, 1973), 1.

1.1
Reenchantment Now

No doubt this talk of enchantment and wonder, so tied to immediate experience, can seem trivial in the face of any number
of environmental crises (global warming first among these) that
do not just appear ominously on the horizon, but loom as never
before. My first task here is thus to pose the same question that
Jane Bennett does at the end of her own work on enchantment:
"How can someone write a book about enchantment in such a
world?"[17] Does this approach really provide, as Latour phrases it,
"a way to bridge the distance between the scale of the phenomena we hear about and the tiny Umwelt inside which we witness,
as if it were a fish inside its bowl, an ocean of catastrophes that
are supposed to unfold"?[18] I will argue throughout this work that
this is precisely what "affective ecologies," properly attended to,
point toward: an open present, one that broadens the horizons
of the "fish bowl" and allows us to imagine engendering futures
that are neither naively hopeful nor hopelessly apocalyptic. This
section begins, however, with the catastrophic futures alluded
to by both those in ecological camps and politics. Although I
have no desire to paint a less bleak picture of what may happen
should we choose to do nothing to alter our engagement with
the ecosphere, and the works examined here do nothing to sug-
ar-coat ecological crisis, I question the efficacy of these tactics.
What I argue for, in place of or as a supplement to this "future-
speak," is a more modest ethics of the present — an exploration
of human ecological potential that might lead to a more fundamental reexamination of our relations with the earth. Essential
to this is not the dripping sentimentalism so characteristic of
approaches that stress, above all else, the future and the figure of
the child, but the "affectively ecological," which both encourages

17 Bennett, *Enchantment,* 159.
18 Bruno Latour, "Waiting for Gaia: Composing the Common World
Through Arts and Politics," Lecture, French Institute, London, November
2011, 2, http://www.bruno-latour.fr/sites/default/files/124-GAIA-LON-
DON-SPEAP_0.pdf.

more fundamental attachments to the world and calls attention
to those that already exist.

1.1.1. Benign neglect: the case against the child

The most basic motivation behind the turn to the affectively
ecological in this project is the idea that the obsessive orientation towards the future that characterizes a great deal of modern ecological calls-to-arms bears no relation to the tools that
might actually assist in averting, or at least softening the blow
of, environmental crisis. Indeed, this refusal to dwell in the ecological present, far from causing us to consider future human
generations in our actions (let alone the organisms that might
win out in deep time), severely limits the horizon of ecological
politics. What if, rather than focusing on the image of the lone
polar bear floating away on the last bits of the polar icecaps, one
poses a different kind of question? What becomes of ecological
ethics and politics, broadly speaking, when one focuses not on
the hourglass that shows our time running out, but the infinite
variety of the sand that marks it?

But the metaphor of the hourglass, perhaps, requires some
contextualizing. Enter Brittany Trilford, the seventeen-year-old
chosen to give the opening address at the 2012 Rio Summit (the
follow-up to the Earth Summit twenty years prior). "You have
72 hours to decide the fate of your children, my children, my
children's children," she proclaimed. "And I start the clock now.
Tick, tick, tick."[19] Very little came of this countdown-as-threat:
no binding policy treaties were signed, but merely an "outcome
document" entitled "The Future we want."[20] This ominous
"tick-tick-ticking," surely also meant to convey the imminence
of environmental crisis and possibly apocalypse, rather than

19 Brittany Trilford, "Are You Here to Save Face — or Us?," *Democracy Now,*
    June 20, 2012, http://www.democracynow.org/2012/6/21/are_you_here_to_
    save_face.
20 "The Future We Want: Outcome Document," United Nations Conference
    on Sustainable Development, September 11, 2012, United Nations Sustain-
    able Development Knowledge Platform, http://sustainabledevelopment.
    un.org/futurewewant.html.

imparting urgency, became the sound of the unfulfilled present — opportunity wasted.

Twelve-year-old Severn Suzuki had made a similar plea in Rio twenty years earlier, in 1992. "You grownups say you love us," she intoned at the end of her speech. "I challenge you, please make your actions reflect your words."[21] This tugging at the reproductive heartstrings hardly constitutes an anomaly. That the primary motivation for acting now is to save the species later is assumed by a great variety of sources, whether grassroots in origin or from more official channels. Sarah Ensor points to the popular environmentalist slogans, "What will your children breathe?" and "We don't inherit the earth from our grandparents. We borrow it from our children."[22] But documents more oriented towards institutional politics, the Earth Charter, for instance, also consistently invoke "future-speak": "We stand at a critical moment in Earth's history, a time when humanity must choose its future."[23] Barack Obama's famously bold statement (at least by American standards), uttered during his second inaugural address, was "We will respond to the threat of climate change, knowing that the failure to do so would betray our children and future generations."[24] In classical texts of environmental ethics, for instance, those by Hans Jonas, the task of securing the future of the species is taken as the most pressing task, without which, supposedly, no other ethics would be possible.[25]

21 Severn Suzuki, "At Rio+20, Severn Cullis-Suzuki Revisits Historic '92 Speech, Fights for Next Generation's Survival," *Democracy Now,* June 21, 2012, http://www.democracynow.org/2012/6/21/at_rio_20_severn_cullis_suzuki.

22 Sarah Ensor, "Spinster Ecology: Rachel Carson, Sarah Orne Jewett, and Nonreproductive Futurity," *American Literature* 84, no. 2 (June 2012): 409–35, at 419.

23 The Earth Charter Initiative, "Download the Charter," *The Earth Charter,* http://www.earthcharterinaction.org/content/pages/read-the-charter.html.

24 Barack Obama, "Second Inaugural Speech," *New York Times,* January 21, 2013, http://www.nytimes.com/2013/01/21/us/politics/obamas-second-inaugural-speech.html.

25 Hans Jonas, "Responsibility Today: The Ethics of an Endangered Future," *Social Research* 43, no. 1 (Spring 1976): 77–97, at 80.

At one level, of course, this is true; there are no ethics, as we currently understand them, without ethical actors. More recent academic texts are hardly immune to this stubborn orientation towards some vague tomorrow, either. Alistair McIntosh asks, "How do we create the means to empathize with people we may never meet, in a future we may never inhabit?"[26] Needless to say, no one bothers to justify why we should, let alone must, cultivate this kind of empathy. These appeals evoke realities different from our own, yet they refuse to articulate these differences and, in so doing, bring us no closer to a "greener future." Notably, neither the Kyoto Protocol[27] nor The Paris Agreement,[28] to date the most significant environmental treaties, appeal to the future or the child.

Nothing can be said against these appeals to the child, unless one joins up with the Voluntary Human Extinction Movement (VHEMT),[29] but no praxis can follow from them either. The problem with "loving our children," with orienting ourselves exclusively towards the generations to come, is that it offers no way to begin, no way to tackle the present. My point is not that we ought to entirely disregard the future — we would certainly be

26 Alastair McIntosh, "Foreword," in *Future Ethics: Climate Change and Apocalyptic Imagination,* ed. Stefan Skrimshire (London: Continuum, 2010), vii–xi, at ix.

27 "Kyoto Protocol to the United Nations Framework Convention on Climate Change," United Nations Framework Convention on Climate Change, December 11, 1997, http://unfccc.int/essential_background/kyoto_protocol/items/1678.php.

28 "The Paris Agreement," United Nations Framework Convention on Climate Change, November 4, 2016, http://unfccc.int/paris_agreement/items/9485.php. Paragraph 19 of the preamble does mention children and intergenerational equity when making the case that "climate change is a common concern of humankind," but these concerns are mentioned alongside the obligation to protect "human rights, the right to health, the rights of indigenous peoples, local communities, migrants" and a number of other historically disenfranchised groups.

29 The slogan for the movement, positioning members as a new Vulcan order, is "May we live long and die out." See "About the Movement," Voluntary Human Extinction Movement, http://www.vhemt.org/aboutvhemt.htm#vhemt.

in trouble if we did — but rather that we ought to question the efficacy of this approach and investigate alternative temporal engagements with and investments in the ecosphere.

There are at least two reasons to oust, or at the very least massively supplement, the oppressively future-oriented approach to environmental ethics. The first is that, far from ushering in a new social and political order, it limits the horizon of ecological ethics and politics. Queer theorist Lee Edelman, although not much of an ecological poster-boy, has brilliantly articulated the conservatism embedded in a politics that leans so heavily on the figure of the child. Even radical or progressive politics, he claims, remains "conservative insofar as it works to *affirm* a structure, to *authenticate* social order, which it then intends to transit to the future in the form of its inner Child."[30] The problem is that this forecloses the possibility of doing anything besides reproducing the social order: "That Child remains the perpetual horizon of every acknowledge politics, the fantasmatic beneficiary of every political intervention."[31] Thus, ecological pleas which rely on the child aim, by and large, to extend as many of the "privileges" we enjoy today as features of modern life to the future but do not necessarily entail any questioning of these so-called privileges. The green consumerist dream involves little more than magically green versions of all of our present technologies distributed (supposedly fairly) among the population. This is a sly operation, and a problematic one, since any kind of ecological provisioning, by most accounts, will likely involve a certain amount of bloodletting. But constant reference to the child as the figurehead allows us to maintain the illusion of seamless continuity with the present. The future, in this way, is endlessly deferred. The minute every thought becomes subordinate to the perpetuity of the species, we dismiss the possibility that it is the contemporary political and economic inertia that may, and in all likelihood will, make the future so unimaginably unpleasant.

---

30 Lee Edelman, *No Future: Queer Theory and the Death Drive* (Durham: Duke University Press, 2004), 2–3.

31 Ibid.

Edelman asks, provocatively, "What, in that case, would it signify not to be 'fighting for the children'?"[32] My investigation poses this same question in light of the popular scientific contribution to the environmental movement. Not to be "fighting for the children" certainly doesn't mean fighting against them or abandoning them altogether, explicitly VHEMT-style.[33] It does, however, involve viewing our present engagement with the ecosphere as more than merely a problem, as containing a great number, an infinite number even, of only partially actualized potentials. The VHEMT's rejection of "reproductive futurism," of the "presupposition that the body politic must survive," provides us with a whiff of fresh air, but no more than that. The ideal of extinction becomes merely another term "that impose[s] an ideological limit on political discourse as such."[34] Any politics implied by the VHEMT consists of only a smooth transition to the end. The future retains its mysterious stranglehold on us, with the empty, ahuman Arcadian vision merely supplanting the figure of the child.

This leads us to the second reason to question an exclusively future-oriented ecological ethics, which Edelman already begins to allude to when he describes the child as "the pledge of a covenant that shields us against the persistent threat of apocalypse now — or later."[35] The constant invocation of the child and the future in the realm of ecological politics has become a kind of mindless mantra, betraying, somewhat counterintuitively, an "endless preoccupation with the end times,"[36] a complete inabil-

32 Ibid., 3.
33 This is where I depart from Edelman; while he might support the VHEMT as a quite literal embrace of the death drive (and this is purely hypothetical), I reject it for this selfsame reason — there is no ecological footing to be found in *No Future*. Nicole Seymour dismisses his work on the same grounds, while, like me, noting its usefulness for a critique of ecological conservatism. See *Strange Natures: Futurity, Empathy, and the Queer Ecological Imagination* (Urbana: University of Illinois Press, 2013), 7.
34 Edelman, *No Future*, 2, 3.
35 Ibid., 18.
36 Sasha Lilley, "Introduction: The Apocalyptic Politics of Collapse and Rebirth," in *Catastrophism: The Apocalyptic Politics of Collapse and Rebirth,*

ity to think ourselves out of the trajectory offered by the present moment. We speak of the children, in other words, like those on their deathbeds.

The hope, the rationale, of course, is that talk of the future, and especially the end times, will change our course of action in the present. This emphasis on disaster scenarios has been termed "catastrophism" by theorists.[37] Lilley, however, observes: "Catastrophists tend to believe that an ever-intensified rhetoric of disaster will awaken the masses from their long slumber — if the mechanical failure of the system does not make such struggles superfluous."[38] Appeals to the future in peril, the child without the privilege of a childhood, become the gospel and the revelation here. Lilley points to the evidence that, far from stirring people to action, warnings about "fixed ecological tipping points typically fall on deaf ears or result in greater apathy."[39] Bucking the system is hard when the threat of apocalypse weighs so heavily, and articulating precisely how heavily these threats weigh can actually become a disincentive for change. Calls to face the future, to save the children, thus overwhelmingly result in us adhering ever more stubbornly to contemporary realities. And yet, time still marches on. Donna Haraway even puts an affective spin on the consequences of catastrophism, writing, "There is a fine line between acknowledging the extent and seriousness of

eds. Sasha Lilley, David McNally, Eddie Yuen, and James Davis (Oakland: PM Press 2012), 1–14, at 1.

37 Catastrophism, it should be noted, first appeared as a nineteenth-century theory of geological change, which, in opposition to the prevailing uniformitarianism, contended that "certain geological and biological phenomena were caused by catastrophes, or sudden and violent disturbances of nature, rather than by continuous and uniform processes" (*Oxford English Dictionary Online,* s.v. "catastrophism," https://en.oxforddictionaries.com/definition/catastrophism). The discussion of the Anthropocene in the last chapter will return to the intersection between theories of the geological and the role of the human.

38 Lilley, *Apocalyptic Politics,* 1.

39 Ibid., 5.

the troubles and succumbing to abstract futurism and its affects of sublime despair and its politics of sublime indifference."[40]

Turning to the dynamics that make up the present, on the other hand, allows us not only to think of radically different investments in the ecosphere (ones that might incidentally end up actually saving "the children") but also potentially allows us to break out of the sense of paralysis that catastrophism produces.

1.1.2. An ethics of the present

This book neither concerns itself with what our children will breathe, nor with condemning contemporary decadences. It is, rather, an exploration of the modes that select works of popular science have given us of opening up the present and allowing us to reconsider our most fundamental relations with that which surrounds us. In this sense, any ethics it espouses are decidedly Spinozan, having "nothing to do with a morality," but rather constituting "an ethology, that is, a composition of fast and slow speeds, of capacities for affecting and being affected on this plane of immanence."[41] The crucial difference between ethics and morality, as Deleuze frames it, is that while a morality "always refers existence to transcendent values," an ethics is "a typology of immanent modes of existence."[42] If anything, then, what the works in this book present us with is an experimental ethics, relying on the uncertainty of "not know[ing] beforehand what good or bad you are capable of; [...] what a body or mind can do, in a given encounter, a given arrangement, a given combination."[43] This is an ethics operating at the microlevel rather than at international summits and in legislation. It constitutes no direct alternative to sustainability-oriented ethics, but it does, I hope, loosen the chains that so much talk of the future and the child has thrown around our collective neck (to the extent that it's even fair to speak of our predicament as

40 Donna J. Haraway, *Staying with the Trouble. Making Kin in the Chthulucene* (Durham: Duke University Press, 2016), 4.

41 Deleuze, *Spinoza,* 125.

42 Ibid., 23.

43 Ibid., 125.

an authentically collective one, but section 1.3.1 below returns to this problem).

Sarah Ensor has already referred to such an approach as "spinster ecology," which she claims amounts to "an avuncular form of stewardship, tending the future without contributing to it."[44] Such an approach does not deny the existence of tomorrow, but problematizes whether it is as simple as deciding you want a future and then magically "making it happen." She continues, "Perhaps the question is not the future, yes or no, but the future, which and whose, where and when and how."[45] Instead of speaking the language of constraint or technological domination, these more fleeting, possibly less responsible spinster ethics concern themselves with maximizing ecological subjectivity.[46]

Indeed, one might better understand this kind of ethics as a disposition, or along with Jane Bennett, as "an embodied sensibility."[47] Bennett argues that the carrying out of any moral code requires an affective basis, the disposition to "enact the code."[48] She insists that, in addition to a sense of duty, the implementation of any kind of ethics involves "bodily movements in space, mobilizations of heat and energy, a series of choreographed gestures, a distinctive assemblage of affective propulsions."[49] This does something to explain, already, why a sustainability ethic alone — an imperative to save the children — is not enough. One might speculate that the mania surrounding slow food, and perhaps other aspects of green con-

---

44 See also the emergence of queer ecologies, many variants of which also question reproductive futurist justifications for "saving" the environment. See *Queer Ecologies: Sex, Nature, Politics, Desire*, eds. Catriona Mortimer-Sandilands and Bruce Erickson (Bloomington: Indiana University Press, 2010).

45 Ensor, "Spinster Ecology," 419.

46 In the sense that Arne Naess refers to "maximum perspective." See his chapter "Spinoza and Ecology," in *Speculum Spinozanum 1677–1977*, ed. Siegfried Hessing (London: Routledge & Kegan Paul, 1977), 45–54.

47 Bennett, *Enchantment of Modern Life*, 131.

48 Ibid.

49 Ibid., 3.

sumerism as well, constitutes efforts to fill precisely this gap. Any ethical praxis, seen this way, cannot follow from duty alone.

But it is not only that affective dimensions are necessary for the enactment of more principled ethics. Bennett also frequently alludes to the idea that ethical behavior begins with "a spirit of generosity" or a joy that "can propel ethics."[50] In this sense, enchantment, or "the cultivation of an eye for the wonderful" (the affective elements of which I will discuss in the next chapter), far from constituting a luxury, becomes a necessity and "an academic duty."[51] Bennett insists, as I also do in Chapter 2, that enchantment, though it may come as a surprise, is also something that may be "fostered through deliberate strategies."[52] This book examines what these strategies of enchantment might look like and how wonder may be instigated. I have chosen to focus on this seemingly narrow spectrum of texts, popular scientific writing from the late 1970s to the early 1980s, because it offers a number of "enchanting techniques" that I argue are more relevant now than ever.

It should be stressed, however, that there is a longer history of reenchantment, and this project engages only with one incarnation of it. There is, for instance, already a rich late nineteenth- and twentieth-century Western (not to mention Eastern) counter-tradition of intensively engaging with the present. Nigel Thrift points to precisely this when he claims that "a go-faster world, in which time takes on an increasingly frenetic future-oriented quality, has been balanced by a series of contemplative practices — many of them to do with a heightened awareness of movement — which have, in fact, produced an expansion of awareness of the present."[53] Although he explicitly focuses on many New Age practices of contemplation, body techniques like the Alexander and Feldenkrais techniques, and the rise

---

50 Ibid., 3, 4.

51 Ibid., 131.

52 Ibid., 4.

53 Nigel Thrift, "Still Life in Nearly Present Time: The Object of Nature," *Body and Society* 6, nos. 3–4 (2000): 34–57, at 35.

of photography ("which is able to capture transience"[54]), one could as easily point to the self-conscious seeking out of pre-dominantly nonhuman environments or wildernesses and the attendant popularization of activities like hiking or literature such as nature writing. But popular science, too, I will argue, can produce "an expanded awareness of present time";[55] if it does anything, it asks us to attend to what is right in front of us, the reader, and forget about its self-evidence. Just as Thrift claims of the practices he examines, the works I focus on work to reen-chant the world by setting up what he terms a *"background of expectation."*[56] The implication is always either that there is far more to be discovered than meets the eye, or, alternatively, that the eye, given free reign, is able to discover far more than we may have thought possible. What is vitally important is this ex-cess of things, living things especially, and, as we will return to in the next chapter, their contingency: There is always more, and this more could always change.

Lest my own or Thrift's approach begin to sound like much of the talk of "slowing down" or "deceleration"[57] found in the media and academia, it should be pointed out that attending to the present does not at all automatically imply a slowness. Thrift contends that the notion that we live in a "speeded-up" world is itself a kind of technological determinism and part of the dis-course of modernism, noting that "nature is actually very fast."[58] Whether attending to the present involves a slowing-down or a speeding-up is as much a matter of scale as that to which one is attending. In the context of this work, the connections between organism and *Umwelt* are more important than a vaguely new age kind of slowing down. Indeed, the authors I focus on would be among the first to point out that on a cellular, not to mention

54 Ibid., 43.
55 Ibid., 35.
56 Ibid.
57 See, for instance, Harmut Rosa's *Social Acceleration: A New Theory of Modernity* (New York: Columbia University Press, 2013).
58 Thrift, "Still Life in Nearly Present Time," 41, 35.

galactic, level, things operate far faster than we can perceive, and often faster than we can even comprehend.

Indeed, what the poet-in-scientists I examine contribute cannot be described as a naïve carpe diem-ism; they do not give directions for seizing time, nor for slowing it down. I am doubtful whether any of them would assent to the conviction that it need be slowed down; Sagan and Lovelock, at least, might be described as careful technological optimists. What they do provide are techniques for allowing time to seize the subject, to participate more conscientiously and attend more fully to the "pure becoming"[59] that Deleuze, via Bergson, argues constitutes the fleeting present. Far from being some kind of stasis that we may fix and inhabit, this vision of the present is flux. When we talk about the "openness of the present," then, it refers to this nonfixity, these infinite varieties of "pure becoming" — not one's ability to control it. And if affect is that which is "experienced in a lived duration that involves the difference between two states,"[60] it is precisely what constitutes this dynamic present.

What may be unique about wonder or reenchantment, as will be discussed in the next chapter, is that it involves a suspension in the general orientation toward the future. Martha Nussbaum, one of the few contemporary authors to theorize wonder, regards wonder as non-eudaimonistic, as one of the only emotions not connected to one's own "goals and projects,"[61] and I hold to this as well. To the extent that wonder involves the attunement to or recognition of new affects and exists, as we shall describe it in Chapter 2 as a kind of primary affect, it directs the wonderer to the present. That a science seeking to reenchant should rely so heavily on wonder is no accident, either. If the disenchanted and disenchanting science of modernity was to usher in the future, Wilson, Lovelock, and Sagan ask us to pay more attention to that which is happening right now in front of us (whether

59 Gilles Deleuze, *Bergsonism*, trans. Hugh Tomlinson and Barbara Habberjam (Cambridge: Zone Books, 1988), 55.
60 Deleuze, *Practical Philosophy*, 125.
61 Martha Nussbaum, *Upheavals of Thought: The Intelligence of Emotions* (Cambridge: Cambridge University Press, 2001), 53–54.

that means in the soil or the skies, or somewhere else entirely). While on one level the texts I investigate here look merely like a series of scientific tricks or unveilings, on another level, they seek to catalog the unseen potentials of the world around us and to provide at least a taste of what techniques of attention can reveal. In so doing, I argue, they set up the kind of background of expectation that would be necessary for any successful long-term sustainability ethic. The poet-in-scientists of this project, in contrast to their more overtly political contemporaries, abandon the child altogether, opting instead for the exploration of the chaotic potentials of the field. Precisely what this amounts to in the context of this work, and how this can be understood in the context of popular science more generally, will be explained in what follows.

1.2
Popular Science and the Affectively Ecological

What are the strange ties that link the works this book examines? It is easy enough to refer to them, at least on a preliminary basis, as works of popular science, but this distinction, without further explanation, reveals very little and does nothing to clarify the relation between the works and the affective ecologies I claim they present.

1.2.1. Popular science: what's left when you take away the facts?
The scattered scholarly attempts to come to terms with popular science begin in the 1980s with the extremely unhelpful assertion that the genre is merely science popularized.[62] Richard

---

62 Not only are scholarly treatments of popular science few and far between, but at the time this project was embarked upon, there had been no substantial volumes dedicated to the subject released in the twenty-first century, despite the continuing popularity of authors such as Richard Dawkins, Stephen Hawking, and Neil deGrasse Tyson. Sarah Tinker Perrault's *Communicating Popular Science: From Deficit to Democracy* (New York: Palgrave Macmillan, 2013) is a welcome addition to the field.

Whitley, in one of the first examinations of the formal features of the genre, points to its startling range (from TV shows to textbooks to articles in popular science magazines to books) and argues that the defining feature of popular science is simply the "transmission of intellectual products from the context of their production to other contexts."[63] The farther these works stray from contexts in which science is being conducted, Whitley argues, the lower the "degree of formalisation and technical precision used to communicate results."[64] For Whitley, to put it bluntly, popular science is merely science dumbed down.

While the language employed in popular science certainly can be described as less technical, scholars in the 1990s take issue with Whitley's idea of popular science as simply watered-down science brought to the masses. Popular science, for Murdo McRae, as well as for the purposes of this work, is not merely science out of context, but something of an entirely different order. McRae argues that, for this reason, we ought to refer to "literature of science" as opposed to "popular science."[65] While I don't feel it necessary to go as far as rejecting the term "popular science" entirely, two features of McRae's "literature of science" are important for the works I examine here. The first is that they are "open to as full a range of contemporary interpretative techniques as any other works of literature."[66] Indeed, if Wilson refers to himself and scientists like him who have a

Nevertheless, it focuses primarily on the manner in which popular science mediates between the public and the scientific academy, largely glossing over the abundance of claims in popular science that are not strictly scientific.

63 Richard Whitley, "Knowledge Producers and Knowledge Acquirers: Popularisation as a Relation Between Scientific Fields and Their Publics," in *Expository Science: Forms and Functions of Popularization,* eds. Terry Shinn and Richard Whitley (Boston: D. Reidel Publishing Company, 1985), 3–30, at 12.

64 Ibid., 14.

65 Murdo William McRae, "Introduction: Science in Culture," in *The Literature of Science: Perspectives on Popular Scientific Writing,* ed. Murdo William McRae (Athens: The University of Georgia Press 1993), 1–13, at 10.

66 Ibid., 10.

popular bent as "poet-in-scientists," he invites this treatment himself. The second reason that McRae employs the term is that "[i]t emphasizes that the literature of science must be read not as mere popular transmission of superior scientific knowledge but as sophisticated production of knowledge in its own right."[67] Popular science may be part science communication, but it is also awash in literary and political strategies that relate to the science itself only peripherally. Thus, while this work focuses on works of popular science, there will neither be much science nor any substantive exploration of the more technical elements of the books.

What is of much more interest here is what Jean Fahnestock, in the same volume, refers to as the epideictic — that which concerns "a judgment over whether something deserves praise or blame."[68] Fahnestock isolates two kinds of epideictic appeals made in popular science: "the 'wonder' and the 'application' appeals, corresponding to the deontological and teleological appeals in ethical argument."[69] While there are some application appeals to be found in popular science relating to, for instance, policy implications of scientific findings, what predominates are the deontological, "wonder" appeals: "In science popularizations, all references to the amazing powers and secrets of nature or to the breakthroughs and accomplishments of the scientists themselves are basically deontological appeals."[70] Wonder, understood very generally, may be regarded in this way as a feature of the genre of popular science itself. The type of wonder I will argue is pursued by Wilson, Lovelock, and Sagan, however, is a unique embodiment of this tendency within the genre. The popular science of these works does something that goes far beyond the communication of supposed scientific fact. As we will see,

67 Ibid., 10–11.
68 See Jean Fahnestock, "Accommodating Science: The Rhetorical Life of Scientific Facts," in *The Literature of Science: Perspectives on Popular Scientific Writing*, ed. Murdo William McRae (Athens: The University of Georgia Press, 1993), 17–36, at 19.
69 Ibid., 20.
70 Ibid., 19.

the celebratory, epideictic element of popular science extends to the scientist's connection to and embeddedness in supposed objects of inquiry as much as to phenomena in the world.

1.2.2. Ecology without catastrophism

But for now the urgent question becomes: How can we connect this epideictic, wonder-filled popular science to the ecological? What I wish to argue is that, when we take the science away from popular science, we are not merely left with pulp, but with strategies and traces of wonder that can be patched together to form affective ecologies. While to an extent the entire book is concerned with this, I would be remiss here if I did not begin to sketch what I mean by the affectively ecological, and what these works of popular science from the 1980s, not all of which are strictly about environmental crisis, have to do with it.

The term "affective ecology" was originally used by the psychologist Giuseppe Barbiero, although my understanding of it departs substantially from his. Barbiero's orientation, in contrast to mine, is overwhelmingly pedagogical. He describes his brand of affective ecology as:

> the branch of ecology that educates people about Nature by bringing them into direct contact with it; indeed, only by immersing oneself within Nature can the energies be rediscovered that can only be restored by establishing the right kind of connection with Nature.[71]

Barbiero never fully explains what this "right kind of connection with Nature" might look like, nor why we aren't already immersed in it. "Nature" in this affective ecology stands apart, and the goal, apparently, is a reunion in which the shackles of culture are thrown off. While I share with Barbiero the conviction that more immediate relations in the present must inform approaches to environmental ethics, what I contend, along with the authors

71 Giuseppe Barbiero, "Affective Ecology for Sustainability," *Visions for Sustainability* 1, no. 3 (2014): 20–30, at 21.

that I examine, is that connection with so-called Nature is inevitable: There is no outside of it. Affective ecology as explored here is about connection, but not to some monolithic entity called "Nature," and the pedagogical takes a backseat to more fundamental questions about the production of subjectivity.

In this I have been influenced by Guattari's "virtual ecology," which he proposes in Chaosmosis.[72] In this work, Guattari links the ecological crisis, on a number of occasions, to "a more general crisis of the social, political and existential."[73] He argues that we now operate with mentalities "based on a productivism that has lost all human finality," when "[t]he only acceptable finality of human activity is the production of a subjectivity that is auto-enriching its relation to the world in a continuous fashion."[74] A tentative solution, for Guattari, involves shifting the discussion of the subject to subjectivity, "taking the relation between the subject and object by the middle and foregrounding the expressive instance."[75] Understood this way, a virtual ecology is not about reconnecting "man and nature," but the exploration of the infinite manifestations of a subjectivity that is auto-enriching.

Taking this up, the ecological as dealt with here is something much broader than that which is typically recognized by green camps. Although the works I explore in this work do often focus explicitly on environmental crisis and the human role in it, *Biophilia* and *Cosmos* do not primarily concern themselves with the havoc humans have wreaked upon Earth systems (although they both touch upon this multiple times). When I group them as ecological, I understand the term in a slightly broader sense. Here, I follow Nicole Seymour in choosing to speak of the ecological rather than, perhaps more concretely, of the environmental. She calls attention to ecology, "in its extended use" as denoting "the relationships between any system and its

---

72 Félix Guattari, *Chaosmosis: An Ethico-Aesthetic Paradigm,* trans. Paul Bains and Julian Pefanis (Bloomington: Indiana University Press, 1995).

73 Ibid., 119.

74 Ibid., 21.

75 Ibid.

environment."[76] Seymour goes on to say that this allows her to take into account relationships between social formations and what we might refer to as "the environment." I conscientiously shy away from the social, both because the texts that I discuss themselves largely steer clear of this dimension and because the scope of this work is already broad enough, but I join Seymour in emphasizing the aspect of interrelation so essential to a broader view of the ecological.[77]

And to the extent that the works I examine aim not only to explain interrelation strictly scientifically but also to transmit *a sense of how interrelation feels,* they offer up affective ecologies. As stated before, I understand affect here with Deleuze (and Spinoza) as something, "experienced in a lived duration that involves the difference between two states."[78] Affect is what transpires between — whether one takes states to mean entities or temporalities — and as such forms the very fabric of experience. Notably, Deleuze and Guattari also describe affect as "nonhuman becomings of man."[79] Affect, in this way, necessarily brings the subject not only to the lived present, but to that outside the self — the very animal, vegetable, or cosmic of which Guattari speaks.

And it is important to recognize that ecological subjects consist, from an affective perspective, of bodies and minds caught in webs, not all of which are immediately obvious to us. Gregory

76 Seymour, *Strange Natures,* 29.
77 Félix Guattari, in his aptly titled *Three Ecologies,* trans. Ian Pindar and Paul Sutton (1989; repr. London: Continuum, 2008), himself divides the ecological into three dimensions — "the environment, social relations, and human subjectivity" (19–20). Limiting my discussion to works concerned largely with the first and third of these dimensions was the only way to make coherent claims about interrelation; that I did choose not to lose myself in ecological webs, and, to a certain extent, did choose to draw artificial lines of demarcation, does not mean, however, that I view the social as insignificant.
78 Deleuze, *Practical Philosophy,* 49.
79 Gilles Deleuze and Félix Guattari, *What Is Philosophy?,* trans. Hugh Tomlinson and Graham Burchell (New York: Columbia University Press, 1994), 169.

Seigworth and Melissa Gregg speak of affect's "open-ended in-between-ness,"[80] which is "integral to a body's perpetual *becoming* (always becoming otherwise, however subtly, than what it already is), pulled beyond its seeming surface-boundedness by way of its relation to, indeed its composition through, the forces of encounter." A body, pulled this way and that, "webbed in its relations"[81] is "as much outside itself as in itself."[82] The turn to affect includes the acknowledgment of corporeal and energetic in-discreteness — the ecological condition itself. That we participate in becoming *with* the environment because we are constituted by it (and in fact contain it within us[83]) is the first lesson of the ecological, and it is the concept of affect that most fully accepts that the situatedness of the body has consequences that one cannot express in terms of physio-scientific discourses alone.

Employing concepts of affect in ecological contexts should shift the discussion of how humans can survive in the ecosphere to how humans are in the ecosphere, to the production of subjectivity. The focus becomes relational and present-oriented. Affect, I will argue, gives us something that begins to do justice to the human (and the organisms, too, in many cases) relation to the natural world; we get a kind of "incorporeal materialism."[84] Massumi writes of "accepting the paradox that there is an incorporeal dimension of the body. Of it, but not in it. Real, material, but incorporeal," of *"the felt reality of relation."*[85] This is a line of thought that fully acknowledges the primacy of the material world, but also its literally transgressive character, the strangeness of visible and invisible flux and energy exchange. Incorporeal materialism contains room for both the virtual (the realm

80 Gregory J. Seigworth and Melissa Gregg, "An Inventory of Shimmers," in *The Affect Theory Reader* (Durham: Duke University Press, 2010), 1–25, at 3.

81 Ibid.

82 Ibid.

83 See Alan Dove, "Microbiomics: The Germ Theory of Everything," *Science* 340, no. 6133 (2013): 763–65. Dove writes, "There are more microbial genomes within us than we have human cells. We're a walking ecosystem."

84 Massumi, *Parables for the Virtual*, 5.

85 Ibid., 5, 16.

of affects and potentials) and the actual (the realm of things), which Deleuze describes as falling "from the plane [of immanence] like a fruit."[86] Put simply, acknowledging something like affect means admitting that sensation cannot necessarily be explained away by or become reducible to the physiological. Massumi phrases affective models as "*abstract enough* to grasp the incorporeality of the concrete."[87]

The "affectively ecological" is thus a way of approaching interrelatedness through experience, and this experience consists not only of that to which we can testify and which is measurable, but, as Massumi puts it, "the felt reality of relation." Indeed, in the texts examined here, the force of reenchantment is very often not what happens per se, but the potential that permeates everything — the virtual as opposed to the actual. While the works here do much to explain interrelation concretely — with other forms of life in the case of *Biophilia,* the earth itself in *Gaia,* and the universe in *Cosmos* — they also seek to describe and evoke the feeling of interrelation, of wonder, and of being (or becoming) at home in the universe. This is, as I will explain more in the individual analyses of the works, their lasting contribution to environmental thought.

1.2.3. Why these works, and why now?
It should be clear by now that I have chosen to focus on these particular works of popular science not because of the way in which they translate science, but because they suggest novel ways of approaching questions of ecological subjectivity. Via popular science, they offer visions of reenchantment that have proven incredibly robust.

This is evident, at the most basic level, in the success of the books themselves and the visibility of their authors, which will be explored in Chapters 3, 4, and 5 in more detail. Cosmos, at the

---

86 Gilles Deleuze and Claire Parnet, "The Actual and the Virtual," in *Dialogues II,* trans. Eliot Ross Albert (New York: Columbia University Press, 2002), 148–59, at 150.

87 Massumi, *Parables for the Virtual,* 5.

very least, was a bestseller, and the other works have not been out of print since their publication. The authors are or were all public intellectuals, appearing for academic debates and lectures as well as on TV. Two of the authors, Wilson and Sagan, are Pulitzer Prize winners (although not for the books discussed here).

Even more significantly, however, the concepts so central to the works, introduced in their respective titles, have stuck around. "Biophilia," in addition to providing the title for Icelandic artist Björk's 2011 album, has entered psychological as well as architectural and design discourses and crops up often in pop-environmental contexts.[88] It has also become a concept taken up by environmental educators, as evidenced by the E.O. Wilson Biophilia Center, established in 2009 in Florida's Longleaf Pine ecosystem.[89] "Gaia," for its part, has gone from a scientific hypothesis to a central part of new age environmentalism and back again. More recently, scholars in the humanities have begun exploring the concept, thanks, in large part, to Bruno Latour's 2013 Gifford Lectures.[90] *Cosmos,* a TV series airing on PBS before it was published in book form, has been remade and broadcast widely in 2014, this time by a major private network and starring Neil deGrasse Tyson. Despite some changes, the structure of the original 1980 series and the unnarrated moments of wonder occasioned by "the cosmos" remain intact. The perseverance of these concepts in the twenty-first century demands that we take more than an anthropological interest in the books that introduced them.

88 See, for instance, Neil Chambers, "How Biophilia Can Improve Our Lives," *Treehugger,* March 27, 2012, http://www.treehugger.com/green-architec-ture/biophilia-can-improve-lives.html.

89 See "About Us," *E.O. Wilson Biophilia Center,* http://www.eowilsoncenter.org/#!-about-us/c20r9.

90 See Bruno Latour, "Facing Gaia: Six Lectures on the Political Theology of Nature," Gifford Lectures: "Facing Gaia: A New Inquiry into Natural Religion," University of Edinburgh, February 18–28, 2013. Adapted versions of the lectures have been published in Latour's *Facing Gaia: Eight Lectures on the New Climatic Regime,* trans. Catherine Porter (Cambridge: Polity Press, 2018).

Indeed, this kind of investigation would not have been possible in the 1980s. This is, first and foremost, because the theoretical landscape that has so crucially informed this project is more recent. Jane Bennett's *Enchantment of Modern Life,* referred to above, as well as her more recent *Vibrant Matter*[91] — both of which connect the affective to environmental issues — were not published until 2001 and 2010, respectively. Moreover, it is only really in the twenty-first century that ecocriticism and the ecological humanities have broadened to include approaches that, in the words of Lawrence Buell, deviate from "the self-intoxicated fetishization of greenery as such" and "save-the-world moral earnestness," and that insist that "the winning move" lies "not in abandoning the concept of nature but in abandoning the idea that culture is something outside *nature*."[92] This book is, of course, not the first that brings affect theory to bear on ecological texts,[93] but it is the first to bring it to this group of texts and, to my knowledge, popular science generally. Certainly, the collision this produces, with wonder and reenchantment, one might say, as the debris raining down in its aftermath, is something novel in popular science studies as well as in the environmental humanities, a field which has only in recent years begun to venture outside of what one might refer to as the environmentalist cannon.

Finally, and connected to this move beyond straight-forwardly green environmentalism, this is a project for the Anthropocene, an age in which the human is not only intricately bound up with its *Umwelt* but influential as never before. The end of this work delves into the connection between the texts I examine here and our historical and geological moment in much more detail. Nevertheless, it is worth saying here that these texts have been selected explicitly because they refuse to pretend that

91 Jane Bennett, *Vibrant Matter: A Political Ecology of Things* (Durham: Duke University Press, 2010).

92 Lawrence Buell, "Foreword," in *Prismatic Ecology: Ecotheory Beyond Green,* ed. Jeffrey Jerome Cohen (Minneapolis: University of Minnesota Press, 2013), ix–xii, at xi, x.

93 See, for instance, Alex Lockwood, "The Affective Legacy of Silent Spring," *Environmental Humanities* 1 (November 2012): 123–40.

it is possible to go back to an era that is less human. They are reconciled to the fact that our sheer numbers and technologies necessitate a more nuanced understanding of our relation with that which surrounds, sustains, and sometimes threatens us.

1.3
The Nature/Culture of My Reading

1.3.1. "We," the human

It bears explaining why I have self-consciously employed the first person plural— the pronouns "we," "our," and "us" — despite recognizing that there are real problems in casually assuming commonalities and/or collective culpabilities among actors on the world stage.

The primary reason I have chosen to speak in these collective terms is practical: the texts examined here, by necessity, make frequent reference to the human as species, and often invoke the first-person plural themselves. Discussing them without myself using these pronouns, i.e. referring to "the human" with "they" and "their" has the uncanny effect of positioning myself as an alien observer. I have no desire, and indeed it would be irresponsible, to assume this level of distance from any discussion of the ecological in which we (!), the human, play a substantial part. One may see already here how the practical rationale for this crucial stylistic choice bleeds into the ideological.

In fact, the "pronoun problem," though it certainly crops up in many academic and pseudo-academic discourses, is of particular significance to ecological discourses. Peter van Wyck identifies what he calls a "'we' shift"[94] occurring in the grassroots environmentalism of the 1960s. According to him, the shift constitutes an "attempt to subsume difference at one level by shifting to a broader, more inclusive category."[95] The problem for

---

94 Peter van Wyck, *Primitives in the Wilderness: Deep Ecology and the Missing Human Subject* (Albany: State University of New York Press, 1997), 9.
95 Ibid.

him is that any attempt to speak of the "people," creates a "new and total position."[96] He writes, "Moving from profits, technology and political ideologies to the level of 'all people,' ignores the fact that people are (in varying degrees and combinations) *about* profits, technology and political ideologies."[97] For van Wyck, collective pronouns only create fictions of solidarity and actually serve to silence dissent. He refers to them as "a means of establishing the guise of a community — Gaia, the ecosphere, spaceship Earth — that leaves no possible space for difference.[98] The use of them is, in other words, merely an obstacle to talking about the "real" problems, the more concretely political.

To some extent, I agree with the critique, although I view it as an insufficient reason to abandon the collective form altogether. The "we" form camouflages the forms of power and the technologies so bound up with it — that, in short, which divides. It is important and in fact crucial, to remember that "we" have not all had an equal share in creating the current ecological crisis. I would never claim that the "profits, technology and political ideologies" dividing up the collective ought to be disregarded in favor of an establishing an impossible ecological happy family.

With all of this in mind, a number of ideological reasons still prevent me from abandoning collective pronouns. The first is that, despite being brought on by what we can only call a global elite and subsequently perpetuated by this elite's own "ideologies, technologies and profits," our predicament is an authentically collective one. Climate change may not affect all evenly, or even directly, but the distinct possibility that it might have such deleterious consequences for the world's poor (who have not yet engaged as intensively in activities we consider environmentally damaging[99]), combined with the highly unpredictable second-

96 Ibid.
97 Ibid.
98 Ibid., 25.
99 See the concept of "ecological debt" proposed in Joan Martinez-Alier, "Distributional Obstacles to International Environmental Policy: The Failures at Rio and Prospects after Rio," *Environmental Values* 2, no. 2 (May 1993): 97–124.

ary and tertiary effects that will resonate far from the coasts, should at least be enough to consider it a problem in which we all have a stake. Those touting the benefits of global warming for, just to cite one example, growing peaches in Canada, have, like the rest of us, only the foggiest idea of what effects might accompany the tropical breeze in decidedly non-tropical latitudes.

Secondly, the "we" allows us to consider the human ethologically as its own kind of animal. This is not an assumption of universalism per se, but it does acknowledge that there is something peculiar about the human. If one follows Uexküll, the human is a range of affects, of possibilities unique to the organism. With Agamben, it is merely the recognition of oneself as human, as not animal.[100] Latour, for his part, describes the human as the "weaver of morphisms"[101] or the ultimate conjugator. What does in fact distinguish the human need not necessarily be worked out. Invoking the "we" here merely entails that we can talk about *Homo sapiens* as animal and does not necessitate an exhaustive "fleshing out" of precisely how we might understand the human. This work considers the human from a number of angles, but it is enough at the beginning to recognize the simple fact of shared strangeness in this strange animal.

Pointing to this condition of shared animality again and again with collective pronouns, I hope, also directs attention to "an emancipatory politics of bare life."[102] Both Thrift and Jameson have connected the expansion of the present to the animal-in-human,[103] and I wish to continue this project in my analyses. As Thrift so succinctly puts it, "'bare life' is not bare. It is most

---

100 Giorgio Agamben, *The Open: Man and Animal,* trans. Kevin Attel (Stanford: Stanford University Press, 2004), 26.
101 Bruno Latour, *We Have Never Been Modern,* trans. Catherine Porter (Cambridge: Harvard University Press, 1993), 137.
102 Thrift, *Object of Nature,* 48.
103 Although Jameson, in contrast to Thrift, insists that "the historical tendency of late capitalism — what we have called the reduction to the present and the reduction to the body — is in any case unrealizable; human beings cannot revert to the immediacy of the animal kingdom (assuming indeed the animals themselves enjoy such phenomenological immediacy)." He does not say why this phenomenological immediacy is denied to the hu-

of what there is."[104] Although biopolitics that reduce the human to bios are much maligned in critical literature, the potential inherent in *bios* has been less explored.[105] The "we" may thus be seen as directing the reader away from the endless entanglements of *zoē* (most notably the social), and toward the very different entanglements of *bios*.[106]

Finally, I would like to suggest that collective pronouns, rather than referring to "the guise of a community," as van Wyck would have it, themselves call forth collectives that cannot be said to yet exist. Deleuze, in "Literature and Life," identifies this as the function of literature itself: "[T]he writer as such is not a patient but rather a physician, the physician of himself and of the world. The world is the set of symptoms whose illness merges with man."[107] He continues, "Health as literature, as writing, consists in inventing a people who are missing. It is the task of the fabulating function to invent a people."[108] I make no claims for the world-therapeutic value of this work, but the authors with which it engages are certainly physicians of a sort. Lovelock even advocates a "planetary physiology." The world consists of more than ecological crisis, surely, but ecological crisis is nothing if not "the set of symptoms whose illness merges with man." These authors consistently write in the first-person plural, I believe, not because they already maintain the existence of some authentic global community, but because they wish to summon

man. See Frederic Jameson, "The End of Temporality," *Critical Inquiry* 29, no. 4 (Summer 2003): 695–718, at 717.

104 Thrift, *Object of Nature,* 35.

105 See also Thrift, *Object of Nature,* 53.

106 Agamben defines *zoē,* synonymous in his work with "bare life," as "the simple fact of living common to all beings (animals, men, or gods)." *Bios,* on the other hand, is "the form or way of living proper to an individual or group" and understood in most texts as specific to the human. See *Homo Sacer: Sovereign Power and Bare Life,* trans. Daniel Heller-Roazen (Stanford: Stanford University Press, 1998), 9.

107 Gilles Deleuze, "Literature and Life," in *Essays Critical and Clinical,* trans. Daniel W. Smith and Michael A. Greco (Minneapolis: University of Minnesota Press, 1997), 1–6, at 3.

108 Ibid., 4.

one. Far from wishing to dismiss this summons, I view my taking up of these pronouns as a kind of forwarding action.

The invocation, and, hopefully sooner than later, the building of such collectives is especially necessary if we are to grapple with the enormity of ecological crisis. Bruno Latour describes the collective dilemma especially succinctly: "How could it be 'us' who did 'all this' since there is no political, no moral, no thinking, no feeling body able to say 'we' — and no one to proudly say 'the buck stops here.'"[109] This is what drives his call for the "work of assembly": "Right now there is no path leading from my changing the light bulbs in my home straight to the Earth's destiny: such a stair has no step; such a ladder has no rung. I would have to jump, and this would be quite a *salto mortale*!"[110] The authors I engage with sought to build the rungs of this ladder, to render this jump less lethal, and these collective pronouns are essential to their effort. Even if the only ones to break the "salto mortale" are those who have read and been persuaded by the same literature, the authors at least promise and hope for some sort of collective with global aspirations. I write in the same hope, although I think we (!) ought to constantly scrutinize what and who is implied in the summoning of a global human collective.

1.3.2. The reparative disposition

It should also be becoming increasingly clear that this work is not one that attempts to unmask and demystify, and, indeed, although the scientist-humanists I focus on could certainly be taken to task for any number of things, I have chosen not to do so. To approach these works, written by three male scientists who believe so strongly in what science can accomplish that it often blinds them to what it does not, with anything but suspicion, may be seen by some as unforgivable, and yet that is precisely what I've set out to do. This stance owes as much to Eve Kosofsky Sedgwick's critique of paranoid reading as it does to

109 Latour, "Waiting for Gaia," 4.
110 Ibid., 7.

the vision of an essentially productive criticism, propounded by Bruno Latour.

This is not to say that I do not acknowledge some of the criticisms leveled at the authors (and the individual analyses will touch upon these), but I do not allow that the "hidden historical violences that underlie a secular, universalist liberal humanism"[111] necessitate the dismissal of the texts entirely. There is too much, in any case, in the texts of Wilson, Lovelock, and Sagan that eludes the kinds of metanarratives a paranoid or critical reading would zero in on; these are the traces through which this book attempts to sift. There is always something that escapes, a micropolitical dimension that may emerge if one only attends to it.[112]

I would like to maintain, moreover, that, particularly in the ecological humanities, attempting to approach texts in the reparative mode is essential in order to begin to depart from the catastrophism that is only reinforced by readings that are merely paranoid. If one wishes to emerge from a crisis, in short, not every form of expression can be seen as of that crisis. Perhaps the question is not the one that I followed Bennett in posing at the beginning, "How can someone write a book about enchantment in such a world?" but rather, why is it that attending to enchantment is seen by a great many scholars as "so sappy, aestheticizing, defensive, anti-intellectual, or reactionary"?[113] This work does not necessarily position me to answer that question, but it does join Kosofsky Sedgwick in saying that there is nothing "mere" about "pleasure and amelioration."[114] Ethics, as Bennett insists at the beginning, is as much a matter of rules, perhaps arising from

---

111 Eve Kosofsky Sedgwick, "Paranoid Reading and Reparative Reading; or, You're So Paranoid, You Probably Think This Introduction Is about You," in *Novel Gazing: Queer Readings in Fiction,* ed. Eve Kosofsky Sedgwick (Durham: Duke University Press 1997), 1–37, at 16.

112 See Gilles Deleuze and Félix Guattari, "1933: Micropolitics and Segmentarity," in *A Thousand Plateaus,* trans. Brian Massumi (London: Continuum 1987), 229–55.

113 Sedgwick, "Paranoid Reading and Reparative Reading," 31.

114 Ibid.

negativity, as dispositions, and pleasure and amelioration are part and parcel of this. Kosofsky Sedgwick continues:

> No less acute than a paranoid position, no less realistic, no less attached to a project of survival, and neither less nor more delusional or fantasmatic, the reparative reading position undertakes a different range of affects, ambitions, and risks. What we can best learn from such practices are, perhaps, the many ways in which selves and communities succeed in extracting sustenance from the objects of culture — even a culture whose avowed desire has often been not to sustain them.[115]

That many have extracted and continue to extract sustenance from *Biophilia, Gaia,* and *Cosmos* should become abundantly clear in the following chapters, and I insist that, even if some find the brand of sustenance provided distasteful, there is something to be gained from understanding what may draw the reader in to begin with. Here I have attempted to, in line with Latour,[116] multiply the possibilities of the text rather than subtract and debunk. Looking at these works as embodiments and enactors of affective wonder, moreover, brings us far closer to understanding the popularity and lasting impact of these texts (and perhaps even to mobilizing their tactics in ecological politics) than paranoid readings ever could.

৵৯

This first chapter has endeavored to explain the motivations behind a project which, consisting of an examination of popular science books from the 1980s, may sound esoteric, but which is at heart just as much about ecological subjectivity today.

115 Ibid.
116 See Bruno Latour, "Why Has Critique Run Out of Steam? From Matters of Fact to Matters of Concern," *Critical Inquiry* 30, no. 2 (Winter 2004): 225–48, at 248.

Not only do the works in question fly in the face of the cata-strophism and the future-talk I argue plagues much of ecologi-cal thought, but they gesture toward ways of inhabiting an open, dynamic present, and thus to alternative kinds of ecological en-gagement. I am not the first to argue that popular science is not merely science popularized, but in fact consists of claims and anecdotes about the intrinsic value of science that also point to the wonder inherent in the world. The next chapter (Chapter 2) will investigate the reenchanting functions of popular science in much more detail. Rather than presenting the reader with inert depictions of life and the life-like, the earth, and the cosmos, the works I discuss can be understood as quasi-vitalist. In the manner in which they insist on the animatedness of material, they fall in much more neatly with more contemporary vital and incorporeal materialist frameworks, which I will also go on to examine. Chapter 2 also explores and explicitly defines affective wonder, outlining, finally, how a reading that seeks to examine how the texts embody and transmit this wonder might proceed.

The other function of this chapter was to begin to outline the work's own stylistic and critical (or rather reparative) dis-positions. These dispositions have crucially informed the analy-ses of the texts appearing in the chapters on *Biophilia* (3), *Gaia* (4), and *Cosmos* (5). What one encounters in these works are a series of attempts to confront the reader with novel affects, with wonder, operating, as a rule, on increasingly larger scales. Biophilia, Gaia, and Cosmos here are not merely the titles of the works that form the core of my corpus but are themselves explored as concepts central to the affective ecologies woven by their respective authors. "*Biophilia:* Affiliation and the Infinite Unseen" begins small but explodes the very idea of smallness. Here, with Wilson, a mere handful of dirt, in its inexhaustibility, constitutes a source of wonder. As we will see, Wilson constantly employs technologies (even if they are merely literary) of scale that put a new cast on the mundane and our relation to it. What this amounts to in the end is, perhaps, the most anthropocen-tric conservation ethic of them all: We must conserve in order to preserve the infinity of the reservoir of affects that nurture the human. "Gaia: The Affects of the Earth" presents not only a larger vision of the living earth rather than individual ecosystems but also one which is far more indifferent to the human. By way of the 1985 BBC mini-series *Edge of Darkness*,[117] which features of a group of scientist-activist who call themselves Gaians, the chapter focuses on the manner in which the very concept of Gaia radically reenchants and draws us into the planetary present. Finally, with "*Cosmos:* 'The Subtle Machinery of Awe,'" we turn to Sagan's massively successful book and series. The declaration that we are star-stuff, far from being merely a statement about the distant origins of matter, also insists that we share something with the extraterrestrial and, indeed, feel with it. Although *Cosmos* shares a great deal with *Gaia* and *Biophilia* in celebrating the infinity and excess of life on Earth, it is also fundamentally about the potential for reenchantment in an age in which we are just beginning to realize the vastness of that which we have not yet experienced in the universe.

The final chapter, "The Poet-in-Scientist in the Anthropocene," begins by looking back at the analyses of *Biophilia, Gaia,* and *Cosmos*. Pitting the larger claims they make about reenchantment and the place of the human against one another, the chapter reveals that, although they share a great deal in their general orientation towards reenchantment and the place of the affective in science, they diverge in important ways. Here, as well, the figure of the poet-in-scientist is brought into the present, and specifically into what we will discuss as the Anthropocene. It ends by asking how the role of the poet-in-scientist has changed in an era in which everything has become at least a little bit human: What becomes of wonder when our day-to-day activities have, less than overnight in geological time, rendered former affective treasure troves so familiar?

117 *Edge of Darkness*, DVD, dir. Martin Campbell (1985; London, United Kingdom: BBC Worldwide, 2003).

2

Wonder, or
Reenchantment on High

Lest this talk of reenchanting science be associated with a "haze of romantic nostalgia,"[1] either in the sense of a lack of clarity or a kind of preciousness, the concept of wonder must be made more concrete. This chapter endeavors to do just that, exploring, first of all, why it makes sense to talk about wonder in the context of the popular science of the 1980s. One cannot fully understand *Biophilia, Gaia,* or *Cosmos* without looking at the narratives of disenchantment, beginning, arguably, with Weber, and reaching a fever pitch in the 1970s and the 1980s with calls for a less alienated science. Against this backdrop, a reenchanted and reenchanting popular science can be understood as a way of negotiating what comes "after" disenchantment, refusing both a return to the naïve animisms of the past, as well as a no-holds-barred glorification of technoscience.

As I explain in the second section of this chapter, these works align themselves much more comfortably with the quasi-vitalist frameworks found in contemporary vital and incorporeal materialisms, as well as Karen Barad's agential realism. The frame-

---

1   Rita Felski, *Uses of Literature* (Oxford: Blackwell Publishing, 2008), 76. Felski here is referring to the enchantment occasioned by a text — a style of reading made suspect by, for instance, Frankfurt School thinkers, but the suspicion towards it can be thought of more broadly as well.

works are united by their rejection of mechanist views, understanding reality as a perpetual unfolding of potentials and as teeming with organic and inorganic life arising from and embedded in the interaction of matter. Affect, as the "felt reality of relation," is also central to these accounts, and the more detailed exploration of it within these frameworks gives us a vocabulary with which we might begin to define affective wonder and distance ourselves from the sentimental.

This, indeed, is the task taken up by the third section of this chapter, which argues that wonder can be usefully conceptualized in an ecological sense as the attunement to new affects, or with Jacob von Uexküll, as the expansion of the *Umwelt* via the experience of new affects. As Uexküll elaborates on the nature of the *Umwelt*,[2] he returns again and again to the figure of the scientist, and it is in his discussions of the inquiring subject, in particular, that one gets a sense of wonder's potential to take the human beyond itself.

The final section of this chapter turns at last toward the works themselves and identifies how a reenchanted science operates in practice. Here, I outline what guided the readings of the works in the following chapters. Although the analytic portions of the readings focus on wonder's many manifestations within the texts, what gives texture and, ultimately, meaning to them are the connections to be drawn between affective wonder, the enchanted science they present, and ecological praxis. To this end, I will propose a framework for the series of very non-hermetic close readings that I embark on in the following chapters.

2   Most prominently in "A Stroll Through the Worlds of Animals and Men: A Picture Book of Invisible Worlds," trans. Claire Schiller, *Semiotica* 89, no. 4 (1992): 319–91.

2.1
Disenchantment and Its Discontents

Rather than conceiving of the popular scientific works of the 1980s in a vacuum, one ought to keep in mind that their engagement with affective wonder might be seen as a larger project to, in Morris Berman's words, "reenchant the world,"[3] to undo the disenchantment Max Weber argued was accomplished by modernity. This project may be seen as much as an effort that followed naturally from sciences that no longer perceived the same disconnect between the observer and the observed as an attempt to overcome a conception of science as only serving the most narrowly anthropocentric interests.

This section begins by outlining the story of disenchantment, first as articulated by Max Weber, and then as taken up by others like Morris Berman, explaining, along the way, how we might understand a disenchanted science. But, as Jane Bennett reminds us, "The modern story of disenchantment leaves out important things."[4] The disenchantment story may be seen as just that — a story — and here we examine how it might easily be described as a fantasy or, at best or perhaps worst, self-fulfilling prophecy. This section asks, in other words, that the self-evidence of disenchantment be done away with, and that we turn, ultimately, to those enchantments "already in and around us."[5]

2.1.1. Disenchantment demystified

The story of disenchantment cannot be disentangled from the scientific and industrial revolutions. Max Weber argued, famously, that these had triggered the "intellectual process of rationalization through science and a science-based technology."[6]

---

3   See Morris Berman, *The Reenchantment of the World* (Ithaca: Cornell University Press, 1981).

4   Jane Bennett, *The Enchantment of Modern Life* (Princeton: Princeton University Press, 2001), 159–60.

5   Ibid., 159–60.

6   Max Weber, "Science as a Vocation," in *The Vocation Lectures,* trans. Rodney Livingstone, eds. David Owen and Tracy B. Strong (Indianapolis:

This, for him, did not mean that individuals could necessarily explain the working of the world any better, only that the forces behind lived reality were, in theory, no longer mysterious (and therefore no longer enchanting), because an explanation *could* be sought out. It is not as if, in other words, the advancement of science and technology implied with it "a growing understanding of the condition under which we live."[7] Weber argued that we hardly possess "a greater knowledge of the conditions determining our lives than an Indian, or a Hottentot," and that, "[u]nless we happen to be physicists, those of us who travel by streetcar have not the faintest idea of how the streetcar works."[8] Indeed, the notion that, at least potentially, all explanations of our physical surroundings are available to us, even if we do not know them offhand, could only have become more entrenched in the Internet age.

Where the full force of disenchantment is felt here, however, is in the emergence of an anthropocentric cosmos in which we attribute more agency and power to the human than we ever have before. Weber continues:

[I]n principle, then, we are not ruled by mysterious, unpredictable forces, but [...], on the contrary, we can in principle control everything by means of calculation. That in turn means the disenchantment of the world. Unlike the savage for whom such forces existed we need no longer have recourse to magic in order to control the spirits or pray to them. Instead, technology and calculation achieve our ends.[9]

If this sounds familiar, and it should, it is because so many since Weber have repeated some version of this: We have become as gods.[10] Weber himself was deeply ambiguous about this "ration-

Hackett Publishing Company, 2004), 1–31, at 12.

7   Ibid., 12.

8   Ibid.

9   Ibid., 12–13.

10   Stewart Brand's version of this, appearing on the first page of every *Whole Earth Catalogue,* was, "We are as gods and might as well get good at it." See

alization and intellectualization," stating, "Its resulting fate is
that precisely the ultimate and most sublime values have with-
drawn from public life. They have retreated into the abstract
realm of mystical life or into the fraternal feelings of personal
relations between individuals."[11] If disenchantment is the emptying of mystery (and therefore meaning) from the world, it is also
the destruction here of a sacred commons. For Weber, as well,
modern religion offers "[r]elease from the rationalism and intel-
lectualism of science."[12] Enchantment, in his world, has retreated
fully to enclaves in the private sphere.

The historian Lynn White takes up a number of these themes
up in the late 1960s, in an article appearing in *Science* entitled
"The Historical Roots of Our Ecological Crisis."[13] For White,
notably, it is not merely the "rationalization and intellectualization of science" that has brought about an all-pervasive disenchantment; he describes a fatal cocktail involving the rise of
Christianity, which for Weber still constituted something of a
refuge, and the wedding of technology to science accomplished
by democracy. White explains, "Science was traditionally aristo-
cratic, speculative, intellectual in intent; technology was lower-
class, empirical, action-oriented." The democratic revolutions of
the mid-nineteenth century and the dissolution of many social
barriers that went along with them, White claims, created a
"functional unity of brain and hand." Very much ahead of his
time, White then states: "Our ecologic crisis is the produce of an
emerging, entirely novel, democratic culture."[14]

In this narrative, the investment of science with *telos,* via the
fusion with "low" technology, destroys its speculative character,
which one might assume allowed it, at one time in history, to

Fred Turner, *From Counterculture to Cyberculture* (Chicago: University of
Chicago Press, 2006), 82.

11 Weber, "Science as a Vocation," 30.

12 Ibid., 16.

13 Lynn White, Jr., "The Historical Roots of Our Ecologic Crisis," *Science* 155,
no. 3767 (1967): 1203–7.

14 Ibid., 1204.

possess some degree of enchantment.[15] White recognizes that, while this "unity of brain and hand" was part and parcel of democratic culture, it had devastating consequences in terms of the damage that could now be inflicted upon the earth; technoscience not only pretended, and arguably still pretends, to comprehend the world, but also to make it bend to its will. One need only think back to the nuclear science occupying so many scientists during World War II and the Cold War era in order to imagine just how much the unity of brain and hand had both accomplished and devastated, or could at least in theory devastate. It is no accident that the scientists examined in this work attempt to turn back to this more speculative science (and were, in fact, heavily criticized by those within the academy for this). They had all at least experienced the nuclear era, and Sagan and Lovelock have spoken and written at length about both nuclear weapons and power. Although at no point in time do these scientists argue for the divorcing of science from technology, what they offer is an ethically guided science for its own sake.

In subsequent articulations, in the 1980s, this vision of disenchantment becomes less nuanced and more focused on the consequences for the individual. It is the emergence of scientific consciousness, as Berman phrases it, at the beginning of modernity that allows participants in the cosmos to imagine themselves as somehow separate from it:

> Scientific consciousness is alienated consciousness: there is no ecstatic merger with nature, but rather total separation from it. Subject and object are always seen in opposition to each other. I am not my experiences and thus not really a part of the world around me. The logical end point of this world view is a feeling of total reification: everything is an object,

15 Richard Holmes in fact insists on a second scientific revolution: the dawning of a "Romantic science," which he also refers to as "The Age of Wonder." See Richard Holmes, *The Age of Wonder: How the Romantic Generation Discovered the Terror and Beauty of Science* (New York: Pantheon Books, 2009).

alien, not-me; and I am ultimately an object too, an alienated "thing" in a world of other, equally meaningless things.[16]

Scientific consciousness and the attendant disenchantment thus entails a double alienation — from the world, and the ability to conceive of oneself as part of it, and from subjectivity itself. Always accompanying this disenchantment of experience, moreover, is a "disenchantment of nature,"[17] as David Ray Griffin terms it. He describes this as, "the denial to nature of all subjectivity, all experience, all feeling. Because of this denial nature is disqualified — it is denied all qualities that are not thinkable apart from experience."[18] And "apart from experience" here already means apart from the disenchanted experience of the scientist, the limitation, in Uexküll's terms (which we will discuss later in this chapter), to one tiny sector of nature. There is no room for the Deleuzian virtual in a disenchanted science, for that net of relations that itself comprises the subject; the scientist, impossibly, stands apart.

This begs the question: what was it like *before?* How do these authors describe an enchanted world? White, for one, makes reference to the *genius loci,* the guardian spirit of antiquity, claiming, "These spirits were accessible to men, but were very unlike men [...]. Before one cut a tree, mined a mountain, or damned a brook, it was important to placate the spirit in charge of that particular situation, and to keep it placated." He goes on to say that, "By destroying pagan animism, Christianity made it possible to exploit nature in a mood of indifference to the feeling of natural objects."[19] The world, prior to the ascent of modern science and religion, is suffused with spirit — in a word, animist.

Berman paints a similar picture of a cosmic garden of Eden, writing, "The view of nature which predominated in the West

16 Berman, *Reenchantment of the World,* 17.
17 David Ray Griffin, "Introduction: The Reenchantment of Science," in *The Reenchantment of Science,* ed. David Ray Griffin (Albany: State University of New York Press, 1988), 1–46, at 2.
18 Ibid., 2.
19 White, "Historical Roots," 11.

down to the eve of the Scientific Revolution was that of an enchanted world. Rocks, trees, rivers, and clouds were all seen
as wondrous, alive, and human beings felt at home in this
environment."[20] Before the advent of scientific distance, "A
member of this cosmos was not an alien observer of it but a
direct participant in its drama."[21] The world before the scientific
revolution is framed as a kind of pleasure garden. That some
members of this cosmos may not have found it so benign is, of
course, never presented as a possibility. The point is that, prior
to the development of scientific consciousness, there could be
no clash, and certainly no distance, between human and environment. Humans had not yet learned to be directors but were
still actors in a drama. And not only was there no separation
between subject and object, but no part of this world could be
described as object, or inert, at all. This leads many theorists,
unsurprisingly, to trace the contemporary disregard for the
earth and environmental crisis itself to the disenchantment of
the world accomplished by science.

Jane Bennett gives her own, lengthier overview of disenchantment narratives in *The Enchantment of Modern Life,* together with a rather wryly administered disenchantment quiz
intended to gauge one's own degree of disenchantment. After-
ward, she summarizes the features of the concept:

(1) our modern, highly rationalized world, characterized by
calculation, stands in stark contrast to a magical or holistic
cosmos, a cosmos toward which we have a double orientation of superiority and nostalgia; (2) although this world
opens up a domain of freedom and mastery, we pay a psychic
or emotional toll for demagification in the form of a lack of
community and a deficit of meaning; (3) the idea of progress
through science inspires both hope and despair; (4) even in
societies in which rationalization has advanced the furthest,
recalcitrant fugitives from rationalization persist, and these

20 Berman, *Reenchantment of the World,* 12.
21 Ibid.

errant forces are understood through the categories of the mystical and the erotic.[22]

Here, Bennett articulates the ambiguity surrounding disenchantment well. Disenchantment involves the supposed victory of reason over the mysterious forces of the world, and this is attached both to a triumphalism over these forces and despair at what has been lost. No longer viewing ourselves as part of the cosmos, we invest these former energies in a kind of cease-less scientific march forward, but cannot adequately answer the question, "What for?" Finally, Bennett, crucially, points out that even the theorists of disenchantment themselves acknowledge leaks; these are the "recalcitrant fugitives of rationalization," and are especially important for this project. In the writings of Wilson, Lovelock, and Sagan, it is argued here, science attempts to outrun its own shadow, to return to the possible, the speculative, as opposed to that which can be verified and rationalized.

2.1.2. The disenchantment fantasy
The question is, of course, how much credence one ought to grant the grand narrative set out by those describing disenchantment. My contention is that, even though the narrative itself is essential to understanding the climate in which the popular science of the 1980s operated, one ought to regard it with suspicion.

The first and primary reason to do this is that the very embeddedness of the narrative itself has now become inseparable from any disenchanting effect that modern science or its fusion with technology may have had or continue to have. In short, in its pervasiveness, disenchantment has become, at least in part, a self-fulfilling prophecy. Bennett puts it especially succinctly when she writes, "For me the question is not whether disenchantment is a regrettable or a progressive historical development. It is, rather, whether the very characterization of the world as disenchanted ignores and then discourages affec-

22 Bennett, *Enchantment of Modern Life,* 57.

tive attachment to that world."[23] The disenchantment narrative, in a strange twist, itself disenchants, and it becomes irrelevant whether the disenchantment precedes the narrative or not. What is especially important in Bennett's critique of disenchantment, moreover, is her mention of affective attachment. The very notion that there is a separation between the human and the world limits, in many ways, the kinds of relationships that can transpire between them. Bennett thus argues that "the enchantment effect," this intense affective attachment to the world, rests on the ability "to resist the story of the disenchantment of modernity."[24] She asks, again and again, and in a way that echoes the wonder-inducing strategies in popular science to be discussed later, "But what if the contemporary world is *not* disenchanted?"[25] If disenchantment is a self-fulfilling prophecy, the first step to "recovering" enchantment, regardless of how or even if we have lost it, is asking this question.

The disenchantment narrative, furthermore, is described by both Bennett and Latour as a self-indulgent fantasy. What, they ask, makes us so special as to be the only ones who have conceived of themselves as being ripped from the cosmos or abandoned in an empty universe? Bennett observes, "After all, a sense of insecurity and the spectre of meaninglessness are not specific to modernity; experiences of undeserved suffering and inexplicable evil have regularly called into question the safety and viability of the universe for humans."[26] We have no way of knowing that the lives of those that lived before us were suffused with meaning, and we have many methods that allow us to point to how cruel they may have been. Latour is even more severe in his assessment of the forces driving the disenchantment tale, musing that Westerners "like to frighten themselves with their own destiny."[27] "Why," he asks, "do we get so much pleasure out

23 Ibid., 3.
24 Ibid., 3–4.
25 Ibid., 34.
26 Ibid., 66.
27 Bruno Latour, *We Have Never Been Modern,* trans. Catherine Porter (Cambridge: Harvard University Press, 1993), 114.

of being so different not only from others but from our own past? What psychologist will be subtle enough to explain the morose delight in being in perpetual crisis and in putting an end to history?"[28] Here, disenchantment is a kind of masochism, a kind of "poor me" that multiplies with every development we decide is modern. Latour adds disenchantment, in fact, to a list of modern woes we simultaneously decry and relish, exclaiming,

> Haven't we shed enough tears over the disenchantment of the world? Haven't we frightened ourselves enough with the poor European who is thrust into a cold soulless cosmos, wandering on an inert planet in a world devoid of meaning? Haven't we shivered enough before the spectacle of the mechanized proletarian who is subject to the absolute domination of a mechanized capitalism and a Kafkaesque bureaucracy, abandoned smack in the middle of language games, lost in cement and formica? Haven't we felt sorry enough for the consumer who leaves the driver's seat of his car only to move to the sofa in the TV room where he is manipulated by the powers of the media and the postindustrialized society?![29]

It is not as if Latour dismisses these woes entirely, but he questions here whether endlessly bewailing the state of the world does more to reinforce these woes than to provide the kind of critique necessary for imagining other modes of living. The catastrophism spoken of in this volume's introduction might be taken as another instance of this; while its roots are material, we often conceive of it as a straightforward description of what is and a lament for what has been lost.

As an alternative to perversely pretending to dwell in a disenchanted world, Latour suggests, like Bennett, that we direct ourselves to the enchantments "in and around us." To do this, he points to the wonders both science and industry themselves

28 Ibid., 114.
29 Ibid., 115.

produce, asking, "How could we be capable of disenchanting the world, when every day our laboratories and our factories populate the world with hundreds of hybrids stranger than those of the day before?"[30] In attending to the nonhuman biological, earth systems, and outer space, the authors discussed here take a slightly different track from Latour's; what drives enchantment for them are not the strange man-made hybrids Latour alludes to, but the experience of forms and processes that can never be entirely rationalized.

2.1.3. What becomes of the disenchanted

It is not as if debunking or casting doubt on disenchantment, however, magically resurrects the "holistic, or participating, consciousness"[31] theoretically possible before the scientific revolution. Resisting the great disenchantment narrative also means resisting the idea of the cosmological garden of Eden in which a fully holistic, participating consciousness may have dwelled. It is, perhaps, better to accept that disenchantment lives side by side with enchantment in the lives of most and that the great disenchantment narrative is now simply in need of counterbalancing. If, after all, the disenchantment narrative is powerful enough to constitute a self-fulfilling prophecy, as Bennett suggests, counter-narratives have the potential to alter the manner in which we engage with and conceptualize reality.

The disenchantment theorists writing in the 1980s had interesting ideas for how one might overcome large-scale disenchantment, and even if one does not buy into the idea of disenchantment as a fall from an ecological and spiritual state of grace, they are worthy of attention. Berman suggests, for instance, that Gregory Bateson's work and cybernetic thought provide a possible avenue for bridging the canyon between subject and object created by this disenchantment. Others suggest that we learn to tell new, scientifically informed creation stories,

---

30 Ibid.
31 Berman, *Reenchantment of the World,* 32.

partaking in what Brian Swimme calls "cosmic storytelling."[32] In these accounts, science itself possesses the ability to reenchant and usher in a community of "Earthlings."[33] What many seem to agree on is Stephen Toulmin's assertion that, within a postmodern science, "the pure scientist's traditional posture as *theoros,* or spectator, can no longer be maintained."[34]

More recently, sociologist William Gibson has spoken of a number of counter-disenchantment currents he refers to as "the culture of enchantment."[35] For him, this new culture revolves around the "reinvestment of nature with spirit"[36] through environmental movements that seek to re-sacralize nature. The way in which they do this is not unproblematic, however, and he mentions the strategy of "tying a piece of land to a large, charismatic animal species — particularly animals nearing extinction" as a not terribly successful case in point, as the attempt to "restore the connection"[37] can lead to laughably shallow or specific relations to environments and environmental issues that are actually very complex.

Gibson also calls attention to efforts to replace religious cosmologies with "evolutionary epics," and cites E.O. Wilson himself as claiming that they are "as intrinsically ennobling as any religious epic."[38] The story of evolution, which many have argued is *the* story that science has to tell, is potentially a powerful counter-narrative, perhaps especially because it operates in biological and not human time. The scientific and industrial revolutions, at least in most accounts, do not constitute an evolutionary leap in and of themselves. In this sense, the biological,

32 Brian Swimme, "The Cosmic Creation Story," in *The Reenchantment of Science,* ed. David Ray Griffin (Albany: State University of New York Press, 1988), 47–56, at 47.

33 Ibid., 47.

34 Stephen Toulmin, *The Return to Cosmology: Postmodern Science and the Theology of Nature* (Berkeley: University of California Press, 1982), 255.

35 William Gibson, *A Reenchanted World: The Quest for a New Kinship with Nature* (New York: Holt Paperbacks, 2009), 11.

36 Ibid., 11.

37 Ibid., 73.

38 Ibid., 235.

religious epic can take us away from the anthropocentric narratives that are so essential to, for instance, a Weberian understanding of disenchantment.

But in this project I want to question whether science does not also and especially have something of a non-narrative nature (and culture) to contribute to reenchantment, or at least resisting the crippling disenchantment narratives. What I will present in the following chapters contains very little of the cosmological epic, but does, again and again, conjure up a world that is very much alive and brimming with potential. Unlike with the evolutionary or religious epic, however, these fabulous worlds, as Bennett terms them, are not purposive.[39] Although they often marvel at the miracle of intelligent life, for instance, it is a statistical miracle, and generally not cast as the work of a divine power or the inevitable result of billions of years of evolution. The authors I discuss may allude to the evolutionary epic, but the real power of the texts to enchant comes when they set this aside for a moment and focus on the immediacy of experience and the contingency of life. The enchantments are fragmentary, coming and going, much as in everyday life. Their lack of purposiveness and narrative cohesion does not make them any less engrossing, and, on the contrary, if this fragmentariness more closely resembles something like day-to-day experience, there are good reasons to claim that it "out-enchants" more narratively oriented texts. The type of enchantment these texts conjure up is that of "a window onto the virtual secreted within the actual."[40] It is not as if the enchantments we will confront in the following chapters refer us to an unseen transcendent realm. Instead, they look at the miraculous, contingent unfolding of the life processes that surround us. We will return to the notion of enchantment or wonder as a glimpse of the virtual later in this chapter.

For now, it is important to remember a number of things about the disenchantment story. The first is that it is deeply embedded in our understanding of modernity and the scientific

39 Bennett, *Enchantment of Modern Life*, 10.
40 Ibid., 131.

and industrial revolutions. As such, we can hardly think about the role of a supposedly enchanting science without seeing it as a response to this all-pervasive narrative of disenchantment. Secondly, the disenchantment story is just that — a story — and it is one we should take with a grain of salt. There are not only good reasons to doubt a cosmological garden of Eden succeeded by a rapid and violent spiritual fall, but given the pervasiveness of the narrative itself, it is likely that, as Bennett claims, it discourages the kind of investment in the world that might resemble enchantment in the first place; it is, in short, a self-fulfilling prophecy. The reason I have gone to such lengths to outline the disenchantment tale is not that I grant it any legitimacy, but rather because it is so pervasive. It is impossible to think through the texts in the following chapters without having any idea of *why* they pursue the strategies that they do. Popular science, I will argue, helps us to negotiate what comes after disenchantment, or at least the debunking of the disenchantment tale. Neither looking back with nostalgia on the animisms of the past nor viewing technoscience as the be-all, end-all of humanity, they insist on a third way, on affective investments in the world that are enriched and deepened by scientific worldviews.

2.2
One Way Out: Vital Materialism(s)

This third way could go by many different names, but in this work, I link it explicitly to Jane Bennett's "vital materialism," Brian Massumi's "incorporeal materialism," and Karen Barad's agential realism.[41] What they hold in common is a commitment to apprehending the world as a continuous unfolding of poten-

---

41 It should be noted that these texts also acknowledge much older "natural philosophical" precedents; see, for instance, Jane Bennett's discussion of Lucretius in *The Enchantment of Modern Life* (81–84). For reasons of economy, this book limits itself to more contemporary works.

tials, populated by entities that are simultaneously stubbornly indiscrete and in possession of agentic capacities. Everything in these worlds, organic and inorganic, pulses with something vital, with the capacity to become otherwise. Rather than locating this vitality in any substance or higher power, however, Bennett, Massumi, and Barad insist that the potential for transformation lies in the interaction (or, according to Barad, intraaction) of matter.

To jump back briefly to what was covered in the introduction: Affect is central here because it is, by definition, what interrelation feels like — that "experienced in a lived duration that involves the difference between two states."[42] Affect, as that which transpires between, forms the very fabric of experience. If the ecological takes the centrality of interrelation as its starting point, affective approaches, following Massumi, focus on *"the felt reality of relation."*[43] To this end, the virtual — the potential that permeates reality as it unfurls — is as significant as the measurable and material: the actual. Enchantment and wonder, as we will discuss in the next section, rely precisely on this potential that is no less real for being unlocatable, and we might recall here Massumi's description of the paradox of a phenomenon being "[r]eal, material, but incorporeal."[44] Attending fully to affect means admitting that sensation, though of the body, is not reducible to the strictly physiological.

This section fleshes out the understanding of affect and the quasi-vitalist frameworks in which one might situate affect, beginning with one of the thornier questions raised by incorporeal materialism: How can we discuss the immediacy of affect, unfolding in the present, when attempts to make sense of it necessarily impose a certain distance? It also looks at the related question of the distinction between affect and emotion and explains why this work concerns itself primarily with the

42 Gilles Deleuze, *Spinoza: Practical Philosophy,* trans. Robert Hurley (San Francisco: City Light Books, 1988), 49.

43 Brian Massumi, *Parables for the Virtual: Movement, Affect, Sensation* (Durham: Duke University Press, 2002), 16, emphasis in the original.

44 Ibid., 5.

former. The second part of this section, "Immanent subjectivity" examines the way in which a vital materialism or incorporeal materialism problematizes more discrete notions of subjectivity, and elaborates how we might understand the inter- and intra-connected ecological subject. The last subsection, "Scientific entanglements," brings this understanding to bear on the figure of the scientist, who, according to Barad, is but another entangled actor among many. The scientist is not only a key figure in this project, which, after all, revolves around the writing of three scientists, but also one essential to understanding these strange materialisms, in which the subject is always already caught up in that which he or she has deemed object.

2.2.1. Mediated immediacy

We may as well confront the fact that we can never speak of affect in any pure, unadulterated sense. As Annie Dillard observes, "The present of my consciousness is itself a mystery which is also always just rounding a bend like a floating branch borne by a flood."[45] And in the context of this work, there are at least two bends: I am writing about authors that are writing about experience. It would be folly to think immediacy is being dealt with directly. Affect is always already mediated, but this neither means that we should dismiss what happens in the present, nor entirely give up hope of discussing it.

Massumi acknowledges fully that even before we talk about affect, before we filter phenomena via language, the very process of becoming cognizant of it complicates matters. We are warned: "[S]ensation is never simple. It is always doubled by the feeling of having a feeling. It is self-referential. […] It is an immediate self-complication. It is best to think of it as a resonation, or interference pattern."[46] This has implications for this work, first of all, in that I make no claim to access affect directly. Indeed, as will be seen, I accord to wonder the status of affect which precedes

---

45 Annie Dillard, "The Present," in *Pilgrim at Tinker Creek* (New York: Harper & Row, 1974), 9–28, at 93.
46 Massumi, *Parables for the Virtual*, 13–14.

and makes way for other affects. This resonance, far from being a conceptual hurdle, is essential to it. But this "interference pattern" inherent to affect also means that looking at affective elements of writing is as good a way as any of investigating affective engagements in the ecosphere. The sooner one reconciles oneself to the idea that consciousness, let alone communication, of even the most basic sensations inevitably involves mediation, the more comfortable one becomes contenting oneself with affective traces in writing that may be picked up, followed, but that have no proper end to their reverberation or origin. Certainly, the texts here not only attempt to conjure immediacy but also contain meta-reflections on affective experience.

The second implication of the inevitable mediatedness of affect concerns its place in nature/nurture discussions. Our affective engagements with the environment can neither be described as entirely pre-cognitive (innate) nor entirely conscientious, because of this very doubling-back of sensation described by Massumi. This allows us here not only to view approaches that insist on the naturalness of particular modes of human/environment interaction, such as Wilson's own sociobiology, suspiciously, but also those that are perhaps overly constructivist. Following Spinoza, we do not know beforehand what a body or mind can do, we cannot circumscribe the range of affects, yet we also cannot say that with everybody, not to mention every body, everything is possible. Potentials are neither fully ours, nor assigned to us, neither fully innate nor learned. This project does not concern itself with why we attend to certain things, or to what end, only with the fact that we attend to them in the first place. The focus shifts, then, from the nature/nurture dichotomy, from origins, to the relation itself.

It is also important to note that this understanding of affect is not synonymous with emotion, although emotion must of necessity possess an affective basis. Massumi has described "perception and cognition" as the "capture and closure of affect," and writes that "[e]motion is the most intense (most contracted expression of that *capture*)."[47] We may, then, differentiate affect from emotion based, first of all, upon the idea that emotion involves a becoming-conscious of sensation or affect, and, secondly, the notion that emotion is somehow a more concentrated, perhaps even a more coordinated, manifestation of affect. If affect is fleeting, emotion is, in other words, less so.

The distinction between affect and emotion becomes even more meaningful when we consider emotion as affect interpreted, or "the ideological attempt to make sense of some affective productions."[48] Massumi defines emotion as "the sociolinguistic fixing of the quality of an experience which is from that point onward defined as personal," and for this reason, it is always "qualified intensity," "intensity owned and recognized."[49] Emotion is thus of the subject, while affect, strictly speaking, cannot be confined to it. Certainly a whole arsenal of words for wonder and enchantment do something to fix them as emotions, as qualified intensities that persist in time, but I will argue that the texts in this work focus on a more impersonal, incoherent, unsentimental wonder — not as romantic indulgence in superficial emotion, but a more fleeting feeling or sensation. What is of primary interest, then, is wonder as affect rather than emotion.

An important question is whether one might discuss pre-emotional affective productions without recourse to the language of emotion. In other words, we ought to critically assess whether the immediacy of affect might somehow find semiotic preservation. To imagine that writing does not ideologically invest affective productions is certainly naïve, and yet this project loses meaning if we cannot somehow make reference to the world of sensation and the virtual. But what we find in the corpus is not simply writing that references particular "affective assemblages." It may take this as a starting point, but it then turns to concepts like attentiveness and attunement, and often openly

47 Massumi, *Parables for the Virtual*, 35.
48 Lawrence Grossberg, "Affect's Future: Rediscovering the Virtual in the Actual," in *The Affect Theory Reader*, eds. Gregory J. Seigworth and Melissa Gregg (Durham: Duke University Press, 2010), 309–38, at 316.
49 Massumi, *Parables for the Virtual*, 28.

refuses the task of fully communicating the individual affective experience. By and large, then, these texts make a concerted attempt to avoid the emotional or sentimental, and opt, rather, to serve as a guide to exploring intensities, whether those happen to be microscopic or cosmological.

2.2.2. Immanent subjectivity

What's most significant about the affective encounter for ecological ethics is its disruptive or transformative potential. Rather than reassuring of us of our human relation to the ecosphere, affect ought, at least sometimes, to challenge it. Davide Panagia, in the realm of the political, casts affective experiences as "moments of breakdown," which "interrupt the assurances that guarantee the slumber of subjectivity."[50] These stand in stark opposition to, for instance, pleas to save the children, which, as Edelman reminds us, rely on the belief that the contemporary social order is worth perpetuating. It bears mentioning, however, that despite the potential affect possesses for spurring us to revise our conceptions of the world, it does not do so in any way that is uniform or predictable. Affective ecologies, on their own, cannot form the basis for the kind of ecological ethics that could, for instance, be legislated. They do form, however, an ideal position for exploring the depth and breadth of human relations to the ecosphere.

A focus on affective dimensions of the ecological thus frees us from the binds of a future-oriented ethics because it does not make the same assumptions about the human, let alone the subject, that more traditional ecologies do. These are ecologies that no longer speak the language of responsible citizenship, that place no special focus on the children or the perpetuation of the species. Affective ecologies address registers that undeniably passionate cries to save the future, *à la* Trilford or Suzuki, leave entirely unaddressed. Although these pleas are nothing if not intensely emotional, they rely on very limited notions of the

---

50 David Panagia, *The Political Life of Sensation* (Durham: Duke University Press, 2009), 3–4.

human, drawing, at one and the same time, on an idea of the *anthropos* as the selfless creature with a (perhaps rather cavalier) faith in the ability and desire to maintain and perpetuate the Western progress narrative, and notions of the human as merely a biopolitical entity that must continue to proliferate at any cost. The study of affect, on the other hand, is not limited strictly to the human and certainly does not make the same assumptions about legitimate reasons to act. It may not, in fact, help us immediately to act at all, but it does illuminate precisely how narrow our definition(s) of the human have become. Michael Hardt, in a spin on the classic Spinozan dictum, states, "We do not know in advance what a body can do, what a mind can think — what affects they are capable of. The perspective of the affects requires an exploration of these as yet unknown powers."[51] The "perspective of the affects" is not interested in entirely abandoning the human, but enlarging it, providing, "a new ontology of the human or, rather, an ontology of the human that is constantly open and renewed."[52] Indeed, it is the very acknowledgment of our creatureliness that contains the potential for the transformation of the human. Traditional environmental ethics preclude this radical ontological shift.

2.2.3. *Scientific entanglements*

Given that so much of this project rests on scientists who are profoundly mixed up in that which they examine, scientific inquiry ought also to be placed in this vital/incorporeal materialist or agential realist framework. Karen Barad, herself trained as a scientist and the originator of the term "agential realism," does just this. Knowing, for her, is entirely tangled up with experience, and the activity of "wondering at" slips ceaselessly into "wondering with." Indeed, she questions the very models of objectivity and distance the scientists in this project hold dear,

51 Michael Hardt, "Foreword: What Affects are Good For," in *The Affective Turn: Theorizing the Social,* eds. Patricia Ticineto Clough and Jean Halley (Durham: Duke University Press, 2007), ix–xiii, at x.
52 Ibid., x.

but boldly elucidates the entangled science that, at least in their most popular works, they appear to practice.

The agential realist ontology is, in its emphasis on perpetual becoming and broadening of the category of agency, strikingly similar to incorporeal and vital materialist accounts. Barad writes, "phenomena — whether lizards, electrons, or humans — exist only as a result of, and as part of, the world's ongoing intra-activity, its dynamic and contingent differentiation into specific relationalities."[53] "'We humans,'" it follows, "don't make it so, not by dint of our own will, and not on our own. But through our advances, we participate in bringing forth the world in its specificity, including ourselves."[54] Barad explains, again and again, that there is no such thing as human exceptionalism. We do not wander a globe that, were it not for us, would operate *just so*; we participate fully in the formation and co-creation of what we call nature. In this way, too, agential realism calls for a radical non-anthropocentrism: We do not merely do things to matter. Barad insists, "Bodies are not of the world; they are part of the world."[55] She goes on to clarify:

The world is an ongoing intra-active engagement, and bodies are among the differential performances of the world's dynamic intra-activity, in an endless reconfiguring of boundaries and properties, including those of spacetime. Technoscientific and other practices entail space-time-matter-in-the-making. Nothing stands separately constituted and positioned inside a spacetime frame of reference, nor does there exist a divine position for our viewing pleasure located outside the world. There is no absolute inside or absolute outside. There is only exteriority within, that is, agential separability. *Embodiment is a matter not of being specifically*

---

53 Karen Barad, *Meeting the Universe Halfway: Quantum Physics and the Entanglement of Matter and Meaning* (Durham: Duke University Press, 2007), 353.
54 Ibid.
55 Ibid., 176.

situated in the world, but rather of being in the world in its dynamic specificity.[56]

This is another way to describe the condition of immanence, which, after all, Deleuze described as "a life."[57] We are not only of the world (are not only brought forth by it), but we, too, bring it forth. We do not only watch the actual drop like a fruit from the virtual, but ourselves cause it sometimes to drop.

But there is more to Barad's agential realism than the contention that we, the human, participate constantly in making, re-making, and un-making the world. She also insists that other actors, known and unknown to us, continually accomplish the same thing. As a result, there is no properly passive object of human knowledge. She writes, "There is more to nature than 'nature-as-the-object-of-human-knowledge. The latter constitutes a re-veiling (which provokes the seeming need for revealing) of nature, yet again."[58] Making discrete actors or phenomena the object of human knowledge entails the impossible task of cloaking only them, followed by a prestige in which they are, as if by magic, brought back into the world. The way in which we know is not only very selective for Barad, then, but neglects the intra-activity of that which we deem "object." Barad observes:

> Boundary-making practices do not merely pick out the epistemic object, backgrounding the rest. And scientific practices are not merely practices of knowing, and the knowledge produced is not ours alone. Even in direct challenges to Western philosophy's traditional conceptions of epistemology, there is a tendency to continue to think of knowers as human subjects, albeit appropriately hooked into our favorite technological prostheses."[59]

56 Ibid., 376–77, emphasis in original.
57 See Gilles Deleuze, "Immanence: A Life," in *Pure Immanence: Essays on A Life*, trans. Anne Boyman (New York: Zone Books, 2001), 25–34, at 27.
58 Barad, *Meeting the Universe Halfway*, 378.
59 Ibid.

Knowing is not nature revealing herself to us, but a set of material practices that give us limited insight into the world ongoing intra-activity. Subject and object, therefore, are not pre-existing categories, but emergent ones "that are enacted."[60]

This alternative epistemological and ontological account already has important implications for science as a way of knowing. The most obvious is that "To the extent that humans participate in scientific or other practices of knowing, they do so as part of the larger material configuration of the world and its ongoing open-ended articulation."[61] Knowing occurs through intra-action. This becomes important for the works in this project because they present the human and especially the scientist as not only deeply embedded in the field and the world, but as themselves part of what is so often viewed merely as background for human dramas. As we will see, wonder and enchantment often "happen" at precisely the moment that object is revealed as possessing agentic capacities. In these instances, the boundaries are redrawn; the scientist ceases to occupy a fixed and defined position from which he or she can be observed and, instead, dissolves in the world's intra-activity. And Barad insists, time and time again, that we, the humans, the animals, the strictly "living," do not possess a monopoly on agency. For her, "agency is understood as an enactment and not something someone has."[62] Science, at its most progressive, involves the recognition of nonhuman agencies — those enactments that happen because of, but just or more often, despite us, which we in turn struggle eternally to understand with our own intricate agency. Knowing is possible not only because we choose to manipulate matter in the world, but because that matter is active to begin with.

The second implication Barad's agential realism holds for science is that it means we do not always "murder to dissect."[63] While Barad adheres to a realist conception of science in main-

60 Ibid., 359.
61 Ibid., 379.
62 Ibid., 214.
63 William Wordsworth, "The Tables Turned," in *The Complete Poetical Works of William Wordsworth* (London: Moxon, Son, & Co., 1869), 361.

taining that it involves the investigation of things *really* happening (She speaks of "the objective existence of particular material phenomena"), she also maintains: "Objectivity is a matter of accountability for what materializes, for what comes to be. It matters which cuts are enacted: different cuts enact different materialized becomings."[64] Objectivity is not a stance, but a practice, and one that must be negotiated and adjusted again and again in order to produce phenomena that cohere to or build upon previous bodies of knowledge. As a scientist, one does not merely operate on inert material in order to reconfirm what was previously thought. Rather, "different cuts enact different materialized becomings." We do not merely murder to dissect, or kill in order to know; we also vivisect, create and nurture life, in order to see what is possible, to know more.

This entangled science, as we shall see, is a profoundly useful complement to Massumi and Bennett's vital/incorporeal materialism. What Barad succeeds so well in doing is exploding the myth of knowledge creation happening above and apart from the object of that knowledge without wholly discounting science itself. Science explains and discovers phenomena, but not by dint of its apartness. It may seek to understand "the world's ongoing intra-activity," but it cannot do so away from or above it. Scientific practice involves actualizing potential just as much as it involves the study of the actualization of these potentials.

What is striking about both Barad and Bennett's work is that ontological claims are nearly always followed by ethical ones. Understanding intra-activity and vitality always entails the recognition of and respect for the nonhuman, and vice-versa. Barad writes: "Learning how to intra-act responsibly as part of the world means understanding that "we" are not the only active beings — though this is never justification for deflecting our responsibility onto others."[65] Recognizing nonhuman agency, inevitably, plants the seeds for a non-anthropocentric ethics. Bennett explores this even more explicitly:

64 Barad, *Meeting the Universe Halfway,* 361, 214.
65 Ibid., 391.

Why advocate the vitality of matter? Because my hunch is that the image of dead or thoroughly instrumentalized matter feeds human hubris and our earth-destroying fantasies of conquest and consumption. […] The figure of an intrinsically inanimate matter may be one of the impediments to the emergence of more ecological and more materially sustainable modes of production and consumption.[66]

Recasting the world as dynamic becoming, of which we the human are only a part, means that we have no choice but to care about the other actors. Certainly, what it means to "meet the universe halfway, to take responsibility for the role that we play in the world's differential becoming"[67] is far from a straightforward matter. But Barad and Bennett both insist that the first step is to care. The enchanting tactics employed by the works of popular science discussed here, I will argue, aim to accomplish this first step. They do so by exploring and inducing wonder, a phenomenon that involves a temporary suspension of subjectivity and with it, the specter of objectivity.

2.3 New Attunements: Understanding Affective Wonder

Already, then, one might see how "a science that meets the universe halfway" — that takes up a vital materialism — might run counter to the disenchantment narrative. To understand how this operates in the works investigated here, however, it first bears examining how we can understand wonder as the action of reenchantment. This section begins with a broad approach to wonder, using its loosely phenomenological articulation to connect it provisionally with affect, and to explore it as both a

---

66 Jane Bennett, *Vibrant Matter: A Political Ecology of Things* (Durham: Duke University Press, 2011), ix.
67 Barad, *Meeting the Universe*, 396.

disruptive phenomenon and something cultivatable and related to habit. The second section then focuses more explicitly on scientific wonder, taking up Uexküll's notion of the Umwelt as a way to understand the novelty with which wonder confronts us.

2.3.1. Wonderstruck, again and again?

That "wondering" happens in the present takes no great effort of imagination, but tracing its precise relation to the affective involves some work. As the introduction touched upon, Martha Nussbaum refers to it as one of the only emotions that does not qualify as eudemonistic, or connected to one's own "goals and projects."[68] Instead she claims it is a responding to "the pull of the object,"[69] when the "subject is maximally aware of the value of the object, and only minimally aware, if at all, of its relationship to her own plans."[70] Although, as will be shown, subject and object become problematic divisions when speaking about wonder, particularly in an ecological context, one can at least take away from this that wonder forms a kind of intense engagement with the present, in which our orientation towards the future ("goals and projects") is at least partially suspended.

Indeed, in many accounts, that of the seventeenth-century painter Charles Le Brun included, wonder is a kind of paralysis in the face of the new or exceptional. In a 1668 lecture, Le Brun refers to wonder as "the first of all passions," continuing:

Wonder is a surprise which causes the soul to consider attentively objects which seem to it rare and extraordinary, and this surprise is sometimes so powerful that it pushes the spirits towards the place whence the impression of the object is received, and they are so much occupied in considering this

---

68 Martha Nussbaum, *Upheavals of Thought: The Intelligence of Emotions* (Cambridge: Cambridge University Press, 2001), 53–54.
69 Ibid., 54.
70 Ibid.

impression that there are none left to pass thence into the muscles; the body therefore remains motionless as a statue.[71]

My contention here, and this aligns well with Le Brun's account, is that wonder constitutes a special kind of affect, a kind of primary affect that enables the experience of a whole host of others.[72] Affective wonder as dealt with in this work may be expressed as *the realization that the affects one is undergoing are new,* or, expressed in slightly different terms, it might be called *a sudden attunement to affects that one had not been attuned to before.* More Deleuzian vocabulary, which we will return to in the next subsection, might cast it as something like a sensitivity to new becomings. As such, wonder is precipitated as much by transformative experience as by intention and practice. I have chosen, in this section, to focus on the work of phenomenologist Howard Parsons, largely because he is one of the few theorists to mention wonder, at least its more immediate variants, more than peripherally,[73] and Jakob von Uexküll, who provides a much more explicitly affective framework and upon whom Deleuze and Guattari also drew heavily.[74]

---

71 Charles Le Brun, "Le Brun's Lecture on Expression," trans. Jennifer Montagu, in Jennifer Montagu, *The Expression of the Passions: The Origin and Influence of Charles Le Brun's "Conference sur l'expression generale et particulare"* (New Haven: Yale University Press, 1994), 125–40, at 127.

72 In this it is also distinctive from the sublime, which signals the supposed triumph of reason over the unassimilable — when "the mind has been incited to abandon sensibility" (see Kant's *Critique of Judgment,* trans. James Creed Meredith [Oxford: Oxford University Press, 2007], 76). This work has attempted to avoid, as much as possible, language related to the sublime, insisting rather on the manner in which the subject does not entirely come to terms with the infinite.

73 Nussbaum, despite claiming to discuss wonder in *Upheavals of Thought,* actually does so on precious few occasions. We will return to a few of her remarks at the end of this chapter, however.

74 Doubtless a much more exhaustive history of the concept, especially concerning Renaissance conceptions of wonder and the *Wunderkammer,* would be possible, but time forces a certain amount of selectivity. See Lorraine Daston and Kathrine Park, *Wonders and the Order of Nature, 1150–1750* (New York: Zone Books, 2001).

But before delving into the philosophical treatment of wonder, the lay definition also bears mentioning. In the *Oxford English Dictionary,* "wonder" as a noun may be:

the emotion[75] excited by the perception of something novel and unexpected or inexplicable; astonishment mingled with perplexity or bewildered curiosity. Also, the state of mind in which emotion exists; and an instance of this; a fit of wonderment.[76]

Already a dual character of wonder is implied here: It involves, on the one hand, a certain distance from the stimulus, a realization of novelty, but this also constitutes, on the other hand, an experience in and of itself. One might think back to Brian Massumi's assertion that sensation "is always doubled by the feeling of having a feeling," and, as such, is more accurately a kind of resonating than a phenomenon discretely captured.[77]

More speculative etymology links wonder to the Old English *wundor,* which Parsons writes "might be cognate with the German *Wunde* or wound."[78] Though Parsons published his "Philosophy of Wonder" in 1969, his rhetoric, at times, appears strikingly similar to more contemporary theorists who, like Davide Panagia, insist on the disruptive nature of affect. Parsons continues the discussion of wonder as wound:

It would thus suggest a breach in the membrane of awareness, a sudden opening in a man's system of established and expected meanings, a blow as if one were struck or stunned.

75 Although the word "emotion" is employed here, my contention is that wonder, as affect, can just as easily be described as a sensation. Certainly ideological investment renders it something more like an emotion, but it may also describe states that are less coherent.

76 See *Oxford English Dictionary Online,* s.v. "wonder," https:// en.oxforddictionaries.com/definition/wonder.

77 Massumi, *Parables for the Virtual,* 13, 14.

78 Howard L. Parsons, "A Philosophy of Wonder," *Philosophy and Phenomenological Research* 30, no. 1 (1969): 84–101, at 85.

To be wonderstruck is to be wounded by the sword of a strange event, to be stabbed awake by the striking.[79]

Wonder, here, consists of something distinctly different from "wondering." Although curiosity may render the perception of a "strange event" more likely, wonder as wound involves a precognitive element, although it is never an exclusively pre-cognitive phenomenon. Wonder, here, speaking figuratively, "happens" not merely when some aspect of the world knocks, but also when it steals in, and subsequently comes face to face with the subject. (This does not necessarily mean, as we will see in a moment, that wonder comes unbidden.) Wonder can thus be termed precognitive only to the extent that, in whatever way, we cannot account for or order it, but it generally involves a retrospective recognition of the limits or inadequacy of the cogito and some process of assimilation that must be cognitive in character. For Parsons, this initial shock is always followed by an attempt by the cogito to assign meaning to and assimi-late the experience.[80] While I do not necessarily disagree with this sense-making process, this book and this chapter concern themselves with this first and more elemental stab: "the spark of excitation leaping across the gap between man and the world."[81]

Parsons is certainly not the only author to frame wonder as an instance of the nonhuman world invading what is popularly perceived as human. Rachel Carson, the famed author of *Silent*

79 Ibid., 85.

80 Significantly, however, it is not the assimilation, the "aha" moment, as with Cartesian models of wonder, that produces or motivates the phenomenon itself. For an exhaustive description of Cartesian wonder, which I will not deal with substantively in this work, see Philip Fisher's *Wonder, the Rainbow, and the Aesthetics of Rare Experiences* (Cambridge: Harvard University Press, 1998). In connection with these very different under-standings of wonder, Robert Fuller makes a distinction between the dis-positions of curiosity, always oriented in some way towards mastery of the surroundings, and wonder, which focuses on "intrinsic value or meaning." See Robert Fuller, *Wonder: From Emotion to Spirituality* (Chapel Hill: The University of North Carolina Press, 2006), 8–9.

81 Parsons, "Philosophy of Wonder," 85.

Spring, refers to wonder as a "recognition of something beyond the boundaries of human existence."[82] Here, with Carson's attempt to articulate a particularly non-anthropocentric phenomenon, we draw close to Deleuze and Guattari's "non-human becomings of man," in which we "are not in the world, we become the world; we become by contemplating it."[83] Wonder, in other words, involves the suspension of the systems that we so often believe constitute us as discrete subjects — language and culture — even if it is these same systems that sometimes allow the experience of wonder to begin or help to make sense of it later. It is no accident, then, that experiences of wonder often precede a more principled engagement with ecological interconnectedness; it flies in the face of our anthropocentrism.

Parsons, notably, also recognizes degrees of wonder. At the one end, and exhibiting a milder form, is a type that elicits merely a "signifying interest."[84] It invites the subject to make sense of the contents of the experience, to place it in some sort of signifying framework. The other end of the spectrum is composed of the basically unassimilable, and "may be so affectively unifying and overmastering that the symbolic meaning cannot grasp or accommodate it; it becomes, in the report of the mystic, ineffable."[85] Parsons makes the further distinction between these two types or degrees: the wonder associated with a "signifying interest" involves an active, fully conscious subject. This more profound kind of wonder, involving an element of surprise, is, on the other hand, described as follows:

> To be surprised (*super* + *prehendre*) is to be taken over and taken up. It is to be subjected to an innovating experience or creation whose occurring or novelty is beyond one's con-

82 Rachel Carson, *The Sense of Wonder* (New York: Harper & Row, 1998), 100.

83 Gilles Deleuze and Félix Guattari, *What Is Philosophy?* trans. Hugh Tomlinson and Graham Burchell (New York: Columbia University Press, 1994), 169.

84 Parsons, "Philosophy of Wonder," 93.

85 Ibid.

scious control and is felt vividly. Within such wonder, however, lies the disposition to act and to take a part in the forming of one's experience. Wonder of this type is thus a kind of suspended animation, a balance and a tension between a passive mood and an incipiently perceptual and active mood. In some mystical experience the latter mood appears to be more or less nullified.[86]

Wonder, as the experience of the ineffable, I would like to suggest, not only means that the "passive mood" acquires the upper, or at least equal, hand in experience, but that it shakes the very foundations of the "active mood" itself. This becomes especially pertinent when discussing ecological wonder, where revelations regarding energetic and material interconnectedness swiftly undermine supposedly commonsense notions of human agency and discreteness.

It is no accident, either, that Parsons associates at least some varieties of wonder with mystic experience. Varadaraja Raman argues that mystic experience includes a "mysterious plunge into an aspect of the world that is sometimes described as oceanic" and that "the becoming conscious of a normally inaccessible aspect of the universe," also noting that it need not be tied to religion in the traditional sense (i.e. those systems concerned with prophetic revelation).[87] This is not far at all from our working definition of wonder as a sudden attunement to affects that one had not been attuned to before. Mystic experience seems to constitute, or be constituted by, especially dramatic or intense experiences of wonder.[88]

86 Ibid., 94.
87 Varadaraja Raman, "Vielfalt in der Mystik und Parallelen zur Naturwissenschaft," in *Biomystik,* ed. Christoph F.E. Holzhey (Munich: Wilhelm Fink Verlag, 2007), 61–79, at 63, 64, translation mine.
88 In order to limit the scope of inquiry, this work does not engage with Eastern philosophy; nevertheless, there are doubtless countless connections to be drawn between descriptions of mystic experience found within any number of Eastern sources and the affectively novel and wonderful. Robert Fuller, for instance, points to the concept of darshan in the Indic tradition, or "the ritual act of seeing divinity," which goes far beyond the emotions

And it should also be noted that the second kind of wonder mentioned by Parsons, the one akin to mystic experience, is not always "wondrous" in the sense of pleasant. The nature writer Annie Dillard has made a career in masterfully articulating moments when articulation fails and either terror or exaltation sets in. She describes the witnessing of the total eclipse, for instance, as "like dying, [...] like the death of someone, irrational, that sliding down the mountain pass. It was like slipping into fever, or falling down that hole in sleep from which you wake yourself whimpering."[89] In this particular episode, she regains her composure only when another witness describes the obscured sun as looking "like a Life Saver up in the sky."[90] The eclipse may have allowed her to glimpse, and indeed become aware of, the goings-on of the cosmos, but the force of it overshadows terrestrial life. Negative experiences of wonder may indeed be alienating or nullifying.

What is key to Dillard's encounter, as well, is the relation between the precognitive, here the ineffable experience of the eclipse, and the cognitive, here the attempt to place it back within the realm of the social, within language. Dillard encounters relief only when the event's immediacy, its affective dimensions, become expressible, declaring, "All those things for which we have no words are lost."[91] She does not specify what might be lost in the attempt to find words for things, i.e., whether the ability to subsume the event linguistically lessens its initial impact.

Parsons, on the other hand, claims that it does, arguing that the physical and metaphorical flattening out of experience is responsible for the ordinary. Ordinary experience is accomplished by "the flattening out of the wild, erratic flora and protruding peaks and outcroppings — by blueprints, bulldozers,

of curiosity or surprise popularly associated with wonder today (*Wonder*, 10–11).

89 Annie Dillard, "Total Eclipse," in *Teaching a Stone to Talk* (New York: Harper Collins, 1982), 9–28, at 9.

90 Ibid., 23.

91 Ibid., 24.

superhighways."[92] It does not take too much effort to imagine that this "wild, erratic flora" and these "protruding peaks" are conceived of as major sources of wonder. Mechanisms for understanding phenomena can also constitute a kind of flattening here; Parson remarks that, before they became well understood by a large percentage of the population, thunderstorms, eclipses, and comets also elicited wonder.[93] The effort to draw an experience into the signifying system, for Parsons, also inevitably constitutes an effort to render it ordinary.

Where Parson's argument becomes most interesting, however, is when he talks about habit. It is not as if ordinary experience is synonymous with habit, and wonder always disruptive of it, but "fits of wonder" are themselves often determined by habitual mechanisms: "Thus the conditioning effects of habit tend to determine not only what we regard as ordinary, but also what we are ready to respond to as wonderful."[94] Thus, a writer such as Dillard, who has staked her existence on the experience and subsequent articulation of "fits of wonderment," might be much more likely to experience wonder during an eclipse (despite understanding the mechanics of it perfectly well) than someone who is not accustomed to looking up at the sky.

As I will discuss later, the notion that explicability detracts from the wonderful is expressly challenged by both Sagan and Wilson.[95] The two authors, in fact, argue that understanding increases wonder. My argument forms a kind of compromise. I contend not that understanding is a flattening out, nor that it possesses the ability to make experience more wondrous, but that it is always more complex than that. Understanding, like the experience of wonder, can itself alter habits and forms of attention. One must acknowledge that the ability to place expe-

92 Parsons, "Philosophy of Wonder," 86.
93 Ibid.
94 Ibid.
95 Not to mention Richard Dawkins. His *Unweaving the Rainbow* (New York: First Mariner Books, 2000) is a lengthy refutation of Keats's poetic claim that "Newton had destroyed all the poetry of the rainbow by reducing it to the prismatic colours" (x).

riences of the ineffable, the marvelously precognitive, in a signifying framework, might preclude a certain intensity in future
experiences along these lines. But the authors I deal with also
consistently imply that, both in terms of scale and intricacy, life
and the cosmos are inexhaustible. There is no such thing as fit-
ting "it all" into a signifying framework, and the drive to discover and place the ineffable may in fact put one more often in contact with it. One may, in other words, talk about "the practice of
wonder" non-oxymoronically. If we return to the affective, this
means that "transformation and sedimentation"[96] are not always
at odds with one another. Wonder may indeed beget wonder,
and the habits that allow us access to that outside ourselves do
not necessarily detract from the intensity of the experience.

But still, although Parsons gives us an idea of how we might
conceive of the concept of wonder and the experience of it, however passive or active, extraordinary or conditioned by ordinary
experience, he does not exactly give us a way to think novelty, of
precisely how the subject encounters something outside itself.

2.3.2. When Umwelten collide: wonder with Uexküll
One may bypass these binaries of the active versus passive
subject and ordinary experience, or sedimentation, versus the
experience of wonder, or transformation, by looking back to
the work of Jakob von Uexküll, an ethologist active in the late
nineteenth and early twentieth centuries who was revived by
Deleuze and Guattari. Uexküll himself never discusses wonder
explicitly, but his notion of the dynamic *Umwelt,* or the subjective surroundings of an organism, serves to ground the notion
of wonder more effectively in the affective and allows us a way to
conceive of new affects. Indeed, wonder may be further elabo-
rated in Uexküll's terminology *as the experience of the expansion*

---

96 See Lisa Blackman, "Habit and Affect: Revitalizing a Forgotten History,"
    Body & Society 19, no. 186 (2013): 186–216, at 188.

of the individual Umwelt[97] via the experience of new affects. For Uexküll, this is a natural, and mostly inevitable, process:

> As the number of an animal's performances grows, the number of objects that populate its *Umwelt* increases. It grows within the individual life span of every animal that is able to gather experiences. For each new experience entails an adjustment to new impressions.[98]

Thus, the *Umwelt* of the tick, supposed by Uexküll, with its three limited affects (climbing toward the light, dropping from a branch upon smelling mammalian sweat, burrowing and latching on where it is warm)[99] is extremely small, and the capacity for the expansion of this *Umwelt,* or wonder, is likely limited at best. While nonhuman animals could certainly also experience wonder in this framework, the human is perhaps the most interesting subject because there are, at this point in time, virtually no restrictions to the boundary of the human *Umwelt.* This does not mean that we possess the capability to expand our actual territory and colonize the planets of faraway suns, but it has rather something to do with the fact that objects and phenomena in space may strike us. Though a comet may be oblivious to the whole episode, any number of humans may have an encounter with it (whether with the naked eye or with the aid of technologies) that produces wonder.

Indeed, Uexküll firmly insists on the significance of virtual *Umwelten.* These "magic *Umwelten*" not only exist for chil-

---

97 It must be noted, however, that despite using the word "expansion," this does not entail any traditional kind of expansionism. Rather than only, or even necessarily, including growth in the sphere of perception in spatial terms, expansion of the individual *Umwelt* can mean increased attunement at any level. New affects may be experienced on the micro-level, just as on the cosmic, and over longer stretches of time just as easily as in fleeting microseconds.

98 Jakob von Uexküll, "A Stroll Through the Worlds of Animals and Men: A Picture Book of Invisible Worlds," trans. Claire Schiller, *Semiotica* 89, no. 4 (1992): 319–91, at 359.

99 Ibid., 322–26.

dren and "primitive peoples," but also for the "highly cultured European"[100] and potentially many nonhuman animals. To illustrate how magic *Umwelten* operate, Uexküll examines the same subject, an oak tree, as viewed by various actors: For the forester, the oak tree is merely a resource, "a few cords of wood,"[101] despite the fact that its knobs look like a human face. For a little girl, however, "[t]he whole oak has become a threatening demon."[102] But Uexküll does not stop at the human. For the fox, the oak tree's roots provide a roof and protection.[103] The owl, similarly, seeks shelter under the branches, whereas for the squirrel, the oak is many things, including, "a wealth of comfortable jumping boards"[104]while for the ant the oak is an entire hunting ground. For the bark-boring beetle, which eats the oak, and the woodpecker, which eats the beetle, the oak is different still. Uexküll's point, in the end, is this:

> Should we attempt to epitomize all the contradictory properties which the oak tree as an object displays, only chaos would result. And yet they are all but parts of a subject firmly structured in itself, which bears and harbors these *Umwelten* — not comprehended and never discernible to the builders of these *Umwelten*.[105]

Umwelten are virtual environments populated by actual objects that themselves inevitably possess virtual dimensions. That they are not transparent to those who live them does not mean that changes within or to them go unnoticed, however. Thus it is with wonder, which is the expansion of the boundaries of the magical or virtual *Umwelt* made perceptible. In many cases, in fact, it is when the subject, or explorer-scientist, discovers one of the other manifold properties of a familiar object that wonder

100 Ibid., 376, 378.
101 Ibid., 378.
102 Ibid., 384.
103 Ibid., 386.
104 Ibid., 386–87, 387.
105 Ibid., 388.

"sets in." The human may marvel at the squirrel's acrobatic use of the oak tree as much as the woodpecker's efficient drilling of it for food.

The very end of Uexküll's essay concerns the *Umwelten* of scientists, and, as the remainder of the chapter examines the attempts of two select scientists to share the expansion of their own *Umwelten,* the passage is worth quoting at length. The *Umwelten* of scientists reveal, perhaps, just how radically different the *Umwelten* of members of a single species may become. Uexküll writes:

> High on his tower, as far as possible from the earth, sits a human being. He has so transformed his eyes, with the aid of gigantic optical instruments, that they have become fit to penetrate the universe up to the most distant stars. In his Umwelt, suns and planets circle in festive procession. Fleet-footed light takes millions of years to travel through his *Umwelt* space.
>
> And yet this whole *Umwelt* is only a tiny sector of nature, tailored to the faculties of the human subject.
>
> With slight alterations, the astronomer's image can be used to gain a conception of the deep-sea researcher's *Umwelt*. Only here, instead of constellations, the fantastic shapes of deep-sea fish wheel around his sphere with their uncanny mouths, long tentacles and radial light organs. Here again, *we glance into a real world, which constitutes a small sector of nature.*[106]

The figure of the scientist may be unique, insofar as he or she is trained to recognize the constraints of his or her *Umwelt*. The scientist's supposition must routinely rest on the idea that, however valid the "real world" observed may be, it only "constitutes a small sector of nature." Thus scientific work consists, in countless different ways, of the expansion of this small sector: the collection of data, the refinement of instruments of observation,

106 Ibid., 389–90, emphasis added.

cooperation with other scientists, and methods of synthesiz-
ing data. When this small sector, the individual or collective
scientific *Umwelt,* is expanded, it is indeed a cause or occasion for wonder. This affect, especially given the heavy literal
and figurative public investment in science, is not limited to
the researchers themselves. As a dramatic case in point, one
might cite the enormous public interest in space exploration,
which "can be identified even in national contexts lacking direct access to spaceflight before the late 1970s,"[107] and the twentieth-century romantic identification of the Space Age as "the
greatest age of all."[108] One need not even experience new affects
firsthand in order to wonder. An image, a report, even an inkling that someone, or something that will report to someone (in
the case of a probe), is glimpsing or sensing something that has
never before featured in a human *Umwelt* suffices in the context
of space exploration.

Moreover, Uexküll's own invitation to explore the worlds
of nonhuman creatures on their own terms, to expand the
human *Umwelt* by stepping into the *Umwelten* of others, also
provides occasions for wonder. Brett Buchanan, a scholar of
Uexüll, says of his *Stroll through the Environments of Animals
and Humans,* "No, it may not be a new science, not nearly so
ordinary and pedantic, but it is indeed something wondrous.
New worlds arise before our eyes, through our sensations, in
our imaginations."[109] Uexküll asks us, at the very least, to imagine new affects; who is to say, then, that one does not experience them? This is, in the truest sense, an anti-anthropocentric
effort. Buchanan continues:

Rather than conceiving of the world according to the param-
eters of our own human understanding — which, histori-

107 Alexander C.T. Geppert, "Rethinking the Space Age: Astroculture and
    Technoscience," *History and Technology* 28, no. 3 (2012): 219–23, at 222.
108 Ibid., 219.
109 Brett Buchanan, *Onto-Ethologies: The Animal Environments of Uexküll,
    Heidegger, Merleau-Ponty, and Deleuze* (Albany: State University of New
    York Press, 2008), 1.

cally, has been the more prevalent approach — Uexküll asks us to rethink how we view the reality of the world as well as what it means to be an animal. So not only does he multiply the world into infinite animal environments, he also seeks to transform our understanding of the animal away from its traditional interpretation as a soulless machine, vacuous object, or dispassionate brute.[110]

Uexküll asks us, in other words, to conceive of other intelligences, by which we must understand something far different than simply other modes of cognition. These are entirely alien affective worlds, in which sights and smells (not to mention a host of other senses that humans likely do not possess) do not cohere with what is familiar to us. Even at an early age, for instance, the realization that even one's own cat or dog sees differently is an occasion for wonder.

But the acquaintance with and recognition of other *Umwelten* goes even further than this; it is not only a matter of familiarizing oneself with other realities, other modes of "being," but also a matter of seeing that the organism and its affects are inseparable. This is what Deleuze & Guattari take from Uexküll, and also what they mean, potentially, when they declare in *A Thousand Plateaus* that "[t]he organism is the enemy."[111] Buchanan elaborates:

It is a curious call to arms and one that has nothing to do with a dislike of organisms or animals. It is nothing of the sort. Rather, it is more an issue of "going beyond the organism" [...], of penetrating past the phenomenological interest in the "lived body" and "being-in-the-world," in order to discover the ontological processes that create what we are accustomed to calling the "organism." The organism is the enemy.[112]

110 Ibid., 2.
111 See Gilles Deleuze and Félix Guattari, *A Thousand Plateaus: Capitalism and Schizophrenia*, trans. Brian Massumi (New York: Continuum, 1987), 176.
112 Buchanan, *Onto-Ethologies*, 151.

Like all revolutionary cries, this calls for an assault on small-mindedness. The interest in other modes of being is not enough here, because it assumes, at least on some level, that we exist in the same *Umwelt*. Deleuze & Guattari, along with Uexküll, invite us not only to encounter radical difference but also to incorporate it into our own modes of moving and perceiving in the world — hence the emphasis on becoming(s). This, at last, fully accounts for the wound Parson locates in wonder, and the notion that, even when we do manage to encase wonder in some sort of signifying framework, to craft an adequate explanation, we no longer encounter the same subject. Wonder, even accompanied or perhaps enhanced by understanding, as the experience of new affects through new *Umwelten,* means that the subject never comes out the same.

It does not require a great deal of effort to imagine how a biologist, namely Wilson, writing a work of popular non-fiction, might mobilize this kind of wonder in his own writing, particularly when he investigates that most alien of creatures, the leafcutter ant. What perhaps requires slightly more of a stretch is the effort to understand how Sagan's much less earthly or Lovelock's much more systemic engagement is also wonder-driven. I argue here that, as focused as Wilson is on revealing the importance of *Umwelten* that are not our own, Sagan and Lovelock are equally focused on what may be made of the human *Umwelt*. Wilson and Lovelock ask us primarily to protect, Sagan to maintain the spirit of exploration, but each of the scientists insists on these activities because they allow us to wonder. Wonder here is never simply instrumental but constitutes an end in and of itself.

2.4
Navigating the Affectively Ecological

The works dealt with here discuss wonder and its analogs[113] nearly perpetually. The popular science writer, the post-in-scientist, becomes in these works especially a machine built for wondering. The mundane and inert are exploded as unscientific myth, and the reader is ceaselessly, at times exhaustingly, presented with a world teeming with an infinity of singular affects. What the next chapters present are the unique but interrelated ways in which the texts engage with wonder and reenchantment, interrogating, in each of these cases, how these practices are linked back to an environmental politics.

Although there is certainly plenty to keep one busy on the formal level in these texts, I have conscientiously shied away from approaches that would have me dwell exclusively or mostly on this.[114] Instead, in pursuit of a framework that would allow

113 A more technical distinction could certainly be made between wonder, marvel, awe, and enchantment, particularly on etymological grounds. The authors I deal with, however, use these concepts interchangeably, and, for purposes of not making my own investigation impossibly narrow, I do, too. Nevertheless, it is interesting to note that while the exact derivation of wonder is unknown (see the OED entry for "wonder, *n.*" cited in note 76 above), marvel is linked etymologically to the miraculous, awe to fear, and enchantment to magic. See, respectively, *Oxford English Dictionary Online,* s.vv. "marvel," https://en.oxforddictionaries.com/definition/marvel, "awe," https://en.oxforddictionaries.com/definition/awe, "enchantment," https:// en.oxforddictionaries.com/definition/enchantment.

114 I allude here to reader response theory, which, in theory at least, has fascinating applications with regard to popular science, in which the reader is so often addressed directly and involved in the text, as well as narratological approaches. As previously stated, however, while these works do have some narrative aspects, this investigation is much more concerned with where these narratives, understood in a very conventional sense, are interrupted by the affective — by experience that does not quite fit into the conventional stories of cosmic or biological evolution. I have also avoided deconstructive approaches, despite their potential for exploring the places in which the narrative ambitions of the texts fail. In the interest of pursuing strategies that would allow me to connect meaningfully with vital materialist concerns and avoid getting bogged down by the strictly formal,

me simultaneously to do justice to the strategies pursued in the works, open them to vital materialisms, and connect them to more contemporary ecological concerns, I have devised my own focal points for the close readings that follow. What this amounts to is a schemata that structures to what, in particular, a reading of these works concerned with affective wonder and how it connects with the ecological and, to a lesser extent, the scientific, should attend. There are thus six categories that have guided my reading — the first four relating explicitly to manifestations and references to wonder and the latter two providing useful connecting points to enchanted science and the ecological.

Before proceeding, the categories are worth outlining here:

1. The first, and I would imagine least, controversial category involves either the implicit or explicit mention of wonder or its analogs (awe, marvel, (re)enchantment). Attending explicitly to wonder is simple enough, in that one simply awaits a keyword like wonder or a variation of it, but "detecting" implicit wonder quickly becomes more complicated. An episode relating the poet-in-scientist's own experience serves well here, but just as often implicit wonder crops up in the inability to successfully relate an experience (as we will see in Chapter 3 with Wilson's experience in the Surinamese jungle). More fragmentary references to novel sensations and affiliations, even if posed as hypotheticals, also fall into this category. One may think of Sagan's mention of "a tingling in the spine, a catch in the voice"[115] associated with the contemplation of the cosmos. This first category, then, contains both attempts to both articulate and discuss affective wonder reasonably directly.

2. The second category involves references to the infinite, intricacy, and complexity. It includes, in most cases, the poet-in-scientist's attempt to articulate their engagement with *the*

close readings guided carefully by my theoretical concerns allowed me more freedom than these other approaches.

115 Carl Sagan, *Cosmos* (New York: Ballantine Books, 1980), 1.

field, a swarm of potential affects — in short, the virtual. This is the realm of *Umwelten* that one could, in theory, encounter. Here, often, the language of the author's becomes unusually figurative: Wilson's "light-points," which he uses to imagine the unthinkably complex arrangements of life in the rain forest, will provide a good case in point in the next chapter.

3. The flip side of these references to the virtual consists of references to what one might refer to as the actual — in this case to the singularity and precarity of life. While at times this takes the form of descriptions of individual creatures and their *Umwelten,* such as Wilson's descriptions of the leafcutter ant, it is just as often about singularity and precarity in the abstract. Lovelock, for instance, likens life on earth to a sandcastle that has miraculously assembled itself on an empty beach.[116] Something I refer to as the "affective statistic" also belongs to this category, and crops up often in texts by all three authors: these are back-of-the-envelope calculations (relying on orders of magnitude) geared, most often, at emphasizing the unlikelihood of life developing, or encountering life, in the vast universe. The statistics are affective not because they themselves emphasize affect, but because, if effective, they occasion in the reader an immediate sense of the novelty and improbability in which, merely by living, he or she necessarily participates. As we will see, the affective statistic already overlaps with the territory marked out by the fourth category.

4. The final guiding category dealing with wonder and enchantment itself has been labeled "fits of wonder," and deals with attempts to expand the readerly Umwelt. One example of this, certainly, is the affective statistic, but it also involves addressing the reader directly, particularly with the use of the first-person plural (we/us/our) and second-person (you/your). Sagan tells us, "Every cell of *your* body is a kind of commune [...]. We are, each of us, a multitude."[117] These "fits

---

116 James Lovelock, *Gaia* (Oxford: Oxford University Press, 1979), 31.
117 Sagan, *Cosmos,* 21, emphasis added.

of wonder," in many cases, are also marked by the attempt to bridge the world of the reader and that being discussed by the poet-in-scientist, and thus involve explorations and manipulations of scale. As if operating magical instruments, space and time, here, are expanded and contracted, to suit the poet-in-scientist's purpose. Ants become as large as people in *Biophilia,* the development of the universe can be mapped onto one calendar year on earth in *Cosmos,* and, in order to explain the complex mechanisms that regulate the chemical content and temperature of our biosphere in *Gaia,* the earth becomes a human body.

5. The fifth category attended to in my readings involves discussions of science. In works of popular science, this may seem hopelessly broad, but, in effect, this pertains to meta-scientific commentary. This is about what science can accomplish, what science as a vocation entails, and what, in the end, looking at the world scientifically means. In a number of places within the texts I focus on, the disenchantment associated with modern science is addressed directly. In a work claiming that these texts are answers to the disenchantment narrative, these discussions are crucial.

6. Finally, I have paid special attention to discussions of ecological ethics and subjectivity, as well as conservation practice. While Sagan deals with the topic slightly more gingerly and broadly, both Lovelock and Wilson make very concrete recommendations for what they believe can and should be done to protect life on earth. I have made a point, in each of the chapters, to try and connect their brands of vital materialism to what they recommend as ecological praxis. In many cases, as we will see, however, the sophistication with which they discuss subjectivity does not translate very well to real-world praxis. It has become necessary, in many cases, to present scenarios that problematize the perhaps hasty recommendations made by the writers, while, at the same time, exploring what, in their more abstract discussions of subjectivity, they may have left untapped.

In practice, of course, these categories, particularly the first four, are not entirely discrete. They have, however, served to structure my readings in a way that has allowed me to articulate the affective ecologies offered by each work, as well as to draw comparisons between them. The last two categories have also served to open up what might ordinarily come off as a hermetic, purely analytic exercise to the overarching questions posed by this work: what kind of reenchanted science is offered by these works? What, potentially, do they have to contribute to thinking ecological ethics and politics? And what kinds of people are being summoned with the "we" that permeates all of these texts? Thus, while on one level, these categories have allowed me to select, to pick and choose what is relevant in the texts and subtract the rest, the last two, in particular, have allowed me, in line with a reparative reading, to vastly multiply the possibilities offered by these works.

And what they offer, although they are responses to the disenchantment narratives most famously articulated by Weber and continuing even today, goes far beyond a mere counter-disenchantment narrative. These authors, at least at their most persuasive, have eschewed narrative altogether. What they confront us with, instead, are tinglings of the spine, catches of the voice, and very, very large numbers. They describe *Umwelten,* worlds, universes teeming with affect and potential, and offer a vision of the human as up to the task of exploring all of these. That these are scientists, and not artists or (at least primarily) environmentalists, that do this is important: time after time, these authors confront us with a science that refuses to separate itself from its object of inquiry. There are no laboratories to be found in these texts, no empty field on which the scientist does his work, but logs crawling with ants, atmospheres populated with innumerable gasses, and a "spaceship of the imagination." What they give us is an enchanted science because it is an immanent science, of the world. As we will see, their ecological orientation comes from the fact that they have abandoned the notion that science ought to be geared toward mastery. On the contrary, science within these works becomes a way to sense and attempt to get beyond one's "tiny sector of nature." Affective wonder, here, becomes both the engine and byproduct of an enchanted science. But, despite the fact that all of these works can be said to possess an ecological orientation and to offer an enchanted science in which affective wonder plays the key role, each work here offers its own version of the affectively ecological. The following chapters seek, then, not only to trace the various manifestations of affective wonder in the three works but also to articulate the specificity of each of the affective ecologies to which they amount.

3

Biophilia

AFFILIATION AND THE INFINITE
UNSEEN

3.1

*Two Biophilias:
A Prologue*

Decades after its initial articulation by E.O. Wilson, biophilia's heritage is a divided one. On the one hand, it survives as an evolutionarily driven hypothesis circulating in the fields of architecture and design, diagnosing (and offering a cure for) most modern ills. "Evolution has made us predisposed to want and need nature,"[1] it is claimed in a series entitled "How Biophilia Can Improve Our Lives" on the popular environmental blog *Treehugger*. The article continues, "The jump to high-rises, concrete and curtain walls could be the cause of most disorders present in society today. As a species, we are unaccustomed to these

---

1   Neil Chambers, "How Biophilia Can Improve Our Lives – Part I," *Treehugger,* March 27, 2012, https://www.treehugger.com/green-architecture/biophilia-can-improve-lives.html.

new non-biological environments."[2] This strain of biophilia resembles, in suspicious ways, the theories of disenchantment that trace nearly every conceivable ill plaguing the individual and society to the nomad's fall from grace and the rise of civilization.

The other biophilic strain is more tenuous, less reductive, and focuses on the depth and breadth of human affiliation to life and the lifelike, rather than, for instance, how forest bathing prevents cancer.[3] One might point here to the biophilia of the Icelandic artist Björk, who released an album entitled "Biophilia," inspired by Wilson's work, in 2011.[4] More than an album, "Biophilia" was an experimental, multimedia extravaganza, requiring programmers to cooperate with musicians and artists in order to release not only the songs themselves but also interactive material to accompany them. Scientists also cooperated with instrument-makers in order to produce the most distinctive sounds on the album, rigging, in the case of "Thunderbolt," a Tesla coil so that it functioned as a baseline. Björk's biophilia explores Nature writ large — not as a design concept, but as a set of potentials and enactments, affects and precepts.

That Björk's biophilia is more than the insistence that we were made to saunter through the savannahs and stare up at the intricate leafy patterns of trees is evident throughout the album, but the song "Crystalline" illustrates this particularly well. The song's first verse and chorus also provide an especially good launching point for this chapter:

Underneath our feet
Crystals grow like plants
(Listen how they grow)
I'm blinded by the lights
(Listen how they grow)
In the core of the earth

2 Ibid.
3 See Part IV of the same series, also by Neil Chambers, published April 2, 2012, https://www.treehugger.com/green-architecture/how-biophilia-can-improve-our-lives-part-iv.html.
4 Björk, "Crystalline," *Biophilia*, CD, Polydor, 2011.

(Listen how they grow)
Crystalline
Internal Nebula
(Crystalline)
Rocks growing slow-mo
(Crystalline)
I conquer claustrophobia
(Crystalline)
And demand the light

This is a biophilia that is unmistakably affective, a symphony of images that blend into light that blend into sound. "Crystalline" points to what I will later, in the analysis of Wilson's biophilia, call the "infinite unseen": the sense of there always being something growing (and dissolving) beneath, above, everywhere around us, even if that something is not strictly alive. "The infinite unseen" is the richness and complexity of life that surrounds one at any given time, of which one can only perceive a minute fraction. Moreover, underscored by the otherworldly sounds of the sharpsicord (a harp nestled in a giant music box), Björk, like Wilson, works to defamiliarize the supposedly natural. Apparently mundane or familiar phenomena, in this way, acquire novelty and singularity. When Wilson does pluck one organism from the unfathomably deep well of life for examination, he casts the group as "aliens among us," as fundamentally different life forms, with fundamentally different *Umwelten* or even haecceities in their own right. Finally, "Crystalline" calls attention to the various scales at which processes unfold and bodies live. Rocks grow "slow-mo" here, and yet one is asked repeatedly to "listen how they grow." "I conquer claustrophobia" might well refer to the effort required to affiliate with things that occupy cramped spaces underground. On a more profound level, however, to be discussed in greater detail in "Scale and the Readerly *Umwelt*," this conquering of claustrophobia echoes the expansion of the readerly *Umwelt* occasioned by wonder.

It is important to state that, although both Björk's biophilia and the evolutionarily charged *Treehugger* variety can be found in Wilson's own text, this chapter is all about the former. The latter, as will become clear in the following sections, drains biophilia of its richer, affective dimensions, and, along with it, presents a reductive vision of the human. The first section here, in addition to defining biophilia, thus also critically examines its evolutionary basis, arguing it functions much better as a label for affiliation with the nonhuman than as a hypothesis in evolutionary biology. It proposes a definition of biophilia that operates more explicitly on affective terms. The bulk of the chapter, however, revolves around wonder as a theme and strategy in *Biophilia*. This is the terrain alluded to above, where the affective biophilic strain, which "Crystalline" picks up on so well, becomes apparent. "The infinite unseen," examining references to the intricacy and infinity of experience in the nonhuman world, "The aliens among us," looking at wonder occasioned by particularity, and "Scale and the readerly *Umwelt*," investigating Wilson's inventive interfacing with the reader, are all attempts to "tease out" this affective biophilia from the text. The last section of this chapter turns to praxis, complicating Wilson's own conservationism with a look at Project Isabela, an ecosystem restoration project implemented in the Galapagos Islands. Despite the effort in *Biophilia* to escape anthropocentric approaches to wildernesses and other creatures, I argue that the work's plea, at the end especially, to preserve environments in order to preserve human wonder, forms one of the most anthropocentric conservation ethics of all.

3.2
Biophilia and Its Discontents

Biophilia, penned by the famed myrmecologist E.O. Wilson,[5] has spawned a word and an idea that has, since 1984, gained ever more circulation, if not traction. The book and its eponymous coinage has had a deep and lasting influence in ecological

5   E.O. Wilson, *Biophilia* (Cambridge: Harvard University Press, 1984).

circles. More recently, biophilia has been taken up by the fields
of architecture and design, as well as the evolutionary psychological fields to which the previous section alluded.[6] That the
concept of biophilia has survived to at least the first decade of
the twenty-first century is evident not only in Björk's adoption
of it in her 2011 album and its continued circulation in the blo-
gosphere but also in the 2009 establishment of the E.O. Wilson
Biophilia Center, located in Florida's Longleaf Pine ecosystem,
for which Wilson has long been an advocate.[7]

It is unsurprising that Wilson is the originator of the term.
Although trained as an entomologist and recognized by the end
of the 1960s as the world authority on ants, he was also one of
the early systems ecologists, coining the wildly successful term
"biodiversity" in a 1988 edited volume.[8] Wilson began to write
books intended for popular audiences in 1975, with the highly
controversial *Sociobiology: The New Synthesis*.[9] It was here that
he first dared to write about the biological basis of human behavior, taking this up again in *On Human Nature* (1978), for
which he also won the Pulitzer Prize. In the course of the next
two decades, he would write seven more books for popular audiences, including *Biophilia,* winning another Pulitzer along the
way. Continuing to produce best-sellers,[10] he was and continues

6   See, for instance, Yannick Joye, "Architectural Lessons from Environmen-
    tal Psychology: The Case of Biophilic Architecture," *Review of General
    Psychology* 11, no. 4 (December 2007): 305–28, and Stephen Kellert, Judith
    Heerwagen, and Martin Mador, eds., *Biophilic Design: The Theory, Science,
    and Practice of Bringing Buildings to Life* (Hoboken: Wiley, 2008). See also
    the *The Biophilia Hypothesis,* coedited by E.O. Wilson and prominent
    social ecologist Stephen Kellert (Washington, DC: Island Press, 1993).
7   See "About Us," E.O. Wilson Biophilia Center, https://www.eowilsoncenter.
    org.
8   See E.O. Wilson and Frances M. Peter, eds., *Biodiversity* (Washington, DC:
    National Academy Press, 1988).
9   E.O. Wilson, *Sociobiology: The New Synthesis* (Cambridge: Harvard Uni-
    versity Press, 1975).
10 Notably *Letters to a Young Scientist* (New York: Liveright Publishing Co.,
    2013) and *The Social Conquest of Earth* (New York: Liveright Publishing
    Co., 2012). See the *New York Times* Non-Fiction Bestseller Lists from May
    to July 2013 and April 2012, respectively.

to be a key figure in the conservation movement, serving as the director of the American Museum of Natural History, Conservation International, The Nature Conservancy, and the World Wildlife Fund.[11] He is, in short, as popular as scientists get, and also an important figure in environmental circles.

Although reference will be made to some of Wilson's other works, I focus on *Biophilia* here not only because of the concept it advances but also because it is, I would argue, the least sociobiologically driven of Wilson's books. One may, as I will suggest here, dispense with the "innate" part of its definition altogether, and still retain an incredibly vibrant concept. More than that, the concept becomes far more dynamic when unleashed from the confines of the sociobiologically innate.

Biophilia has never lent itself particularly well to exacting definitions. The original 1984 articulation[12] cast it as "the innate tendency to focus on life and lifelike processes."[13] Later, in the '90s, it became "the innately emotional affiliation of human beings to other living organisms."[14] This phrasing, especially considering Wilson's background as a biologist, lacks a certain amount of theoretical rigor, although, as deep ecologist Arne Naess reminds us, "Being more precise does not necessarily create something that is more inspiring."[15] Indeed, the natural scientists who have acted as proponents of the term, among them Lynn Margulis and Dorion Sagan, have largely abandoned the attempt to express it in more precise or reductive terms — in other words, in the language of modern science. Sagan and Margulis readily admit that "biophilia and biodiversity are scientifi-

11 Academy of Achievement, "E.O. Wilson Biography," 2013, http://www. achievement.org/achiever/edward-o-wilson-ph-d/.

12 It should be noted here that Erich Fromm was the first to use the word "biophilia," although he did not explore it at length. See Erich Fromm, *The Anatomy of Human Destructiveness* (1971; rpt. New York: Holt and Company, 1992).

13 Wilson, *Biophilia*, 1.

14 E.O. Wilson, "Biophilia and the Conservation Ethic," in *The Biophilia Hypothesis*, eds. Wilson and Kellert, 31–41, at 31.

15 Arne Næss, *Ecology, Community, and Lifestyle: Outline of an Ecosophy*, trans. David Rothenberg (New York: Cambridge University Press, 1989), 8.

cally sanctioned catchwords calling for us to attend seriously to nature and our responses to nature — forms of attention already more fully developed in traditions less nomadic and technologically expansive than those of the west."[16] The words "catchwords calling for us to attend to" should already give us some inkling that biophilia, rather than constituting a reductive description of human behavior and a testable hypothesis, is much more a loose ecosophical concept and a vision for a richer engagement with the nonhuman. It is also, as we shall see, intimately entangled with a vision of an enchanted science that is capable of multiplying, rather than reducing, the number of ways we can relate to the world. *Biophilia* itself contains so many highly impressionistic anecdotes about Wilson's experience in the field that it defies attempts to categorize it as natural science, philosophy, or memoir. Too meandering and conscientiously subjective to constitute a scientific work, but too inexact to lend a new ecological philosophy firm foundations, it becomes interesting to us here precisely when it is most "pop," when Wilson attempts to reach out from the field or the page and infect the reader with the urgency of an environment.

With the concept of biophilia, Wilson transforms wonder from a mere accident in life, a kind of aesthetic excess perhaps, into the very stuff from which our spiritual fabric is woven. He says of biophilia: "To an extent still undervalued in philosophy and religion, our existence depends on this propensity, our spirit is woven from it, hope rises on its currents."[17] The wondrous, for Wilson, is not transcendent, but immanent, found in the things growing, chirping, multiplying, and digesting around us, and of utmost importance is the activity of exploration, the pushing of the boundaries of one's own small *Umwelt*. "The brain is prone to weave the mind from the evidence of life," Wilson writes, "not merely the minimal contact required to exist, but a luxuri-

16 Lynn Margulis and Dorion Sagan, "God, Gaia, and Biophilia," in T*he Biophilia Hypothesis*, eds. Wilson and Kellert, 345–64, at 349.
17 Wilson, *Biophilia*, 1.

ance and excess spilling into virtually everything we do."[18] This "luxuriance and excess," which Wilson continually attempts to capture, is the affective. This is the realm of the incorporeal material—that which cannot be jotted down in field notes.

One can certainly experience a "naive," "unmediated" biophilic wonder within Wilson's framework, but he also makes a case for connecting biophilia to scientific endeavors. He asserts throughout *Biophilia* that scientific knowledge, for instance his own impressive knowledge of the leafcutter ant, does nothing to undermine wonder and, in fact, may increase it.[19] Indeed, Wilson writes, "Humanity is exalted not because we are so far above other living creatures, but because knowing them well elevates the very concept of life."[20] For Wilson, we as a species are not so much defined by peculiarities or our superiorities of physical biology, as much as we are by our curiosity and remarkable attunement to that which is not strictly necessary for survival—in other words, by wonder. Sue Thomas, author of *Technobiophilia,* emphasizes the "catalytic" aspect of biophilia, which she describes as a "process of attraction, forever renewing itself," and, in this way, it functions as a particular type of inexhaustible wonder, focused, above all, on life.[21]

It should be noted that although Wilson claims that the rationalizing of the inexplicable and puzzling can render "it," whatever "it" may be, more wonderful, his prose is sometimes at odds with this. At the very beginning of the book, when he is speaking of his memories of the tiny village of Bernhardsdorp in Surinam, he says this:

For reasons that were to take me twenty years to understand that moment was fixed with uncommon urgency in my

18 Ibid., 118.
19 Ibid., 10. Nearly twenty years later, Wilson still insists adamantly on this, referring to Faraday's statement that "nothing in this world is too wonderful to be true." See E.O. Wilson, *The Future of Life* (London: Little, Brown, 2002), 16.
20 Wilson, *Biophilia,* 22.
21 Sue Thomas, *Technobiophilia* (New York: Bloomsbury, 2013), 10.

memory. The emotions I felt were to grow more poignant at each remembrance, and in the end they changed into rational conjectures about matters that had only a distant bearing on the original event.[22]

He thus confesses, from the beginning, that he cannot exactly think this "uncommon urgency," this immediacy. His attempt to do so, twenty years later, is the concept of biophilia, but it is a much less technical concept than he would have perhaps liked, and that is, in large part, because much of what he hopes to capture is a kind of sensation or intensity. This may go some way to explain his recourse to the lightly evolutionarily charged "tendency," a slippery concept if there ever was one.

There are good reasons for framing biophilia as an ecosophical concept, as I have begun to do here, rather than a scientific hypothesis. The first is its imprecision, which is evident from vocabulary like "emotional affiliation" and "tendency." The second is that Wilson's claim that biophilia is innate or instinctive, somehow "coded for" in our genes, remains highly controversial. Yannick Joye and Andreas de Block, in one of the most exhaustive critiques of biophilia, point out that the claim is a very convenient one, insofar as it renders a conservation ethic a natural feature of human life: If we are indeed programmed to care for nature, it is culture, and particularly Western culture, that subverts this. To create a biophilic ethic, we need only unlearn what is, in any case, unnatural behavior.[23] This, however, becomes just another incarnation of the extremely suspect figure of the ecologically noble savage.[24] Indeed, even if one merely wants to claim that some aesthetic aspects of biophilia are innate, one runs into problems. While it is easy to prove, for in-

22 Wilson, *Biophilia*, 1.
23 Yannick Joye and Andreas de Block, "'Nature and I Are Two': A Critical Examination of the Biophilia Hypothesis," *Environmental Values* 20, no. 2 (May 2011): 189–215, at 190.
24 See Raymond Hames, "The Ecologically Noble Savage Debate," *Annual Review of Anthropology* 36 (January 2007): 177–90.

stance, that we pay more attention to lifelike movement,[25] and that natural landscapes do a better job at alleviating anxiety than artificial ones resembling natural ones,[26] preference for certain landscapes and creatures does not necessarily align with what is evolutionarily advantageous."[27] The "innate" part of the definition is thus riddled with problems.

Wilson, in fact, softened his own evolutionary claims for biophilia in 2002's *The Future of Life,* stating that "[t]he relative indifference to the environment springs, I believe, from deep within human nature."[28] Here he points to our ancestors, "a limited band of kinsmen," emotionally committed "only to a small piece of geography." He then concludes, "To look neither far ahead or far afield is elementary in a Darwinian sense," effectively admitting that an instinct to ignore life runs as deep as any to affiliate with and protect it.[29] Later in the same work, he also writes, "To say that there is an instinct, or more accurately an array of instincts, that can be labeled biophilia is not to imply that the brain is hardwired." He explains rather that "we are hereditarily *prepared* to learn certain behaviors and *counterprepared* to learn others."[30] We may, according to Wilson twenty years later, be innately *prepared* to focus on life and lifelike processes. As one might imagine, distinguishing between a behavior one is prepared to acquire and one that one can acquire is not very easy. For all intents and purposes, it is best to dismiss the evolutionary part of the hypothesis altogether.

Margulis and Sagan, moreover, point to a third and related reason to be suspicious of biophilia as an evolutionary given, emphasizing that it may be just as prevalent as biophobia and

---

25 See Gunnar Johansson, "Visual Perception of Biological Motion and a Model for its Analysis," *Perception & Psychophysics* 14, no. 2 (June 1973): 201–11.

26 See Roger S. Ulrich, "Visual Landscapes and Psychological Well-Being," *Landscape Research* 4, no. 1 (March 1979): 17–23.

27 Joye and de Block, "Nature and I Are Two," 201.

28 Wilson, *The Future of Life,* 40.

29 Ibid.

30 Ibid., 137.

that one may articulate a whole spectrum of responses to life, "varying from disgust (maggots, bacterial infection), care (kittens, puppies), horror (spiders, snakes), awe (tigers), and well-being (magnolia trees, actinobacteria with their woodland scent) to longing or envy (birds in flight)."[31] Biophilia, according to Sagan and Margulis, is only one very particular way of relating to life and the lifelike. They go on to refute Wilson's claim to biophilia's uniqueness among humans, stating that both biophobia and biophilia are examples of a "prototaxis that extends throughout not only the animal but also the plant, fungal, protocist, and bacterial kingdoms."[32] Sagan and Margulis's critique of the original concept is important because it helps to distance the concept from the facile figure of the "animal lover," connecting it not only with less sentimentalized kinds of affiliation, but also making clear that this affiliation is far from one-sided or uniquely human. It points, rather, to the importance of complexity in biophilia. It is not the creaturely, necessarily, to which we are drawn, but that which confronts us with reservoirs of affects beyond those that typically constitute our own *Umwelten*.

And, indeed, despite his sociobiological claims about the concept, Wilson alludes to biophilic attitudes throughout the work in ways that seem as if they are engendered, rather, through techniques of attention. Whether these techniques are innate or learned is beside the point. It is the techniques themselves and what they yield that are of real interest. Wilson, rather than painting the hackneyed picture of scientists as domesticators of wonder, insists that their methods are built upon the same disposition that allows us to experience it in the first place. Thus:

Scientists do not discover in order to know, they know in order to discover. That inversion of purpose is more than just a trait, it is the essence of the matter. Humanists are the shamans of the intellectual tribe, wise men who interpret knowl-

31 Sagan and Margulis, "God, Gaia, and Biophilia," 346.
32 Ibid., 357.

edge and transmit the folklore, rituals, and sacred texts. Scientists are the scouts and hunters.[33]

The emphasis here is on the broadening of the realm of perception, the expansion of the *Umwelt*. As with Uexküll's scientist, Wilson advances a notion of the scientist (and he urges us all to adopt the traits of these "scouts and hunters") as acutely aware of the whole host of phenomena which we have not yet or somehow cannot as humans experience, repeating in various forms the following mantra: "So we are drawn to the natural world, aware that it contains structure and complexity and length of history as well, at orders of magnitude greater than anything yet conceived in human imagination."[34] As we will see in the following sections, this exploration of wonder, this plea to pursue novel affects in the "wild," becomes so powerful and persistent that it overshadows the more dubious evolutionary claims. If we go back to our definition of biophilia, then, "innately emotional affiliation" might become something like "affective affiliation," or perhaps even the openness to nonhuman (and even nonbiological) becomings.

The potential of biophilia to operate beyond or at least independent from this narrow evolutionary framework has been recognized by others as well, notably by the literary scholar Dianne Chisholm. In a contribution to the volume *Queer Ecologies,* she elects to speak of Deleuze and Guattari's "involution," rather than "evolution" when discussing the concept of biophilia.[35] In contrast to evolution, "involution" is tied to a becoming that need not be procreative in character and perpetually crosses

33 Wilson, *Biophilia,* 58.
34 Wilson, *The Future of Life,* 146.
35 Dianne Chisholm, "Biophilia, Creative Involution, and the Ecological Future of Queer Desire," in *Queer Ecologies: Sex, Nature, Politics, Desire,* eds. Catriona Mortimer-Sandilands and Bruce Erickson (Bloomington: Indiana University Press, 2010), 359–81, at 369. See also Gilles Deleuze and Félix Guattari, *A Thousand Plateaus: Capitalism and Schizophrenia,* trans. Brian Massumi (London: Continuum, 1987), 263: "Becoming is involutionary, involution is creative."

species lines. "Neither progressive nor regressive," as with typical framings of evolution, Chisholm writes, "creative involution affects bodies of different kinds with the change of time."[36] Instinct becomes of diminished importance when speaking in involutionary terms, while affective elements (which, if we remember the first chapter, always involve a change, a difference between two states), our various modes of affiliating, take center stage.

3.3
The Infinite Unseen

Near the beginning of *Biophilia,* Wilson describes his experience of the field in Surinam:

> I focused on a few centimeters of ground and vegetation. I willed animals to materialize, and they came erratically into view. Metallic-blue mosquitoes floated down from the canopy in search of a bare patch of skin, cockroaches with variegated wings perched butterfly-like on sunlit leaves, black carpenter ants sheathed in recumbent golden hairs filed in haste through moss on a rotting log. I turned my head slightly and all of them vanished. Together they composed only an infinitesimal fraction of the life actually present. The woods were a biological maelstrom of which only the surface could be scanned by the naked eye. Within my circle of vision, millions of unseen organisms died each second. Their destruction was swift and silent; broken apart in clean biochemical chops by predators and scavengers, then assimilated to create millions of new organisms each second.[37]

Much of Wilson's prose follows this pattern: a turn of the head, a conscious effort to focus on something small, a tiny but lush scene that washes over him and perhaps the reader, then the

36 Chisholm, "Biophilia," 369.
37 Wilson, *Biophilia,* 7.

revelation that this is, as Uexküll has it, "only a tiny sector of nature."[38] Biophilic wonder is not just experienced in the singular (as opposed to the plural, but the sense of wonder itself is always singular in the sense of being unreproducible). One may simply admire the web of the spider, but one may also, even simultaneously, "emotionally affiliate" with the community of life. Wilson gave us at least two good reasons for doing as much, the first of which is the notion that "life is an exceedingly improbable state, open to other systems, thus ephemeral."[39] Life here is happy accident, and we may wonder at its improbability and our own improbable participation in it, just as we might wonder at the exceeding unlikelihood of a singular friend discovered among the multitudes.

But we may also wonder at life's intricacy and complexity. Wilson continues: "Despite the fact that living organisms compose a mere ten-billionth part of the mass of the earth, biodiversity is the most information-rich part of the known universe. More organization and complexity exist in a handful of soil than on the surfaces of all the other planets combined."[40] One may see here one of the first samples of what we introduced in the last chapter as the "affective statistic": the declaration of a number that, in so many cases, expresses the collision of infinity and singularity. In this case, as in many others, the unfathomable permutations of life are held up against what we can only guess is its scarcity in the vast, vast cosmos. On the surface of a planet that is finite (in the sense that the atmosphere provides a relatively clear demarcation between it and space), so many manifestations of the intricate assemblage we know as life creep and crawl that we will never fully come to terms with them. The affective statistic, time after time, reasserts the inexhaustibility of wonder. Provided life survives in some form or another, it attests to the fact that there will never be a time at which the

38 Jakob von Uexküll, "A Stroll Through the Worlds of Animals and Men: A Picture Book of Invisible Worlds," trans. Claire Schiller, *Semiotica* 89, no. 4 (1992): 319–91, at 390.
39 Wilson, *Biophilia*, 5.
40 Wilson, "Biophilia and the Conservation Ethic," 39.

individual *Umwelt* cannot expand. On a fertile Earth, at least, there will always be new affects.

This is not to say that experiencing the infinite in this manner is necessarily a wholly positive experience, as we already saw with the passage from Dillard. For instance, Mary-Jane Rubenstein also explores the trauma of the infinite in *Strange Wonder,* writing, "As trauma, infinity takes place as the discomfiting nonadequation of knowledge and the known; infinity is the thought the thinking self cannot think."[41] Wilson continually brushes up against the infinite, oftentimes literally, and it is not science, in these cases, that allows him to begin to articulate these encounters with the unthinkably vast community of life. Instead, as with the description of the forest floor, he asks us to imagine what it is like to stand there "affiliating," and this sometimes means something as abstract as picturing biological order as light.

The tour of Bernhardsdorp, the small village at the edge of the rain forest in Surinam, which is given by Wilson at the beginning of the work, is already highly charged with affect. He inducts us into the energetic view of the rain forest by first introducing us to the decomposers of which he is so fond. "If you close your eyes and lay your hand on a tree trunk almost anywhere in the tropics until you feel something touch it," he writes, "more times than not the crawler will be an ant." He continues, "Kick open a rotting log and termites pour out. Drop a crumb of bread on the ground and within minutes ants of one kind or another drag it down a nest hole."[42] Wilson briefly explains the ants' role in the process of decomposition, then states the following:

Between them they form the conduit for a large part of the energy flowing through the forest. Sunlight to leaf to caterpillar to ant to anteater to jaguar to maggot to humus to ter-

41 Mary-Jane Rubenstein, *Strange Wonder: The Closure of Metaphysics and the Opening of Awe* (New York: Columbia University Press, 2008), 66.
42 Wilson, *Biophilia,* 5.

mite to dissipated heat: such are the links that compose the
great energy network around Surinam's villages.[43]

Here Wilson traces the entire energetic cycle, from solar rays to
"waste energy," the inevitable byproduct of entropic processes.
Every preposition, every "to," in the second sentence implies a
profound energetic and material transformation and reorgani-
zation, and Wilson reminds us, again and again, although it
may be obvious, that this lengthy process is happening all of the
time, at all stages. We cannot begin to fathom it in any way one
might call complete, but the mere effort at least forces one to
become aware of the ceaseless activities of transformation that
occur even when we cannot attend to them. This is the original
ecological thought[44]: We are caught in energetic networks no
matter what and to an extent that we will never fully be able
to comprehend. All this is launched by attending to an ant that
scurries across the hand.

Throughout the text, Wilson struggles to find almost extra-
linguistic techniques of capturing the infinite complexity of life
he finds at Bernhardsdorp. Early on he writes:

At Bernhardsdorp I imagined richness and order as an intensity of light. The woman, child, and peccary turned into in-
candescent points. Around them the village became a black
disk, relatively devoid of life, its artifacts adding next to nothing. The woodland beyond was a luminous bank, sparked
here and there by the moving lights of birds, mammals, and
larger insects.[45]

This is energy made perceptible — the virtual, or at least a portion of it, quite literally come to light. Even, and especially in,
the dark, which normally so severely constrains the *Umwelt,*

43 Ibid.
44 See also Timothy Morton, *The Ecological Thought* (Cambridge: Harvard
    University Press, 2012).
45 Wilson, *Biophilia,* 6.

Wilson allows himself to be overcome by the intensity of the "richness and order" of the life buzzing and growing and trotting around him. And that this echoes an experience that many readers (at least within certain latitudes) remember from their childhood — seeing fireflies as mysterious and alluring points of light in the summer night — is likely no accident. Wilson calls upon our own reservoirs of wonder in order to supply us with a sense of the ineffability of his own experience.

A similar strategy seems to be at work when Wilson reverts to biological metaphors to explain the manner in which energy flows through the rainforest ecosystem. He explains:

> After the sun's energy is captured by the green plants, it flows through chains of organisms dendritically, like blood spreading from the arteries into networks of microscopic capillaries. It is in such capillaries, in the life cycles of thousands of individual species, that life's important work is done. Thus nothing in the whole system makes sense until the natural history of the constituent species becomes known. The study of every kind of organism matters, everywhere in the world.[46]

This is an especially interesting strategy, for it not only allows the reader to vividly imagine solar energy coursing through the ecosystem and the infinitely intricate paths the sun's energy must take to sustain every part of it; it also positions the ecosystem as a kind of body. This transforms what we would ordinarily refer to as the organism into the organ — the parts are made subordinate to the way in which they relate to one another — in other words, to their affects.

The affective intensity that Wilson finds near Bernhardsdorp, among other places, becomes, for him, a variety of religious experience. In this he places himself in a long line of scientists and naturalists:

46 Ibid., 8.

I savored the cathedral feeling expressed by Darwin in 1832 when he first encountered tropical forest near Rio de Janeiro ("wonder, astonishment & sublime devotion, fill & elevate the mind"). And once again I could hold still for long intervals to study a few centimeters of tree trunk or ground, finding some new organism at each shift of focus. The intervals of total silence, often prolonged, became evidence of the intensity of the enveloping life.[47]

For Wilson, it is when he is farthest from the realm of human affects, in "intervals of total silence," that he experiences wonder. A conscious effort draws him into this state, certainly, but it is also quite literally punctuated by moments that shake him. He continues in the same paragraph:

Several times a day I heard what may be the most distinctive sound of the primary tropical forest: a sharp *crack* like a rifle shot, followed by a whoosh and a solid thump. Somewhere a large tree, weakened by age and rot and top heavy from layers of vines, has chosen that moment to fall and end decades or centuries of life. The process is random and continuous, a sprinkling of events through the undisturbed portion of the forest.[48]

These spectacular moments of decay are, for Wilson, equally wonderful. And while this may partially be due to the fact that the toppling of the trees presents so many possibilities for his precious ants, it is also a more elemental matter of a sensation

47 Ibid., 27. Note that although Wilson borrows the language of the sublime from Muir (directly, in fact), what Wilson describes here is actually a much different phenomenon. While both Burke and Kant refer continuously to the role of the object in sublime experience, in the constellations Wilson (and Sagan) describe and conjure up, there is no object to be isolated. Nor is it as if the ecosystem in its entirety comes to replace the sublime object; Wilson never has any illusion of not being caught up in the intensity of enveloping life.

48 Ibid.

that draws one involuntarily into the unthinkably old and varied processes of life and death. The crack of the tree is both a fissure in Wilson's contemplations and the beginning of them. As Rubenstein writes, continuing her discussion of wonder and trauma, "This astonishment interrupts the project of thinking, cores out the self, and redirects it to the other."[49] The next section concerns itself with what comes of that redirection.

3.4
The Aliens Among Us

Wilson's project, despite his insistence on energetic indiscreetness, never attempts to homogenize the radically individual actors in the biological kingdom. He refuses to stay at the level of the (incomprehensible) system, dipping again and again into individual *Umwelten,* all the while staunchly refusing at least more obvious kinds of anthropomorphizing.

Indeed, in stark contrast to other ecosophical traditions, there is no comfort to be found in Wilson's jungle — it is too strange. He writes:

> I was a transient of no consequence in this familiar yet deeply alien world that I had come to love. The uncounted products of evolution were gathered there for purposes having nothing to do with me; their long Cenozoic history was enciphered into a genetic code I could not understand.[50]

Wilson is fundamentally a creature out of place in the jungle. And yet it is the very alienness of the world that attracts him. He is confronted, all at once, with a mass of creatures whose af-

---

49 Rubenstein, *Strange Wonder,* 67. Despite Rubenstein's use of "the other" in this quote, this work will largely attempt to avoid reference to it. This has as an ecological, as well as an affective-theoretical rationale; material and energetic, as well as virtual and affective, indiscreetness demands the use of other vocabulary.

50 Wilson, *Biophilia,* 7.

fects seem so very different from his own. And unlike with the nineteenth-century naturalist,[51] "nature" here is no drama that unfolds for him, but a tight knot of affects that enfold him. Thus, although the world is alien, he cannot be said to be alienated from it. In fact, he admits to loving it for its strangeness, insisting, "Every species is a magic well."[52]

The radical difference between these organisms is what he seeks, for this entails confrontation with ever-new *Umwelten*. He admits: "I opened logs and twigs like presents on Christmas morning, entranced by the endless variety of insects and other small creatures that scuttled away to safety. None of these organisms was repulsive to me; each was beautiful, with a name and special meaning."[53] Specificity (going far beyond the species) is the source of wonder here. Each instantiation of life, for Wilson, is a new source of wonder, for it is also a composition of new affects.

And it is perhaps more productive to understand "life and lifelike processes," which, Wilson claims in the original definition of biophilia, we are so irresistibly drawn towards, and which possesses relatively little meaning in and of itself, as rather haecceity — a singular affective assemblage. Keith Ansell Pearson discusses Deleuze and Guattari's notion of the term, explaining, "it [a haecceity] has no reference to either subject or substance; on the contrary, it endeavours to deprive both of these notions of their efficacy in order to grant primacy to a mode of indi-

51 See, for instance, George Iles, "Nature as Drama and Enginery," *Popular Science Monthly* 45 (August 1894), Wikisource, http://en.wikisource.org/wiki/Popular_Science_Monthly/Volume_45/August_1894/Nature_as_Drama_and_Enginery. The piece is a bizarrely eclectic overview of then-contemporary science, but the one constant is the place of the scientist in each field and his role (Iles's pronoun) as spectator. The author says of "nature": "It is a drama, not a tableau, which the observer to-day sees spread before him; in that drama every actor has been molded by the part it has had to play to maintain itself upon the stage" (par. 2). The scientist, regardless of discipline, is never included among these actors as features in the landscape or animals might be.

52 Wilson, *Biophilia*, 19.

53 Ibid., 28.

viduation that is not of a definite person, determined subject, or a formal substance."[54] Haecceity is the deindividualized individuation, a particular constellation of affects, of degrees and intensities. A haecceity, needless to say, need not be alive in the traditional sense. One can encounter a haecceity in a rock, even in "rosy-fingered dawn," just as easily as, say, a sloth's singularity might hit one. Elizabeth Grosz reminds us, "Individuation is in no sense tied to the human: it is what characterizes cloud formations, the formation of crystals, and ocean currents, as well as the development of cells and the creation of individuals."[55] Biophilic wonder might be conceptualized, then, as something experienced upon coming into contact with a haecceity. It is hopelessly particular, in a way, but also general insofar as it connects us to a world comprised of infinitely varied intensities and forces, the weird world of flux. Massumi goes as far as to call the haecceity "the agent of an infinitive."[56] The haecceity is a particular instantiation of complexity.

Timothy Morton, in his so-called "dark ecology," develops the analogous concept of the "strange stranger."[57] In his work, the living and nonliving world is conceptualized not as tree, not as web, but as mesh. Junctions in the mesh, where we might understand affects as intersecting, are the "strange stranger." Ecological praxis, for him, begins with "loving the strange stranger," and this gesture "has an excessive, unquantifiable, nonlinear, 'queer' quality. There is something utterly outrageous and, at the same time, universal and unavoidable about it, something the phrase 'tree hugger' fails to capture."[58] Encountering the strange stranger, opening oneself up to haecceities, is not about crea-

---

54 See Keith Ansell-Pearson, *Germinal Life: The Difference and Repetition of Deleuze* (London: Routledge, 1999), 181.

55 Elizabeth Grosz, "Thinking the New: Of Futures Yet Unthought," in *Becomings: Explorations in Time, Memory, and Futures,* ed. Elizabeth Grosz (Ithaca: Cornell University Press, 1999), 15–28, at 27.

56 Brian Massumi, *Parables for the Virtual: Movement, Affect, Sensation* (Durham: Duke University Press, 2002), 182.

57 A phrase that initially appeared in Morton, *The Ecological Thought,* 94.

58 Ibid., 79.

ture worship, not about the polar bear at the zoo or adrift on a slab of ice, but the bear's lazy gait, the glint of its teeth, its fishy breath — punctum rather than studium.[59]

Such an approach refuses the sentimentality and pleas for compassion that characterize other approaches. As entangled as we may be in ecological webs, Wilson never makes any claims regarding "higher" emotional connections with flora and fauna, whether on their part or ours. It is always rather a matter of encountering new *Umwelten,* of brushing up against speeds and slownesses, sounds and smells, that are not strictly *of* him. He writes of the ants:

> Does some remnant of psychological continuity exist across that immense phylogenetic gulf? The answer is that I open an ant colony as I would the back of a Swiss watch. I am enchanted by the intricacy of its parts and the clean, thrumming precision. But I never see the colony as anything more than an organic machine.[60]

This does not detract from Wilson's wonder, but, on the contrary, stokes it. Indeed, it is never "naturalness," — some kind of identification with a pre-anthropic Garden of Eden — that attracts Wilson to creatures and environments; it is almost always the clockwork, the mysterious manner in which they compose and reform their own *Umwelten.* "Organic machine," moreover, especially if we take into account Deleuzian parlance, carries no negative connotation here. By imagining everything as process, everything as machine, Wilson is able to avoid positing himself

---

59 See Roland Barthes, *Camera Lucida: Reflections on Photography,* trans. Richard Howard (New York: Hill and Wang, 1981), 27–28, 32–34. In later works, Timothy Morton focuses even more explicitly on rejecting "a rigid and thin concept of life" in order to think up and engage in ecological practices more suited to the melancholy and endlessly recursive loops characterizing our ecological present. See Timothy Morton, *Dark Ecology: For a Logic of Future Coexistence* (New York: Columbia University Press, 2016).

60 Wilson, *Biophilia,* 36.

as "the king of creation," and becomes the much more profound "eternal custodian of the machines of the universe."[61] The rejection of sentimentality in his approach to the nonhuman opens up a whole new range of possibilities for conceiving of his own relation to them.

3.5
Scale and the Readerly Umwelt

But not all of Wilson's efforts are directed primarily toward explaining and exploring his own sense of wonder. He also attempts to induce these fits in the reader, mostly by drawing comparisons between what he assumes to be aspects of the readerly *Umwelt* and aspects of the environment. Far from expounding dryly on radical difference, however, Wilson becomes an ecological magician, shrinking some creatures and processes and enlarging others, inducting the reader, time after time, into *Umwelten* denied to human speeds and scales.

In this way, even the most ordinary, the smallest clump of dirt becomes something at which to wonder. Wilsons instructs his reader to imagine the following seemingly commonplace scenario:

> Think of scooping up a handful of soil and leaf litter and spreading it out on a white ground cloth, in the manner of the field biologist, for close examination. This unprepossessing lump contains more order and richness of structure, and particularity of history, than the entire surfaces of all the other (lifeless) planets. It is a miniature wilderness that can take almost forever to explore.[62]

61 Gilles Deleuze and Félix Guattari, *Anti-Oedipus: Capitalism and Schizophrenia,* trans. Robert Hurley, Mark Seem, and Helen R. Lane (Minneapolis: University of Minnesota Press, 1983), 4.

62 Wilson, *Biophilia,* 13–14.

In the world, however apparently simple, that Wilson shows us, there is no such thing as inertness; everything teems with life. A handful of dirt from the rainforest (or even our own backyards), one may be certain, is already a collision or mishmash of *Umwelten*. Thus, when one bothers merely to look, a "droplet of moisture trapped between root hairs grows into an underground lake, surrounded by a three-dimensional swamp of moistened humus" and "fungi are not formless blobs, but exquisitely structured organisms with elaborate life cycles."[63] With these miniature unveilings, Wilson attempts not only to retrain the eye but also the expectation that everything of interest will display itself on our human terms. Above all, Wilson assures the reader that, wherever one might look, wonder may be found.

And the complexity to be encountered, even at the smallest of levels, Wilson demonstrates as almost unthinkable. Nevertheless, he constantly attempts to translate this complexity into terms, often spatial, with which the modern reader might be more familiar:

> If the information in just one insect — say an ant or beetle — were to be translated into a code of English words and printed in letters of standard size, the string would stretch over a thousand miles. Our lump of earth contains information that would just about fill all fifteen editions of the *Encyclopedia Britannica.*[64]

The reference to the *Encyclopedia Britannica,* while almost comically dated now and likely highly speculative to begin with, at least attempts to illustrate how much we do not know about even the smaller creatures of the Earth, how much a mere quick glance does not offer up. Wilson cannot offer the reader a complete education in other *Umwelten,* a complete inventory of affects with which we have not yet had the occasion to come into

63 Ibid., 14.
64 Ibid., 16.

contact, but he does attempt to illuminate how much always remains to be investigated and wondered at.

With the relatively small leafcutter ants, Wilson makes an exceptional effort to translate their capabilities and the fixtures of their *Umwelten* to human scales. He notes that, to most, the ants are "inconsequential ruddy specks on a pointless mission," but "a closer look transforms them into beings of another order."[65] Wilson, merely by making a few calculations, turns the ants into the terrifying creatures one may encounter in horror films from the 1950s:[66]

> If we magnify the scene to human scale, so that an ant's quarter-inch length grows into six feet, the forager runs along the trail for a distance of about ten miles at a velocity of 16 miles an hour. Each successive mile is covered in three minutes and forty-five seconds, about the current (human) world record. The forager picks up a burden of 750 pounds and speeds back toward the nest at 15 miles an hour — hence, four-minute miles. This marathon is repeated many times during the night and in many localities on through the day as well.[67]

It is immediately clear from this description that these are not merely sub-human animals with an impoverished range of affects. These are *beings of another order,* with entirely different *Umwelten,* as well as entirely different affects. And yet Wilson invites us, as far as it is possible, to learn about the irreducibly strange worlds the ants inhabit, and to allow our own *Umwelten* to expand to accommodate them. Wonder may describe a kind of a stretching of the individual *Umwelt.* Wilson invites the reader into other *Umwelten* almost always by introducing human equivalences. Thus, he describes the fungus cultivated by the ants as food by writing, "This mass ranges in size between a clenched fist and a human head, is riddled with channels, and

65 Ibid., 29.
66 See especially *Them!,* DVD, dir. Gordon Douglas (Warner Brothers, 1954).
67 Wilson, *Biophilia,* 29.

resembles a grey cleaning sponge."[68] And sometimes the comparisons are even more immediate: when explaining the tasks of the "tiny gardener workers," he describes them as "somewhat smaller than this printed letter I."[69] Wilson effectively invites the reader to imagine an ant on the page. He attempts, like any biologist with the gift of narrative (one may note Darwin and Uexküll here, as well), to reenact the *Umwelt* of the creature in the text.

Something about the life of the creatures is never quite captured, however. Part of the mystery of the ants consists of their sheer numbers, which exceed, by leaps and bounds, human scales. Wilson says of the queen in any given colony, "In her lifetime an individual can produce over twenty million offspring, which translates into the following: a mere three hundred ants, a small fraction the number emerging from a single colony in a year, can give birth to more ants than there are human beings on Earth."[70] It is important that, despite Wilson's efforts at translation, he always allows something to escape, to resist even the most valiant efforts at computation and imagination. Not all affects offer themselves up willingly; he cannot communicate antness to us, only give us small glimpses of it. In this way, he guarantees a certain reservoir of novel affects will always remain.

Although Wilson spends much of the time making these micro-worlds come to life for his readers (as if they were not already awash in them), he also attempts the opposite maneuver: condensing the macro-level of the ecosystem into terms more readily digestible by the twentieth- and twenty-first-century reader. Wilson thinks up a "motion-picture projector of magical versatility" that allows one to "explode seconds into hours and days," "condense years and centuries into a few minutes," magnify an image "to reveal microscopic detail," or compress it "to take in broad vistas from a distance."[71] It is a fascinating conceit,

68 Ibid., 32.
69 Ibid.
70 Ibid., 34.
71 Ibid., 40.

this tool that possesses the ability, at least at the visual level, to render the entire natural world perceptible.

Contemporary nature documentaries, in part, make use of slow motion and time-lapse photography to serve similar ends, but it is not as if the viewer possesses any ability to choose what to see in these cases. With Wilson's projector, one may directly encounter nonhuman speeds and slownesses. The projector enables the affective experience of systems and processes that we normally understand exclusively on an abstract, cognitive level.

The following passage, in which Wilson explores the hypothetical functioning of the projector, is worth quoting at length:

As the reel turns ever faster, we rise above Cambridge to view the countryside of Massachusetts, then the full northeastern seaboard. Day and night pass in quickening succession. When the alternation between them reaches the flicker-fusion frequency, ten or more in a second of viewing time, they merge in our brains, so that the landscape is suffused by a continuous but dimmer light. Individual people and other organisms are no longer distinguishable except for a few long-lived trees that spring into existence and enlarge briefly before evaporating. But something new has appeared. We are aware of the presence of whole populations of species, say all of the sugar maples and red-eyed vireos, as they pass through cycles of expansion and retreat across the New England landscape. Ecosystems, formed of combinations of these species, have become the creatures of our vision. A pond is fatigued with larch, fills up with waterweed, and then congeals into a bog. A sand dune sprouts beach grass, then wild rose and other low shrubs, which yield to jack pine and finally hardwood forest. We have entered *ecological time.* Biochemical events have been compressed beyond reckoning. Organisms are no more than ensemble defined by the mathematical laws of birth and death, competition, and replacement.[72]

72 Ibid., 43.

Ecological time, normally so opaque to those not working in ecological fields, becomes suffused with light and actors here. Wilson's projector does indeed show events "which have been compressed beyond reckoning," but we need not necessarily "reckon" with them. The implicit suggestion, and one unexpected coming from a scientist, is that it is enough to feel the changes and transformations that make up deep time. Because we cannot possibly conceive of the workings of systems at the level of the ecosystem over longer stretches of time, our engagement with them, if we are to engage at all, must be affective. This is the ultimate expansion of the *Umwelt,* the placement of the human in deep time, and as such is as wonderful as it is traumatic.

One is forced to think here, as well, of nineteenth-century efforts to come to terms with the knowledge that the human species is a relative ecological newcomer. In particular, Wilson's projector is uncannily reminiscent of the scene in *The Time Machine* in which the narrator speeds in the eponymous device far into the future, through "palpitating greyness,"[73] to the twilight of the Earth. The Time Traveller initially pauses on a red beach to look at the red sky (the result of a dying sun) and absorb the only remaining forms of life with morbid fascination: giant crabs and white butterflies, and lichens that creep over the landscape.[74] But he does not stop there; he rushes on, past the death of the sun, to experience an Earth cloaked in darkness and silence, removed of all traces of "animal life."[75] This is the eerie, overwhelmingly dreary, and affectively empty death of all *Umwelten.*

Wilson asks us to imagine similar scenarios in time that is not quite so deep. While in the nineteenth century life on Earth was seen as threatened almost exclusively by catastrophic extraterrestrial phenomena like the death of the sun, in the twentieth and twenty-first centuries there has been a dawning realization that the end, precipitated by human activity, will come much

---

73 H.G. Wells, *The Time Machine* (Rockville: Phoenix Pick, 2009), 66.
74 Ibid., 67.
75 Ibid., 68. Further, "All the sounds of man, the bleating of sheep, the cries of birds, the hum of insects, the stir that makes the background of our lives — all that was over" (69).

sooner than we had initially envisioned. Here Wilson flips his comparative terms. It is no longer the nonhuman that he translates to human terms, but the entire human species that acquires dimensions comparable to catastrophic interstellar phenomena. He states:

> Human destructiveness is something new under the sun. Perhaps it is matched by the giant meteorites thought to smash into the Earth and darken the atmosphere every hundred million years or so (the last one apparently arrived 65 million years ago and contributed to the extinction of the dinosaurs). But even that interval is ten thousand times longer than the entire history of civilization. In our own brief lifetime humanity will suffer an incomparable loss in aesthetic value, practical benefits from biological research, and worldwide biological stability.[76]

As infinitely varied and productive as forms of life might be, Wilson argues, humans possess a decidedly inhuman or at least suprabiological ability to level these infinitely various registers of life and to create affective deserts. We can wonder at the sheer destructive potential of a single species, certainly, but, at least in the long term, environmental damage on a large scale means the death of *Umwelten,* the death of the affects that comprise them, and thus an extreme limitation of experience and opportunities for wonder. This, in the end, forms the basis of Wilson's (admittedly roughly hewn) ethics, which the next and final section attempts to flesh out.

Before proceeding to the more concrete, however, it bears looking back at what has thus far been established and discussed in this chapter. Beginning by identifying two strains of biophilia — one reductive and evolutionarily charged, the other concerned with cataloging and fostering the richness of human affiliation with the nonhuman — it was argued that, although both can be found in Wilson's 1984 work, there is a much bet-

---

76 Wilson, *Biophilia,* 122.

ter case to be made for adopting the latter. Rather than under-standing biophilia as "the innate tendency to focus on life and lifelike processes,"[77] or as "the innately emotional affiliation of human beings to other living organisms,"[78] I argued we ought to embrace a non-evolutionary biophilia, defined as the "affec-tive affiliation with life and lifelike processes." Life and lifelike processes, in turn, can be understood as encompassing both the community of life and specific instantiations of it — haecceities, that, like Björk's crystals, may not be "living" in the traditional sense. In embracing this definition, biophilia can be under-stood as a particular flavor of wonder: the experience of the expansion of the individual *Umwelt* occasioned by collisions with other *Umwelten.*

Biophilia, therefore, swims in affective wonder, and in the three previous sections, I have attempted to tease out its mani-festations. The first section, "The infinite unseen" examined Wilson's own confrontations and attempts to confront the read-er with the infinite variety of life and the accompanying inex-haustible fields of affects. Wonder, here, is linked to intricacy and complexity and is constantly renewable. The next section, "The aliens among us," looks to the wonder occasioned by par-ticular instantiations of life and assemblages of affects. Rather than establishing our own kinship with other creatures, Wilson focuses on fundamentally different life forms, with fundamen-tally different *Umwelten,* insisting that, despite their alien qual-ity, they are worth investigating and mixing oneself up with. Finally, "Scale and the readerly *Umwelt*" turns to Wilson's ef-forts to direct the reader to deep time and the very small or microscopic — scales, in any case, which are not traditionally associated with the human. Even the exploration of the world of the ant here becomes a way to, in Björk's words, "conquer claustrophobia," to turn oneself to the novel affects central to an affective wonder.

---

77   Ibid., 1.
78   Wilson, "Biophilia and the Conservation Ethic," 31.

3.6
The Most Anthropocentric Conservation Ethic of Them All

Despite Wilson's meticulous efforts to explore the *Umwelten* of animals on their own terms and to avoid anthropomorphizing, his rationale for any kind of ecological action is undeniably anthropocentric. If the living world is such a profoundly important source, or at least cause, of wonder, and wonder can be conceived of as essential to human experience, there arises an ethical imperative to protect the living world. Here the impetus for conservation emerges not so much from the fact that we are dependent on the natural world for our physical survival, but from the idea that, without it, we would be intellectually and spiritually subhuman.

Thus, when speaking of the clear-cutting of the rainforest for agricultural purposes, Wilson makes no appeal to larger concerns like the regulation of greenhouse gasses in the Earth system. Instead, he writes, "This action can be defended (with difficulty) on economic grounds, but it is like burning a Renaissance painting to cook dinner."[79] This likens the destruction of (at least what Wilson conceives of as) our biological heritage to our cultural heritage; the loss is in large part an aesthetic one. But it is also not a shallow aesthetic appreciation that Wilson espouses. It is never about beautiful scenery, for Wilson, but rather the opportunity to see and smell and come into contact with that which is distinctly not of our usual *Umwelt* — that which shakes the very human in us. Wilson's conservationism is inescapably affective.

Wilson's brand of scientific humanism, moreover, of which wonder also forms the foundation, relies on a vision of the human as not a static, enlightened, and Vulcanesque species, but rather as constantly evolving (a less linear approach would call it involving) via new discoveries. Wilson explains.

---

79 Wilson, *Biophilia*, 25.

Now to the very heart of wonder. Because species diversity was created prior to humanity, and because we evolved within it, we have never fathomed its limits. As a consequence, the living world is the natural domain of the most restless and paradoxical part of the human spirit. Our sense of wonder grows exponentially: the greater the knowledge, the deeper the mystery and the more we seek knowledge to create new mystery. This catalytic reaction, seemingly an inborn human trait, draws us perpetually forward in search for new places and new life.[80]

Scientific discovery, propelled by the wonder occasioned by the infinite varieties of life, is inexhaustible, if only biologically rich areas are sufficiently protected. What is essentially human is not the expansion of human settlements, agriculture, and industry into so-called nature, but the expansion of the realm of affective experience and the changes that this engenders. It means, like Uexküll's scientist, glancing again and again into "a real world," and attempting to allow the "small sector of nature" perceived to fully affect the one doing the perceiving. That the small sector perceived grows ever wider is no threat to wonder, Wilson assures us. There is no limit to that which the environment furnishes for us: no limit to affective potentials, and certainly not the relations between and among living things that produce them. "Because biology sweeps the full range of space and time," Wilson assures us, "there will be more discoveries renewing the sense of wonder at each step of research."[81]

And even though a brand of conservationism is inherent in Wilson's ethics, it has nothing to do with future ethics. Indeed, the figure of the child simply never comes up. Instead, Wilson asks a series of questions, for which he provides rather unconventional answers:

80 Ibid., 10.
81 Ibid., 54.

What do we really owe our remote descendants? At the risk of offending some readers I will suggest: Nothing. Obligations simply lose their meaning across centuries. But what do we owe ourselves in planning for them? Everything. If human existence has any verifiable meaning, it is that our passions and toil are enabling mechanisms to continue that existence unbroken, unsullied, and progressively secure. It is for ourselves, and not for them or any abstract morality, that we think into the distant future.[82]

The real question, of course, is what kind of existence Wilson is referring to when he writes of it continuing "unbroken, unsullied, and progressively secure." Given that he spends only very small portions of the book on the strictly material aspects of existence and how it is bound up with natural resources, we might assume he intends something like the "luxuriance and excess"[83] spoken of at the beginning of the section, the province of the incorporeally material. Although for other authors this may emerge primarily from interactions between human actors, for Wilson this always emerges from encountering nonhuman affects.

Wilson's conservationism is, in the end — despite, or perhaps because of, its anthropocentrism — deeply progressive. Far from attempting to cordon off environments and creatures so that their own existence may continue "unbroken, unsullied, and progressively secure," Wilson offers up biologically diverse areas as testing grounds for the human. In order to fully embrace an affective ecology understood this way, however, the new conservationist ethic would have to disabuse itself of a sentimental attachment to life.

More concretely, this entails the following: First, the notion that an environmental ethic must involve "caring" about organisms equally must be put aside. In order for select organisms to

82 Ibid., 120–21.
83 Ibid., 118.

prosper, something must always go. Sagan and Margulis explain this especially succinctly:

> If we were truly serious about saving all other organisms, we would follow Jainist principles and filter our water to save the paramecia. We would surgically implant chloroplasts in our skin in order to photosynthesize ourselves and not uproot lettuce or carrot plants. We would certainly not cavalierly flesh away our solid wastes that serve as a breeding ground for e. coli and other gut bacteria. This *reduction ad absurdum* shows the hypocritical element implicit in the rhetoric of ecological salvation. In fact, part of the reason a predator like the Bengal tiger is so physically arresting is that it feeds at the top of the trophic chain; it is a carnivore, a killing machine, a king unfairly taxing plant and animal pawns. It has been said that all great poems contain an element of cruelty. Perhaps the same may be said of animals in the biosphere.[84]

Biophilia may allow us to revere life in the abstract or occasion us to lobby for manifestations of it, but we are not and cannot possibly be serious about protecting life in a way that is entirely just or equal. The business of living, as ecologists are eager to remind us, is also the business of dying: consuming and being consumed. Biophilia does not merely encompass, then, the gazing at silhouettes of trees in the forest, but can also be present in the tug of a fishing line as a hook works its way into the flesh of a fish. This, too, may be a profound kind of affiliation.

On the other hand, a more generous, affective biophilia can also entail a certain broadening of ecological sympathies. Again, Sagan and Margulis offer a valuable insight:

> "All organisms are equal," we seem sometimes to want to say in the discourse on biodiversity, "yet some animals are more equal than others." Not surprisingly these "more equal" be-

---

84 Sagan and Margulis, "God, Gaia, and Biophilia," 358.

ings are often large mammals either like us or like those found
in the savanna in which human primates first evolved.[85]

Unsurprisingly, we gravitate most readily to creatures like us.
But a more radical biophilia, in addition to refusing the impossible task of protecting all life, also seeks to create different kinds
of identification. If it is about encountering new and radically
different *Umwelten,* experiencing new affects; it is also about attending to more than just charismatic megafauna (although this
may still form a part of it).

Secondly, and following from the first point, an environmental ethic informed by biophilia embraces a generous anthropocentrism, abandoning the idea that deliberate actions are ultimately taken for the creatures, ecosystem, or planet alone. Once
again, Sagan and Margulis chime in: "the strongest argument
for a directed biophilia leading to a general if not all-encom-
passing biodiversity has to do with survival—not the abstract
ethical survival of all sentient entities, but our own survival, the
preservation of a certain quality of human life."[86] This, perhaps,
is what Wilson is attempting to say when he speaks of owing
nothing to our remote descendants, but everything to ourselves
in planning for them. It is not the desire to secure a future for
all life (which is after all impossible) that motivates conservation efforts, but the preservation of the possibility for affiliation.
This is the "certain quality of human life" alluded to by Margulis
and Sagan: a world in which the abundance required for contact
with other *Umwelten,* and not necessarily all of the creatures we
evolved with, remains.

Finally, if an affective ecological ethic necessitates abandoning the notion that we can protect *all* creatures, or even that conservation activities are conducted purely for their sake, it also
involves dispensing with the idea that it is possible or desirable
to "get back to the Garden." We can make decisions about the
way in which we affiliate with the nonhuman, but there is no

85 Ibid., 357.
86 Ibid., 358.

way to blot out affiliation itself, and the attempts to do so involve, in many cases, a level of violence and micro-management
not normally associated with conservation. This raises some
very thorny questions about how "the reservoirs of wonder" can
best be protected. To better understand this, it is useful to turn
to an actual conservation effort in the Galápagos, begun in 1997
and completed in 2006 — Project Isabela.[87]

Project Isabela, at least at the time of its completion in 2006,
claimed to be the "largest, most ambitious ecosystem restoration project in a protected area worldwide."[88] Like so many similar projects, it targeted an invasive species, feral goats, aiming
to eradicate them on three of the islands in order to restore the
habitats of native flora and fauna. The goats, in all likelihood,
had arrived beginning with the first ships to come to the island
in the sixteenth century, when sailors, tired of eating (and likely
living with) the goats on board, would abandon them on the islands and take giant tortoises in their place.[89] On the return trip,
they would often pick up the goats again, but, over the course
of a few centuries, the populations bred and became relatively
established. On the largest island, Isabela, populations had been
held in check by a natural volcanic barrier until the 1970s, but
the goats had finally managed to cross it, and populations (estimated at 100,000 on Isabela alone) and grazing territory had
expanded to such an extent that it seriously threatened many of
the native species, including the tortoises of lore. In 1997, then,
when the decision was made to eradicate the goat populations
entirely, the goal was, in effect, to erase nearly 500 years of human contact with the Galápagos. A 2002 vision document released by the Charles Darwin Foundation, another partner in
the project, "outlined the goal of going 'Back to Eden'" and re-

87 Facts and statistics concerning the project have been collected from the
    website of the Galapagos Conservancy, one of the partners in Project Isab-
    ela. See "Project Isabela," Wildlife & Ecosystem Conservation, Galapagos
    Conservancy, https://www.galapagos.org/conservation/project-isabela.
88 Ibid.
89 See Jad Abumrad and Robert Krulwich, "Galapagos," *Radiolab*, WNYC, July
    16, 2014, https://www.radiolab.org/story/galapagos.

turning "the biological nature of the Galápagos islands almost to the conditions of 1534."[90]

In order to accomplish this, the project hired sharp-shooters to target goat populations from the air via helicopter. When enough goats had been killed that populations became harder to find, they created an army of "Judas goats." The Galapagos Conservancy describes their role as follows: "Being naturally gregarious, sterilized Judas goats, fitted with radio collars and then released into the population, would seek out the remaining feral goats, allowing them to be located through radio telemetry and then removed."[91] Marksmen would proceed to shoot every goat but the Judas goat (repeating the process as many times as proved necessary), and a few hundred of them remain on the islands to this day, fitted with trackers, should any feral goat populations reappear.

At least on the larger islands, the eradication of the goats has been "wildly" successful, and the areas, according to the scientists involved, appear to be recovering rapidly from the toll taken by the heavy grazing. On the smallest island involved in the project, Pinta, however, the goat population actually decimated the native tortoise population entirely. Rather than simply re-populating the island with a tortoise species native to one of the other islands, scientists have turned to selective breeding, and potentially genetic engineering, to repopulate the island with a species resembling the original Pinta tortoise. In the meantime, an army of sterilized tortoises from one of the larger islands has been released to act as lawnmowers and ecological place-holders.[92] Getting "back to Eden," even in an environment like the

90 See The Charles Darwin Foundation and World Wildlife Fund, *A Biodiversity Vision for the Galápagos Islands,* ed. R. Bensted-Smith (Quito, Ecuador: Charles Darwin Foundation, 2002), as cited in Elizabeth Hennessy and Amy L. McCleary, "Nature's Eden? The Production and Effects of 'Pristine' Nature in the Galápagos Islands," *Island Studies Journal* 6, no. 2 (November 2011): 131–56, at 143.

91 Galapagos Conservancy, "Project Isabela."

92 Abumrad and Krulwich, "Galapagos."

Galápagos, thus takes an astonishing amount of tinkering, and, from the perspective of the goats, an all-out war.

Project Isabela is a highly successful example of a conservation project that, in many regards, embraced a non-sentimental conservationism. Scientists understood, for one, that *something had to go* — in this case over 100,000 goats. And, among all this carnage, the project was not dedicated to protecting life in general, but a peculiar vision of it: one of the Galápagos 300 years prior, even, to Darwin's arrival. What is so striking is that most documents related to it preserve a vision of an ahuman Eden, but conservationists have largely abandoned this in practice. The Judas goats remain, just in case someone tries to repopulate the island with goats, and the sterilized turtles will wander Pinta for decades to come. The scientists occupy a world in which we meddle, ceaselessly, in which we make decisions about what stays and what goes, and yet the pretense, almost always, is that a world is being resurrected in which the human element has been entirely subtracted.

A more nuanced affective ecology, informed by biophilia, does away with this pretense entirely, and, while it does not provide any simple way to evaluate Project Isabela, it points to a different set of questions that might have been asked at the beginning of the project in the 1990s. When the self-evidence of getting "back to Eden" is done away with, more questions than I can possibly propose here arise.

An affective ecology would raise questions, first of all, about what is being forsaken with the conservation effort: What, in other words, does conservation destroy? Here one might dwell not so much on the lives of hundreds of thousands of goats as on how these goats relate to us. How do we, the scientists, the inhabitants of the island, affiliate with them? Linda Cayot, a conservationist heavily involved in Project Isabela, noted, for instance, that these were not ordinary goats that were "removed"; they were the descendants of old European stock, isolated on the island for centuries. Cayot refers to them as "beautiful animals"[93] and, indeed, there were no other populations like them. A whole range of affects died with the goats, deemed impoverished because they were not strictly native. This is not to say that the subsequent flourishing of flora and fauna after the removal of the goats does not add enough richness and complexity to "make up" or "offset" that which disappears with the goats. This is something that, with an affective ecology, must certainly be negotiated.[94]

This leads neatly into the next set of questions: what *Umwelten,* what ways of affiliating, are being "restored"? Are creatures such as the Pinta tortoise irreplaceable, or is the effort to revive them, as some scientists have suggested,[95] precious? For that matter, for whom is the restoration actually taking place? Only conservationists, who are able to visit the sites of restoration, and eco-tourists generally refer to "biological heritage"; do these efforts actually increase the quality of life for those outside these groups?

These questions, far from simplifying the decisions made in order to conduct Project Isabela, make them more complicated. When "the Garden" is abandoned, as a rule, this is what happens: Conservation no longer becomes about chasing some specter of

93 Ibid.
94 Elizabeth Kolbert, writing for the *New Yorker,* points to a similar set of concerns at work right now in New Zealand, where there is a grass-roots effort to exterminate the non-native mammals to allow endangered native marsupials and birds to proliferate; she calls their orientation "a bloody, bloody biophilia." One of the conservation groups Kolbert profiles, Predator Free New Zealand, has a log which "shows a kiwi with a surprised expression standing on the body of a dead rat." See Elizabeth Kolbert, "The Big Kill: New Zealand's Crusade to Rid Itself of Mammals," *The New Yorker,* December 22, 2014, http://www.newyorker.com/magazine/2014/12/22/big-kill.
95 "Galapagos," the episode of *Radiolab* cited above, relates an especially memorable story surrounding "Lonesome George," the last of the Pinta Tortoises, who continually frustrated conservationists with his unwillingness to breed. Conservationist Josh Dumlin reports that, at one of the meetings on the Pinta Tortoise project, one scientist finally snapped, suggesting that Lonesome George be shot so that he could "quit wasting our time."

reenchantment, these astounding islands prior to human contact, but about fostering abundance, creating the conditions of
reenchantment in which wonder is possible. And biophilia here,
rather than pointing to easy answers about saving the beautiful
goats or majestic turtles, asks us to rethink our most fundamental relations with life. How do we preserve and enrich that which
ties us to these singular constellations of affects?

4

Gaia

THE AFFECTS OF THE EARTH

The concept of Gaia, although curiously inhumane in its indifference to the billions of hairy bipeds scurrying ceaselessly across its surface, manages, nevertheless, to connect in remarkable ways to the individual human *Umwelt*. How is it that Lovelock manages to draw us into the realm of the impersonal affects of the earth, or, more accurately perhaps, bring us to realize that, despite our posturing, we were never independent of them? This, ultimately, is the question this chapter seeks to answer.

It begins, however, by attempting to lend more substance and clarity to a concept that is curiously hazy, presenting Lovelock's definition of Gaia and outlining it in explicitly affective terms. This sets us up to see, in section 4.2, how Gaia — a living body that is the composite of all other known living bodies — radically reenchants, examining along the way the outlines of a Gaian science. Section 4.3, "Strange Agents: Gaia and the Human," examines in greater detail how we can understand Gaia's vitality and agency, as well as what, if any, role a living, self-regulating planet might grant to the human. It is here that wonder becomes of paramount importance. Lovelock implies that, as far as human relations with Gaia are concerned, it is the affective and virtual rather than the strictly material that is remarkable. And always, when contemplating the role of the human, Gaia's indifference looms. Simultaneously the unlikeliest of paradises and a potential hell for organisms that cross her or are caught in the line of fire, Gaia is described in section 4.4 as "An Indifferent Eden." The next section, "An Affective Ecology for an Indifferent Planet" (4.5) presents a loose Gaian program, a set of principles that Lovelock and the entity he lets loose upon the world encourage. Finally, a postscript (4.6) turns to a cultural artifact that would not have been possible without Lovelock's first book-length articulation of Gaia in 1979[1]: the 1985 BBC mini-series *Edge of Darkness.*[2] *Edge of Darkness,* despite offering at times an (understandably) confused portrait of Gaia, succeeds so well in depicting its impersonality and indifference to conventional understandings of politics that it cannot be overlooked. Detective Ronald Craven, the main protagonist in the series, serves here as the Gaian *par excellence* and a model for affective ecological subjectivity. Rather than exhibiting hostile indifference toward reproductive futurism, like Edelman's queer, Craven's indifference is far more profound. Ultimately, *Edge of Darkness* is not about resisting the child as the horizon of politics, but about going on after the fantasy of reproductive futurism has exploded.

4.1
An Introduction to Affective Gaia

There are many Gaias, some "as old as humankind,"[3] many inspired by Lovelock himself, and this section will begin by sketching the broad outlines of a kind of affective composite of

---

1   James Lovelock, *Gaia: A New Look at Life on Earth* (Oxford: Oxford University Press, 1979).

2   *Edge of Darkness,* DVD, dir. Martin Campbell (1985; BBC Worldwide, 2003). In 2010, an American adaptation starring Mel Gibson was also released, but is irrelevant here, as it cuts out all references to Gaia.

3   James Lovelock, "The Earth as a Living Organism," in *Biodiversity,* eds. E.O. Wilson and Frances M. Peter (Washington, DC: National Academy Press, 1988), 486–89, at 486.

the Gaias spawned by Lovelock's writings. Like biophilia, the Gaia dealt with here can be described more aptly as an approach than a precise concept. What it lacks in clarity, however, it more than makes up for in its fecundity. Gaia itself possesses a biosphere — a mysterious and powerfully attractive field, a sort of gaseous layer, generated by the interaction of the various evolving concepts. Seen from afar, this nebulous field becomes the composite's defining feature. This section thus turns to the affectivity surrounding the genesis and elaboration of the concept first, before moving on to more concrete definitions offered by Lovelock and others. It concludes by returning to the nature of the concept of Gaia itself (or herself, if we are to adopt Lovelock's language[4]), the status of which, just as much as the bolder claims uttered in its name, has been a matter of intense debate.

4.1.1. Gaia's conceptual evolution:
The English countryside as primordial soup
Gaia would be unthinkable without Lovelock, not only as the articulator of the concept but also as a figure who embodies an alternative, more affectively informed science. Born to working-class parents near London in 1919,[5] Lovelock's scientific career was nothing like inevitable, and has, indeed, followed a very strange arc. In his youth, however, Lovelock's scientific interests already revolved around that which he could directly experience. In *The Ages of Gaia* (1984), he writes fondly of bicycling through the chalk cliffs, looking for "wild plants, especially the poisonous ones like henbane, aconite, and deadly nightshade."[6] But it was not enough merely to find and identify them. He writes: "I experimented once by chewing a fraction of a leaf of

---

4   In this chapter, as a rule, "it" or "its" will be used to refer to Gaia as concept, while "she" and "her" will refer to Gaia as more concrete entity. There are, however, cases in which it is impossible to discern whether it is the concept or the entity that is being referenced.

5   James Lovelock, *Homage to Gaia: The Life of an Independent Scientist* (Oxford: Oxford University Press, 2000), 8.

6   James Lovelock, *The Ages of Gaia: A Biography of Our Living Earth* (Oxford: Oxford University Press, 1988), 227.

one of them and learnt the hard way the discomfort of atropine poisoning."[7] By employing taste, that (al)chemical sense now lost to science, Lovelock early on places himself firmly outside any scientific tradition that emphasizes distance between subject and object.

Indeed, during his long career, Lovelock has worked relatively little for institutions of modern science and does most of his work in his private laboratory adjoining his Devonshire home. The notable exceptions include his work for the National Institute for Medical Research at the beginning of his career (1946–1961),[8] and for NASA's jet propulsion laboratory in the early 1960s, where, coincidentally, he shared an office with Carl Sagan and likely made the acquaintance of Sagan's wife at the time, Lynn Margulis. She became an important American advocate for Gaia, as well as for biophilia much later.[9] Before becoming a popular figure with his books, Lovelock earned his living, appropriately for one who fits in much better with an older scientific tradition, as an instrument maker. In the 1950s, during his time at the National Institute for Medical Research, he invented the "electron capture detector" (ECD), a device that made "possible the discovery that pesticide residues were present in all creatures of the Earth, from penguins in Antarctica to the milk of nursing mothers in the USA."[10] Lovelock, fairly, claims: "It was this discovery that facilitated the writing of Rachel Carson's immensely influential book, *Silent Spring,* by providing the evidence needed to justify her concern over the damage done to the biosphere by the ubiquitous presence of these toxic chemicals."[11] Thus, even before Lovelock became a central figure in the environmental movement, he was providing it with feelers. And the electron capture detector did this not once, but twice: It allowed chlorofluorocarbons (CFCs) to be detected in

7 Ibid., 227–28.
8 Lawrence E. Joseph, *Gaia: The Growth of an Idea* (New York: St. Martin's Press, 1990), 20.
9 Ibid., 24–26.
10 Lovelock, *Gaia: A New Look at Life on Earth,* x.
11 Ibid.

the atmosphere at parts per trillion[12] and provided the data that would eventually raise concerns about the role of CFCs in depleting the ozone layer and lead to the banning of the compounds in many products.

Because of the notoriety brought to him by the ECD, Lovelock is described in many publications as an atmospheric chemist and gas chromatographer, but he sees himself primarily as an inventor[13] "whose business is the creation of useful objects and ideas."[14] Gaia is one such invention, a theory that "'is not so much an idea per se as a generator of ideas, something that performs a useful function repeatedly, like a good tool.'"[15] Lovelock constantly emphasizes the essentially productive nature of Gaia. Rather than tending toward parsimony and reduction, Gaia embraces multiplication and thinking across disciplines.

As is so often the case with inventions, Gaia, in its initial incarnation, was the answer to a specific problem, and it would only later become a vision of the earth celebrated by environmentalists. The hypothesis is a product of Lovelock's time with NASA at the Jet Propulsion Laboratory in Pasadena, California, in the early 1960s, where he worked on the problem of detecting life in extraterrestrial atmospheres. Ever the practical thinker, Lovelock first looked to the earth, asking what "its own clear proof of life's activity"[16] consisted of. He arrived at the conclusion that the "significant decrease in entropy — or, as a chemist would put it, the persistent state of disequilibrium among the atmospheric gases" constituted proof that "Earth's highly improbable atmosphere was being manipulated on a day-to-day basis from the surface, and that the manipulator was life itself."[17] Out of his research in Pasadena thus emerged the seeds of the Gaia hypothesis — a new vision of the earth — and a skepticism

12 Lovelock, *The Ages of Gaia,* 164.
13 Joseph, *Gaia,* 4.
14 Ibid., 23.
15 Lovelock, as quoted in ibid., 23.
16 Lovelock, *Gaia: A New Look at Life on Earth,* 6.
17 Ibid.

with regard to the possibility of life on the planets neighboring our own.

Gaia was thus Lovelock's answer to the question: "Why is the earth, miraculously, not dead?" Latour, too, remarks upon the pervasiveness of this question in Lovelock's prose, which, he states, "reads a little like a detective story."[18] The earth, by all accounts, "*ought to be* like Mars, a dead star. It is not. So what force is capable of *delaying the disappearance of its atmosphere?*"[19] There is a curious symmetry in the fact that the very entity that renders the traditional whodunit irrelevant in *The Edge of Darkness,* which we will turn to at the end of this chapter, is itself at the center of a reverse kind of whodunit: Why is the Earth not (yet) bare? For Lovelock, and for those who, like Lynn Margulis, later side with him, the answer is life, abundant and working somehow in concert to maintain the conditions possible for its own existence. The search for extraterrestrial life, in this way, gave way to an understanding of life on earth as wholly remarkable.

It was not long before Gaia, during a chat in the pub with Lovelock's fellow villager and writer William Golding, acquired its name, now so inseparable from the concept itself.[20] The very first public articulation of the concept was in 1969, when Lovelock spoke of it at a "scientific meeting about the origins of life on earth which took place in Princeton."[21] Lovelock readily ac-

---

18 Bruno Latour, "Third Lecture: Gaia, a (Finally Secular) Figure for Nature," in *Facing Gaia: Eight Lectures on the New Climatic Regime,* trans. Catherine Porter (Cambridge: Polity Press, 2017), 75–110, at 91. Latour's interest in Gaia, reflected in his lectures as well as a play entitled *Cosmocolosse* "exploring the disconnect between the dimension of the crisis and the lack of 'feel' for it," is hardly surprising given his prior work on science as a productive rather than reductive force. See Bruno Latour, Chloé Latour, and Frédérique Ait-Touatti, "Cosmocolosse: a Radio Play," 2011, http://www.bruno-latour.fr/node/358.

19 Latour, "Third Lecture: Gaia, a (Finally Secular) Figure for Nature," 91.

20 Lovelock, *Gaia: A New Look at Life on Earth,* 10. Golding, of course, borrowed the name from the Greek goddess and personification of the earth. See Hesiod, *Theogony and Works and Days,* trans. Catherine Schlegel and Henry Weinfeld (Ann Arbor: University of Michigan Press, 2006).

21 Lovelock, *Gaia: A New Look at Life on Earth,* 11.

knowledges that it was far from immediately popular. Only the
Swedish chemist Lars Gunnar Sillen (who died shortly thereafter) and renowned biologist Lynn Margulis, then at Boston
University, took to the concept.[22] Margulis would become an
important collaborator, publishing with Lovelock the first paper
articulating the Gaia hypothesis in 1974.[23] The two had a difficult
time finding a journal that was willing to publish what many
contemporaries described as pseudoscience; in the end, Carl Sagan agreed to publish an article in his journal, *Icarus*.[24]

The book-length articulation of Gaia would not come along
for five more years. By this time, the concept was much more
thoroughly fleshed out and accompanied by several backstories
pointing to Gaia's affective inspiration, grounding it in both entirely mundane experience and the otherworldly. By the end of
the 1970s, Gaia was not just a product of Lovelock's time at the
Jet Propulsion Lab, but of the space age itself: "It took the view
of the Earth from space, either directly through the eyes of an
astronaut, or vicariously through the visual media, to give us the
personal sense of a real live planet on which the living things,
the air, the oceans, and the rocks all combine in one Gaia."[25]
Gaia becomes thinkable, in other words, the moment she can
be glimpsed from afar. This distance, far from allowing us to
sever our ties with the earth (or imagine them severed), gives us

22 Ibid. It is worth noting that Stanisław Lem's *Solaris,* the publication of
    which proceeds the first articulations of the Gaia hypothesis by a good 13
    years, had already proposed not only a planet as a living entity, but also the
    scientific controversy such an entity might occasion: "With the publica-
    tion of this hypothesis [that Solaris was a living entity], the scientific world
    was torn by one of the most violent controversies of the century. Revered
    and universally accepted theories foundered; the specialist literature was
    swamped by outrageous and heretical treatises; 'sentient ocean' or 'gravity-
    controlling colloid' — the debate became a burning issue." See Stanisław
    Lem, *Solaris, The Chain of Chance, A Perfect Vacuum,* trans. Joanna
    Kilmartin and Steve Cox (Harmondsworth, Middlesex: Penguin, 1985),
    27–8.
23 Lynn Margulis and J.E. Lovelock, "The Biological Modulation of the
    Earth's Atmosphere," *Icarus* 21, no. 4 (April 1974): 471–89.
24 Lovelock, *Gaia: A New Look at Life on Earth, 7.*
25 Lovelock, *The Ages of Gaia,* 19.

"the personal sense of a real live planet," on which we, too, live, breathe, and eventually die. Indeed, Gaia, as we shall see — better than earth, or home planet — acknowledges and takes into account that shock of seeing that sphere we inhabit against a backdrop of nothingness. This is Gaia's celestial inspiration.

But Gaia's more mundane roots in the English countryside are just as, if not more, present in Lovelock's books. He claims in the first book that: "Most of it came to mind when walking or sitting on the warm, red sandstone slabs of Hungry Hill."[26] While part of this, surely, is a deliberate folksiness, it is also significant that Lovelock would write of geological formations of the right temperature, rather than, for instance, a conference room at Princeton. It is the world in all its dynamism, he constantly implies, that informs Gaia. This becomes even more prominent in *The Ages of Gaia* (1984), the preface of which begins with Lovelock describing the place in which he writes: a former mill with the River Carey on one side, looking "onto the river valley with its small fields and hedgerows typical of a Devonshire country scene."[27] For a man constantly poised in his writing on the cusp of the human and the (often violently) biologically informed geological, the space is more than adequate. And that the concept was worked out in this setting, rather than a cramped university office in the city, is integral to it: "It was written as part of a way of life that included time to go for walks in the country and to talk with friends, as Korolenko did, about the Earth being alive."[28] Gaia, Lovelock implies again and again, is a product of an immanent science — one that refuses the sterility of the lab and opts, instead, for the country stroll and the warmth of the sandstone on Hungry Hill.

While the concept of Gaia, which we will explore more explicitly in the next section, is intriguing enough on its own, its popularity has been secured by Lovelock firmly embedding it in the world and the affective. Joseph, among others, writes: "The

26 Lovelock, *Gaia: A New Look at Life on Earth,* viii.
27 Lovelock, *The Ages of Gaia,* xii.
28 Ibid., 14.

reproductive power of Gaian ideas soon would astonish critics and proponents alike. Few books, especially those of the arcane scientific variety, spawn their own publishing houses."[29] Joseph is referring here to Gaia Books, Ltd., established after the success of Lovelock's first book (and since acquired by Hamlyn). Gaia, despite the fierce opposition it encountered in the academy,[30] has thrived, so much so that we may speak of it spawning, and this has everything to do with the thousands of small, affectively charged anchors Lovelock has thrown down into the British countryside, into the earth.

4.1.2. Gaia defined
But enough of fanfare and the nebulous cloud that surrounds Gaia. What is it, or what, at least, does Lovelock claim it is? In fact, he offers many definitions, even in the original 1979 book, some more, some less complicated, some relying more or less than others on the rhetoric of science. The first definition, appearing in the preface, describes Gaia as "the hypothesis, the model, in which the Earth's living matter, air, oceans, and land surface form a complex system which can be seen as a single organism and which has the capacity to keep our planet a fit place for life."[31] This is important insofar as it points to Gaia's status as a working model or hypothesis (in later books it will become a theory), its constituent parts ("the Earth's living matter, air, oceans and land surface"), what they do ("keep our planet a fit place for life"), and, finally, how they do it (by operating as a single organism).

---

29 Joseph, *Gaia*, 63.
30 Richard Dawkins and W. Ford Doolittle have been the fiercest critics, claiming that Lovelock's theory amounts to a kind of global altruism. The critiques have little relevance for this project, which is not overly concerned with the scientific plausibility of the theory, but they are nevertheless interesting. See W. Ford Doolittle "Is Nature Really Motherly?" *CoEvolution Quarterly* 29 (1981): 58–63, as well as Richard Dawkins, *The Extended Phenotype: The Long Reach of the Gene* (Oxford: Oxford University Press, 1989).
31 Lovelock, *Gaia: A New Look at Life on Earth*, x.

The official definition, found in the glossary, does not contradict this, but is more cautiously worded (avoiding, for instance, any mention of the earth as organism), and provides more context for why such a hypothesis is needed:

> *Gaia Hypothesis:* This postulates that the physical and chemical condition of the surface of the Earth, of the atmosphere, and of the oceans has been and is actively made fit and comfortable by the presence of life itself. This is in contrast to the conventional wisdom which held that life adapted to the planetary conditions as it and they evolved in their separate ways.[32]

Here, too, life as the force that tames the earth, physically and chemically, is foregrounded. Lovelock contrasts this with the paradigm that insists life adapted *to* rather than simply adapted its environment. Gaia, here, is an abundant and powerful life force capable of remaking, or at least profoundly altering, the globe and gasses surrounding it.

Elsewhere, in more casual definitions, Gaia is made more concrete, and her status as living entity is proclaimed:

> [T]he hypothesis that the entire range of living matter on Earth, from whales to viruses, and from oaks to algae, could be regarded as constituting a single living entity, capable of manipulating the Earth's atmosphere to suit its overall needs and endowed with faculties and powers far beyond those of its constituent parts.[33]

Gaia, like any organism, is more than the sum of its parts and, as we will see, is indifferent to the makeup of these living inhabitants as long as they carry on with the business of making the earth habitable.

---

32 Ibid., 152.
33 Ibid., 9.

There are at least a dozen more definitions provided by Lovelock that could be listed here, but the exercise would soon become repetitive. What is important to remember is that the Gaia hypothesis holds that life's manipulation of its environment has global consequences that are so far-reaching and predictable that one may regard the earth as a living organism. Naturally, these definitions refer to the Gaia hypothesis, and not Gaia herself, which is the living body shaped by masses of life acting, more or less, in concert; however, they are an important starting point.

Further on in *Gaia*, as well as in later books, Lovelock emphasizes the improbability of the chemical disequilibria so tirelessly kept up by Gaia's inhabitants. This is the Gaia of Latour's strange whodunit, the entity that "is able to sustain and keep constant a highly improbable distribution of molecules."[34] In the story Lovelock tells, Gaia's birth, whether happy accident or opportunism or both, saved the earth from the tedium and lifelessness of chemical equilibrium:

At some time early in the Earth's history before life existed, the solid Earth, the atmosphere, and oceans were still evolving by the laws of physics and chemistry alone. It was careening, downhill, to the lifeless steady state of a planet almost at equilibrium. Briefly, in its headlong flight through the ranges of chemical and physical states, it entered a stage favorable for life. At some special time in that stage, the newly formed living cells grew until their presence so affected the Earth's environment as to halt the headlong drive towards equilibrium. At that instant the living things, the rocks, the air, and the oceans merged to form the new entity, Gaia. Just as when the sperm merges with the egg, new life was conceived.[35]

Life, here, becomes an almost magical force that intervenes with "the laws of physics and chemistry." And the actions of

34 Ibid., 38.
35 Lovelock, *The Ages of Gaia*, 41.

life on a planetary level, allowing it to exist in perpetuity, are Gaia — "symbiosis seen from space."[36]

To consider Gaia as a living entity, differing "from other living organisms of Earth in the way that you or I differ from our population of living cells," one must certainly enlarge, even literally, one's view of life. Lovelock writes again and again: "They hate to admit it, but the life scientists, whether the natural historians of the nineteenth century or the biologists of the twentieth, cannot explain what life is in scientific terms."[37] And while Lovelock certainly devotes a large amount of time to how Gaia *might* fit in with these unsatisfactory definitions (particularly by insisting that Gaia exists in a long-term state of chemical disequilibrium with correspondingly lower entropy), the real reason to say that Gaia lives is intuitive and affective. "[W]e all know intuitively what life is," he writes, continuing: "It is edible, lovable, or lethal."[38] Life, with Lovelock, is defined *in situ*. It is no wonder, then, that it took photographs of the earth like those from the Apollo 8 and Apollo 17 missions to resuscitate the idea of a living planet.

It should be noted that the notion "that the biosphere can be modeled as a single giant organism"[39] is often referred to in literature as the strong form of the Gaia hypothesis, with the weak version merely insisting "that life collectively has a significant effect on Earth's environment."[40] Scientists split hairs over precisely how much agency is granted to the earth in the Gaia hypothesis, and mainstream science, as might be guessed, embraces the weak form much more readily. Discussions of this in the literature are legion,[41] and it makes little sense to go over

36 Lynn Margulis and Dorion Sagan, "God, Gaia, and Biophilia," in *The Biophilia Hypothesis,* eds. Stephen Kellert and E.O. Wilson (Washington, DC: Island Press, 1993), 345–64, at 353.

37 Lovelock, *The Ages of Gaia,* 41, 16.

38 Ibid., 16.

39 James Kirchner, "The Gaia Hypothesis: Fact, Theory, and Wishful Thinking," *Climatic Change* 52, no. 4 (2002): 391–408.

40 Ibid., 393.

41 E.O. Wilson, for instance, in *The Future of Life,* articulates a view that seems to be common within the academy: "The concept of the biosphere

them here, where the scientific plausibility of the concept is tangential, but it is important to remember that there are some who place decidedly more or less weight on Gaia's status as organism.

Even those who wholeheartedly support Gaia are hesitant to frame the concept too much in terms of harmony. Kirchner, himself an earth scientist, for instance, refers to "the Gaian vision of global harmony," then goes on to emphasize the importance of attending to "the actual Earth system": "We should get on with it, as free as possible from preconceptions of the way the world ought to work."[42] Interestingly, Lovelock speaks very little of harmony, occasionally opting for the word homeostasis. And Margulis, it should be noted, rejects even the word homeostatic when referring to Gaia, describing it, with Dorion Sagan, as "homeorrhetic — regulated around what engineers call a moving set point, a set point which can change, as when global oxygen rose from a trace gas to a major constituent of the earth's atmosphere 2 billion years ago."[43] The subtext in many of these discussions (and we will return to this in the last section) is global warming: Would a planet "fit for life" allow the icecaps to melt and the oceans, at least metaphorically, to boil? Does the fact that climate appears to be not all that homeostatic after all mean that Gaia is not a living entity? Lovelock and Margulis suggest, in this regard, that we be patient; their claims about the Gaian capacity to regulate itself operate on decidedly extra-human time scales.

as Gaia has two versions: strong and weak. The strong version holds that the biosphere is a true superorganism, with each of the species in it optimized to stabilize the environment and benefit from balance in the entire system, like cells of the body or workers of an ant colony. This is a lovely metaphor, with a kernel of truth, provided the idea of superorganism is broadened enough. The strong version, however, is generally rejected by biologists, including Lovelock himself, as a working principle. The weak version, on the other hand, which holds that some species exercise widespread and even global influence, is well substantiated. Its acceptance has stimulated important new programs of research" (11–12).

42 Kirchner, "The Gaia Hypothesis," 406.
43 Margulis and Sagan, "God, Gaia, and Biophilia," 353.

Despite this, Gaia is remarkable in the immediate way it extends its relations to the human. As we read about Gaia, many authors remark, we realize we already are Gaians. For instance, Volk, a biologist and environmentalist, states the following:

> We need not wait to be shrunk by some futuristic wizardry to witness an exchange of gases from an interior viewpoint. Just walk in the woods. Trees are taking in carbon dioxide and releasing oxygen across the membranes of their leaves. Each of us already has an airhose, the trachea, by which we tap into the atmosphere and inhale what the trees freely offer. Take a deep breath. Or swim amid the living colors of a reef. Lie down in a field of undulating grass. Let a hand bob in a river's eddies. Smell some pungent dirt. We are already fantastic voyagers. All of us are cells within the embracing physiology of what Jim Lovelock has called "Gaia."[44]

There is no need here, if we think back to the last chapter, for Wilson's "motion picture projector of magical versatility." Gaia, nearly miraculously, grants us immediate access to "an interior viewpoint," in which merely by living and breathing we become "fantastic voyagers." The contemplation of Gaia necessarily involves a questioning of the boundaries of the individual *Umwelt*, creating "a delightful sense of being inside a giant metabolism."[45] With this "delightful sense," we begin to careen already towards the affective wonder occasioned by Gaia.

In the work of David Abram, this delightful sense surrounding or immanent to Gaia can be taken literally. Gaia, more than a hypothesis, is a kind of shorthand for our participation in a "vaster physiology":

> So simply by breathing we are participating in the life of the biosphere. But not just by breathing! When we consider the

---

44 Tyler Volk, *Gaia's Body: Toward a Physiology of Earth* (New York: Springer-Verlag, 1998), viii.

45 Ibid., ix.

biosphere not as a machine, but as an animate, self-sustaining entity, then it becomes apparent that everything we see, everything we hear, every experience of smelling and tasting and touching is informing our bodies regarding the internal state of this other, vaster physiology—the biosphere itself. Sensory perception, then, discloses itself as a form of communication between an organism and the animate earth... Perception is a communication, or even a communion—a sensuous participation between ourselves and the living world that encompasses us.[46]

In a familiar environmentalist turn, even the passive becomes active with Gaia. We cannot sense the earth without ourselves being an organ (or cell or organelle) of it. What distinguishes Gaia is that the human is positioned as no exception to the ecosystem, no disrupter of it (as in more conservative environmentalist rhetoric), but as immediate participant in it. At least with the present technology, we cannot refuse to be Gaians. The very contemplation of our role on earth is a kind of "communion"; Gaia as entity already begins to bleed here into Gaia as sensation.

Abram calls attention to this again and again, implying that the concept actually fosters new kinds of attention. He writes that it "enables, quite literally, *a return to our senses.*"[47] He continues:

We become aware once again of our breathing bodies, and of the bodily world that surrounds us. We are drawn out of that ideal, Platonic domain of thoughts and theories back into this realm that we corporeally inhabit, this land that we share with the other animals, and the plants, and the microbial entities who vibrate and spin within our cells and the

46 David Abram, "The Mechanical and the Organic: On the Impact of Metaphor in Science," in *Scientists on Gaia,* eds. Stephen Schneider and Penelope Boston (Cambridge: MIT Press, 1991), 66–74, at 71.
47 Ibid.

cells of the spider. Our senses loosen themselves from the mechanical constraints imposed by an outmoded language. They begin to participate, once again, in the ongoing life of the land around us.[48]

Gaia, for Abram, becomes a way to "return" to immediacy and corporeality and recognize that the so-called cave is only one "tiny sector" of the world. Certainly, some of this language ("return," "back," "begin to participate, once again") revolves around the notion (referred to in Chapter 2) that at some point in the past we had been more aware of our "breathing bodies, and of the bodily world that surrounds us." As always, this Garden-of-Edenism should be viewed critically, but the idea that Gaia invites us to consider and experience that outside of the narrow confines of our own *Umwelten* is a compelling one.

4.1.3. Gaia: the only concept that is also a heavenly body

Before moving on to what Gaia does, it is necessary to explore its conceptual status in more detail. As Deleuze and Guattari remind us, concepts are not "waiting for us ready-made, like heavenly bodies";[49] while Gaia may be a heavenly body, the concept itself was not merely stumbled upon. Deleuze and Guattari suggest, rather, that the concept is "connected to problems without which [it] would have no meaning."[50] Thus, although Gaia is a way of describing the living earth, a heavenly body *par excellence,* it must be understood in relation to Lovelock's initial problem, which is also highlighted by Latour: Why is the earth, like every other planet we know of, not dead? Gaia, as nebulous in many ways as the planet she refers to, becomes the multiplicity that, time and time again, enables life. In this distinct nebulousness, Gaia is perhaps less a hypothesis about the earth (how would we even falsify the claims Lovelock makes

---

48 Ibid.
49 Gilles Deleuze and Félix Guattari, *What Is Philosophy?,* trans. Hugh Tomlinson and Graham Burchell (1994; rpt. London: Verso, 2015), 5.
50 Ibid., 16.

for Gaia?) and more of a dynamic composition, as Deleuze and Guattari describe it:

The concept speaks the event, not the essence of the thing — pure Event, a hecceity; an entity: the event of the Other or of the face (when, in turn, the face is taken as concept). It is like the bird as event. The concept is defined by *the inseparability of a finite number of heterogeneous components traversed by a point of absolute survey at infinite speed.*[51]

Gaia speaks the living earth as composite event, an equally irreducible and unreproducible multiplicity of lives and processes. It is easy to see from this vantage point, even before getting into the scientific debates, why the concept presents problems for scientists. Gaia corresponds not to what we know about the earth, "a finite number of heterogeneous components," but to their inseparability, "symbiosis seen from space."[52]

51 Deleuze and Guattari, *What Is Philosophy?*, 21, emphasis in original.
52 It is in this way, too, that Gaia can be distinguished from similar terms, such as noosphere. Rafal Serafin, referring to Vernadsky's (as opposed to Chardin's) noosphere states: "The concept of noosphere focuses on what we do know and understand about the workings and management of biogeochemical cycles, while the notion of Gaia emphasizes what we do not know and understand" ("Noosphere, Gaia and the Science of the Biosphere," in *The Biosphere and Noosphere Reader: Global Environment, Society, and Change,* eds. Paul Samson and David Pitt, [London: Routledge, 1999], 136–39, at 138). Indeed, Gaia might actually be viewed as a kind of hybrid between Chardin's and Vernadsky's notion of the noosphere. For Chardin, Serafin notes, "the noosphere represents the total pattern of thinking organisms and their activity, including the patterns of their relations" (ibid., 136). For Vernadsky, the noosphere is "a special environment or medium for humanity, consisting of the systems of organized thought and its artefacts among which humans move and have their being — as fish swim and reproduce in rivers in the sea" (ibid.). For Chardin, then, the noosphere is part of a vitalist spirituality, while for Vernadsky "the noosphere was above all the medium in which humanity could find fulfilment…through exercising deliberate and conscious control over its milieu" ibid.). Lovelock's Gaia contains very little of Vernadsky's anthropocentrism, but it does emphasize the necessity for conscious control. And

And despite the amount of attention Gaia has received from new-age spiritualists, Gaia should be understood as a fiercely secular concept. According to Latour, it constitutes "probably the *least religious entity* produced by Western science."[53] Latour contrasts this with "nature," which, he argues, presents a vision of the world as always already unified. He says of Gaia: "it is made up of agents that are not *prematurely unified* in a single acting totality. Gaia, the outlaw, is the antisystem."[54] Latour thus recognizes the necessity of composing its heterogeneous components in order to comprehend the earth as event and haecceity.

In his Gifford Lectures as well as in *Facing Gaia,* Latour gives a number of reasons for why Gaia is nothing like "nature" or, alternatively, Spaceship Earth, a concept introduced by Buckminster Fuller in the sixties.[55] The most significant of these is that "a spaceship does not change all its parts as it goes along. Gaia does."[56] Lovelock speaks and writes constantly of Gaia's volatility (or dynamism, depending on what light you wish to cast on it) and willingness to forsake one group of organisms for another. There is no mistaking Gaia for a static entity with set rules. Indeed, Lovelock states early on, "There can be no prescription, no set of rules, for living within Gaia. For our different actions

the vitalist streak found in Chardin's noosphere, as we will see later in the chapter, is alive and well in Lovelock's prose.

53 Latour, "Third Lecture: Gaia, a (Finally Secular) Figure for Nature," 91.

54 Ibid.

55 Fuller describes the earth as "a mechanical vehicle" that "must be comprehended and serviced in total" in order to be "persistently successful," by which he ostensibly means suitable for human life. See "Chapter 4: Spaceship Earth" in *Operating Manual for Spaceship Earth,* Buckminster Fuller Institute, March 8, 2010 (first published 1969), https://web.archive.org/web/20100823120750/http://www.bfi.org:80/about-bucky/resources/books/operating-manual-spaceship-earth/chapter-4-spaceship-earth.

56 Bruno Latour, "The Puzzling Face of a Secular Gaia," Gifford Lectures: "Facing Gaia: A New Inquiry into Natural Religion," University of Edinburgh, February 21, 2013, http://www.ed.ac.uk/arts-humanities-soc-sci/news-events/lectures/gifford-lectures/archive/series-2012-2013/bruno-latour.

there are only consequences."[57] Gaia is unique in that, unlike our precious and fragile Spaceship Earth or "nature," she does not need protecting. Life will go on, even if it means that some life forms must be extinguished along the way. In this way, too, Gaia is not something to be held up and worshipped, but to be navigated, explored, and tinkered with (at the same time, of course, that she's tinkering with you).

The second justification for Gaia's secularism is that Gaia removes the distinction between organism and environment, presenting us with organisms radically immanent to the earth, rather than framing the earth as an exalted entity on which we tread as guests. Latour outlines more clearly what makes this point of view distinct: "Since all living agents follow their own intentions all along, modifying their neighbors as much as possible, there is no way to distinguish between the environment to which the organism is adapting and the point at which its own action begins."[58] The environment as a stage of inactivity disappears in Lovelock's work, to be supplanted by the more interactive *Umwelt,* which, as Uexküll reminds us, is composed of constellations of affects. The accumulated forces arising from these intersecting *Umwelten* become *"waves of action"*[59] — the affects of the earth.

When I claim here that Gaia is a fiercely secular concept, then, I mean three things, and these are worth recapitulating. First of all, Gaia is a concept, understood as a "finite number of heterogeneous components" *rendered* inseparable. Gaia may be a heavenly body, but, as a concept, it had to be more conspicuously invented and composed than, say, "nature." Secondly, and following from this, in requiring this composition, this piecing together of disparate phenomena, Gaia provides a secular vision of the natural world that is unparalleled. Gaia, rather than existing as essence, is the composite event. Finally, Gaia erases

---

57 Lovelock, *Gaia: A New Look at Life on Earth,* 140.

58 Latour, "Third Lecture: Gaia, a (Finally Secular) Figure for Nature," 100.

59 Latour, "The Puzzling Face of a Secular Gaia," emphasis in the original. See also Latour, "Third Lecture: Gaia, a (Finally Secular) Figure for Nature," 101.

the distinction between organism and environment and in so doing renders biota and the earth continuous, immanent to one another. Earth as a collection of environments or stages populated by creatures drops away, becoming "a living organism of which we are a part; not the owner, nor the tenant, not even a passenger."[60]

4.2.
Reenchantment for the Space Age

At the same time that Gaia insists on this secularism, it also "leads to a radical reenchanting of the world."[61] And as Sagan and Margulis as well as Lovelock note, this has hardly been taken in stride by the scientific establishment. Lovelock has been nothing less than bitter about Gaia's scientific reception, writing, "It is the scientific establishment that now forbids heresy. I had the faint hope that Gaia might be denounced from the pulpit; instead, I was asked to deliver a sermon on Gaia at the Cathedral of St John the Divine in New York."[62] Here, before moving on to the more specific strategies of affective wonder that Gaia engages with, I will take a closer look at Gaia as a tool of reenchantment: How does Gaia seek to reenchant? What criticisms of the scientific establishment, moreover, are made explicit in this effort? Does Gaia present us with a vision for a reenchanted science?

That Gaia seeks to do more than answer questions about the mysterious composition of the earth's atmosphere is made clear from the beginning. Gaia, the living planet, is framed as the fruit of the space age rather than of advances in gas chromatography. Lovelock claims, in fact, that "the outstanding spin-off from space research is not new technology," but that "for the first time in human history we have had a chance to look at the Earth from

---

60 Lovelock, "The Earth as a Living Organism," 488.
61 Margulis and Sagan, "God, Gaia, and Biophilia," 354.
62 Lovelock, *Gaia: A New Look at Life on Earth*, vii.

space, and the information gained from seeing from the outside our azure-green planet in all its global beauty has given rise to a whole new set of questions and answers."[63] Gaia, in this light, describes a new, invigorated, more uncertain orientation towards the earth made possible by new technologies and the images produced by them. Lovelock refers to the images produced by the Apollo missions over and over again in his books. It is worth observing that, at the same time, Stewart Brand, of Whole Earth Catalog fame, was profoundly impressed by the same images. The beauty of the Earth viewed from space inspired two dramatically different orientations towards the "azure-green" ball: While Brand would go on to write, "We *are* as gods and might as well get good at it,"[64] it spurred Lovelock to think anew about immanence with the Gaia hypothesis and raised new questions about our relationship with the earth. That Lovelock's vision is one of reenchantment, and that Brand's is not, is no accident. Brand's vision foregrounds certainty and control, and also valorizes the tools and methods of modern, institutional science. Lovelock's, as we shall see shortly, does anything but. Lovelock states:

The Gaia hypothesis is for those who like to walk or simply stand and stare, to wonder about the Earth and the life it bears, and to speculate about the consequences of our own presence here. It is an alternative to that pessimistic view which sees nature as a primitive force to be subdued and conquered. It is also an alternative to that equally depressing picture of our planet as a demented spaceship, forever

63 Ibid., 8.
64 As cited in Fred Turner, *From Counterculture to Cyberculture: Stewart Brand, the Whole Earth Network, and the Rise of Digital Utopianism* (Chicago: University of Chicago Press, 2006), 82. Turner also highlights Brand's role in persuading NASA to release the images that are now so iconic, Brand began selling buttons at Berkeley's Sather Gate printed with the question, "Why Haven't We Seen a Photograph of the Whole Earth Yet?" (69).

travelling, driverless and purposeless, around an inner circle of the sun.[65]

Already, here we learn that Gaia is for those who "wonder," who do not seek first to subdue and conquer the earth, but to "speculate on the consequences of our presence here"; its non-anthropocentrism and insistence that the human does not exclusively hold the reigns is also significant because it plainly contradicts Weber's disenchantment narrative as outlined in Chapter 2. That Lovelock chooses to so harshly criticize Buckminster Fuller's Spaceship Earth is also important. Gaia, in fact, exists almost entirely in opposition to Spaceship Earth, which collapses an infinite number of *Umwelten* into one globe, and emphasizes the fragility, rather than the robustness, of life on earth. Perhaps even more significantly with regard to Gaia's defiance of the disenchantment narrative, the concept makes it clear that we are not passengers on a "demented spaceship," but *of* the earth. It is hubris to think that there is some kind of connection that has been severed. It is ironic, of course, that it takes physically leaving the earth, or at least photographic evidence of this, to reassert the degree to which we are part of it. The "moon's eye view of our home in space" reenchants, not by virtue of the fact that we are able to attain this perspective, but because "we are suddenly aware of being citizens of no mean planet, however mean and squalid the human contribution to this panorama may be in close up."[66] "Whatever happened in the distant past," Lovelock assures us, "we are undoubtedly a living part of a strange and beautiful anomaly in our solar system."[67]

The words "strange and beautiful anomaly" lead neatly into the second manner in which Gaia reenchants: It asks us to attend to the beauty of the individual parts and how they contribute to the functioning of the earth as organism. On Gaia, nothing is insignificant, and investigation, far from robbing or-

65 Lovelock, *Gaia: A New Look at Life on Earth*, 12, my emphasis.
66 Ibid., 64.
67 Ibid., 64–65.

ganisms and processes of their intrigue, far from disenchanting, constantly reveals the degree to which life shapes even the apparently nonbiological. Lovelock often waxes poetic about diatoms and radiolarians,[68] for instance, types of nearly ubiquitous zooplankton with glassy silicate shells. While, like the Victorians who showcased them in elaborate arrangements on microscope slides, he appreciates their intricate shapes and patterning, the real beauty of diatoms can only be seen from "a planetary engineering point of view."[69] He goes on to explain:

[T]he significance of the life cycle of diatoms and coccoliths is that when they die their soft parts dissolve and their intricate skeletons or shells sink to the bottom of the sea. A constant rain of these structures, which oceanographers call "tests", almost as beautiful in death as in life, has fallen on the ocean floor through the aeons, building up great beds of chalk and limestone (from coccoliths) and silicate (from diatoms). This deluge of dead organisms is not so much a funeral procession as a conveyer belt constructed by Gaia to convey parts from the production zone at surface levels to the storage regions below the seas and continents.[70]

This process does not merely reveal a strange and enchanting scene in which "tests" comprised of hard-shelled zooplankton fall to the ocean floor like snow. Like nearly all the writing surrounding Gaia, it animates the purportedly inanimate; what is, essentially, rock — chalk, limestone, and silicate — is imbued with a living history. Life pervades each and every part of Gaia, and here science does not render features of Gaia inert, but makes them come to life.

It is not just these descriptions of the planet and individual elements of it that implicitly contradict the disenchantment narrative, however. Lovelock also explicitly acknowledges that he

68 Cf. Ibid., 94.
69 Ibid., 97.
70 Ibid.

does not buy into claims "that things were better in the good old days."[71] He continues:

> So ingrained is this habit of thought — which we pass on in our turn as we grow old — that it is almost automatic to assume that early man was in total harmony with the rest of Gaia. Perhaps we were indeed expelled from the Garden of Eden and perhaps the ritual is symbolically repeated in the mind of each generation.
>
> Biblical teaching that the Fall was from a state of blissful innocence into the sorrowful world of the flesh and the devil, through the sin of disobedience, is hard to accept in our contemporary culture. Nowadays it is more fashionable to attribute our fall from grace to man's insatiable curiosity and his irresistible urge to experiment and interfere with the natural order of things. Significantly, both the biblical story and, to a lesser extent, its modern interpretation seem aimed at inculcating and sustaining a sense of guilt — a powerful but arbitrary negative feedback in human society.[72]

What is so interesting here is that Lovelock positions three versions of the fall as variations on the same theme: the ecological fall from the harmony with the earth suffered by "early man," Adam and Eve's expulsion from the Garden of Eden, and the scientific fall that enables us to "interfere with the natural order of things" are all for him equally suspect narratives that serve, in one way or another, to instill guilt and, ultimately, to control.

Two claims that derive from this rejection of the disenchantment narrative clash with more conservative, "green" ecologies. First of all, Lovelock has been adamant about seeing human industrial activities as part of the larger Gaian metabolism, as opposed to merely "fouling the nest and pos[ing] a threat to the total life of the planet which grows more ominous every year."[73]

71 Ibid., 107.
72 Ibid.
73 Ibid.

Pollution, Lovelock assures us at every turn, is not "bad" in and of itself, but, as the disposal of waste from metabolic processes, "natural" and inevitable.[74] As carbon emissions show no sign of abating, however, he has warned readers in no uncertain terms about the potential consequences of global warming.[75] Secondly, "nature," or nonhuman Gaia, is far from benign, and often downright cruel. Lovelock is fond of reminding readers that many of our deadliest chemicals, like the insecticide pyrethrum, which derives from chrysanthemums, have not been synthesized by humans. He also playfully refers to "dirty tricks" (i.e. mimicry) played by human and nonhuman organisms alike in order to gain selective advantages: "There is no Geneva Convention to limit natural dirty tricks."[76] Gaia confronts us with consequences, not morals. And in refraining from moralizing about pollution or portraying nonhuman Gaia (as if such an entity were imaginable) as benign, Lovelock rejects the human exceptionalism that is so crucial to the disenchantment narrative.

The other part of the disenchantment narrative that Lovelock rails against is the idea that science must drain the world of its allure. Scientific inquiry, in Gaia and its sequels, is presented, rather, as a kind of communion with Gaia, a unique way of participating in the global metabolism. Lovelock writes often of his own serendipitous successes in the field, where, he advises, it is "unwise to plan ahead in too fine detail; one must keep one's eyes open and see what Gaia has to offer."[77] Similarly, he celebrates the kind of independent science he has engaged in at his own home as "no penance, [but] rather a delightful way of life that painters and novelists have always known about."[78] At times, independent science becomes a rallying cry: "Fellow scientists join me, you have nothing to lose but your grants."[79]

74 Ibid., 109.
75 See, for instance, James Lovelock, "Forecasts for the Twenty-first Century," in *The Revenge of Gaia* (London: Penguin Books, 2007), 61–83
76 Lovelock, *Gaia: A New Look at Life on Earth*, 108.
77 Ibid., 164.
78 Lovelock, *The Ages of Gaia*, xv.
79 Ibid.

Clearly a grant is not to be underestimated, but Lovelock claims that the professionalization and institutionalization of science brings with it enormous trade-offs. Institutional and university science, he maintains, "more often applies its expertise to the trivial than to the numinous."[80] This is only to be expected, when "most scientists live their lives in cities and have little or no contact with the natural world."[81] What has been taken out of the laboratory at the scientific institution in the city is the affective richness of the world: "Their [institutional scientists'] models of the Earth are built in universities or institutions where there is all the talent and hardware necessary, but what tends to be missing is that vital ingredient, information gathered first-hand in the real world."[82] Lovelock is adamant about an immanent science that takes into account, rather than denies, the degree to which the human, too, is bound up.

Indeed, David Abram goes as far as to suggest a "Gaian science," in which "it would be manifestly evident that one is always already involved, or participant, in that which one studies. The effort, then, would no longer be made to avoid or repress this involvement, but rather to clarify and refine it."[83] This sounds uncannily similar to Karen Barad's insistence, nearly twenty years later, on the ongoing intra-activity of the world that does not cease in scientific practice, but which must be negotiated in order to produce such categories as subject and object (see 2.2.3). Both authors champion an embedded science and view modern science's claim to be somehow "apart" with a degree of suspicion. For Abram, an alternative model, which he also argues would crucially inform a Gaian science, is provided by the alchemical tradition. According to him, this tradition presents

the material world, and indeed matter itself, as a locus of subtle powers and immanent forces, a dynamic network of

80 Ibid., xiv.
81 Lovelock, *Gaia: A New Look at Life on Earth*, 136.
82 Ibid.
83 Abram, "The Mechanical and the Organic," 72.

invisible sympathies and antipathies…material nature was perceived as alive, as a complex, living organism with which the investigator — the natural magician, or scientist — was in relation. ("It is an error," wrote Campanella, "to think that the world does feel just because it does not have legs, eyes, and hands.") The experimental method was developed and honed as the medium of this relation, as a practice of dialogue between oneself and animate nature. Experimentation was here a form of participation, a technique of communication or communion which, when successful, effected a transformation not just in the structure of the material experimented upon, but in the structure of the experimenter himself.[84]

At least in Lovelock's depiction of himself — as consumer of poisonous plants in his youth, and, later, during WWII, burning his own skin in order to check the effects of radiant heat from flamethrowers[85] — he takes the experimental method as a mode of relation and dialogue very seriously. Perhaps, as Abram suggests, this is why he is able, as we will explore in the next section, to so easily accept nonhuman agency. Gaia is a grand vision of a global metabolism of which, since our appearance on the earth (however one takes "our"), we have always been a part. That Lovelock refuses an easy appeal to "return" us to the earth is a testament to him as a thinker. Gaia reenchants, but not by restoring anything, unless we count a science more embedded in the world as a kind of restoration. What Gaia really does is deny the disenchantment narrative altogether. Its mere existence implies there has never been a time in which it was possible to operate independently from the earth.

84 Ibid., 67.
85 Lovelock, *Homage to Gaia,* 80–81.

4.3.
Strange Agents: Gaia and the Human

It is easy enough to accept the inhabitants of the earth as participating in a global metabolism. What is harder to come to terms
with is in what sense Gaia is alive. This section begins by taking
a closer look at Gaia's agency and vitalist bent — the manner in
which it "complicates any facile distinction between living and
nonliving aspects of our world."[86] As we will see, Gaia's insistence on a world comprised of entirely indiscrete *Umwelten*, as
opposed to mere environments that organisms inhabit, is profoundly disorienting. Section 4.3.2 "Human unexceptionalism?"
explores what this multiplication and broadening of agency
means for the human. Gaia is overwhelmingly non-anthropocentric, but Lovelock does flirt with the idea of the human as a
sign of Gaia acquiring awareness. Our capacity for wonder, and
not our agency and power as individual organisms or a species,
is the only distinguishing characteristic of the human in a Gaian
framework.

4.3.1 *Our body which art in heaven: the earth alive*

When attempting to conceive of a global organism, *The Ages of
Gaia* is often much better than the earlier *Gaia* at conveying the
sense of immanent life for which Lovelock is still so famous:
"There is no clear distinction anywhere on the Earth's surface
between living and nonliving matter. There is merely a hierarchy
of intensity going from the 'material' environment of the rocks
and the atmosphere to the living cells."[87] It is not only that Gaia
is composed of organisms and environments, and that organisms cannot be neatly separated from their *Umwelten* (which,
after all, we have also heard before), but that, in terms of Gaia's

86 David Abram, "In the Depths of a Breathing Planet: Gaia and the Transformation of Experience," in *Gaia in Turmoil: Climate Change, Biodepletion and Earth Ethics in an Age of Crisis,* eds. Eileen Crist and H. Bruce
Rinker (Cambridge: MIT Press, 2010), 66–74, at 221.

87 Lovelock, *The Ages of Gaia,* 40.

vitality, there is no difference between the living and nonliving. What Lovelock gives us instead is "a hierarchy of intensity," presumably in which order, or low entropy, is most intense, but one might also think of it in terms of affective intensity.

By refusing to create meaningful distinctions between Gaia's living and nonliving parts, and instead thinking in terms of intensity, Lovelock accomplishes three things. First, and most basically, he resuscitates vitalist discourses in which "materiality is figured not as inert or even passively resistant but as active and energetic, albeit not purposive in any strong sense."[88] If the living cannot be neatly separated from the nonliving, and Gaia as a living entity is composed of this hybrid *stuff* of varying degrees of intensity, then everything acquires "a vitality flowing across all living [and nonliving] bodies."[89]

Secondly, with this vitalism, Lovelock makes way for nonhuman agency. Jane Bennett describes this vitalist agency neatly as an "*impersonal* kind of agency."[90] If we can speak of Gaia's telos, it involves nothing more than guaranteeing its future existence and resisting the entropic spiral that careens, inevitably, towards lifelessness. Thus, Lovelock can write of Gaia's mysterious "ingenuity" in overcoming threats to her own survival in the form, for example, of the oxygenation of the earth two aeons ago: "[T]he biosphere was like the crew of a stricken submarine, needing all hands to rebuild the systems damaged or destroyed and at the same time threatened by an increasing concentration of poisonous gases in the air."[91] Lovelock goes on to describe the organisms that would replace the anaerobic bacteria that had previously populated the globe. Gaia's agency remains imper-

---

88 Jane Bennett, "The Force of Materiality: A Vitalist Stopover on the Way to a New Materialism," in *New Materialisms: Ontology, Agency, and Politics,* eds. Diana Coole and Samantha Frost (Durham: Duke University Press, 2010), 47–69, at 47. Bennett is referring specifically to Driesch's notion of entelechy here, but it is taken as a model for nonreligiously informed vitalisms.

89 Bennett, "The Force of Materiality," 55.

90 Ibid.

91 Lovelock, *Gaia: A New Look at Life on Earth,* 30–31.

sonal here, however, because one cannot exactly consider this kind of move an act of self-preservation. After this oxygen-induced holocaust, nearly all the parts, if we dare to call them that, are switched out. It is vitality, the continuation of life, rather, that Gaia serves. It is also impersonal because, although Gaia can be viewed as an organism, it has no brain. As Latour has stated: "The great thing about Lovelock's Gaia is that it reacts, feels and might get rid of us, without being ontologically unified. It is not a superorganism endowed with any sort of unified agency."[92]

Despite no unified agency being attributed to Gaia, she is often described in terms of a body, and Lovelock later suggests "planetary physiology" or "planetary medicine"[93] as a name for the profession dedicated to the study of Gaia. The global temperature regulation accomplished by Gaia, for instance, is explained time and time again[94] as analogous to the complex way in which the human body regulates temperature. Carbon dioxide and greenhouse gases become, in this framework, "the gaseous equivalent of warm clothing."[95] Oceans, too, act as a kind of circulatory system, or, at other times, "are vital parts

---

92 Bruno Latour, "Waiting for Gaia: Composing the Common World Through Arts and Politics," lecture, French Institute, London, November 2011, 10, http://www.bruno-latour.fr/sites/default/files/124-GAIA-LONDON-SPEAP_0.pdf. The character of Dr. Lovelock in Latour's theatrical take on Gaia explains its agency as follows: "Yes, almost as if there were an intention. But there is no intention whatsoever, I assure you, just a stroke of luck that life has taken advantage of to put the odds on its side thereafter, to load the dice. Yes, a winning formula that Mars didn't come up with. A bit of tinkering, you see. Why did I call it Gaia if there was no intention? So it would stick in people's minds. But it's not a person, no, not a character, either. Just feedback loops that I've grouped together. I've done a bit of tinkering too. You have to dramatize, as you know very well." See Bruno Latour, Frédérique Aït-Touati, and Chloé Latour, *Kosmokolos: Global Climate Tragi-Comedy*, trans. Julie Rose, http://www.bruno-latour.fr/node/358.

93 Lovelock, *The Ages of Gaia*, xvii.

94 Cf. ibid., 20, 53.

95 Ibid., 20.

of the global steam engine."[96] Indeed, throughout *Gaia* and its sequels, metaphors for the body appear side by side with mechanical metaphors. The formation of the coral and stromatolite reefs is described as "an engineering task well beyond human capabilities."[97] Lovelock cannot or will not decide whether Gaia is body or machine. Perhaps if the earth is "the great unengendered stasis," "the surface on which the whole process of production is inscribed,"[98] Gaia names this process of production — the machine that molds the surface of the great heavenly body. On this level, the organism, or individual agencies, disappear and are supplanted by "biochemical guilds whose members share a commitment to universal enzymes."[99] Hence Gaia's orientation is toward becoming, toward creative maintenance of the conditions necessary for life, rather than the individual lives of the organisms on its surface. Were these organisms to be granted more of a starring role on Gaia, rather than what they take up and what they emit, Lovelock would run the risk of creating a caricature of life and depriving Gaia entirely of intelligence and agency. Gaia could have easily gone the way of the bodies in the popular children's program *Once upon a time...life,*[100] which are nothing more than shells populated by strangely anthropomorphic automatons we are supposed to see as cells and proteins.

Finally, perhaps because it refuses to grant something like a unified agency but is nevertheless so fixated upon the agency of life, Gaia, particularly as described by Latour,[101] has a strange way of inverting background and foreground. Latour writes of Lovelock's "introduction of new invisible characters capable of reversing the order and the hierarchy of the agents."[102] Clouds

96 Ibid., 84.
97 Lovelock, *Gaia: A New Look at Life on Earth*, 98.
98 Gilles Deleuze and Félix Guattari, *Anti-Oedipus: Capitalism and Schizophrenia*, trans. Robert Hurley, Mark Seem, and Helen Lane (London: Continuum, 2004), 140–41.
99 Volk, *Gaia's Body*, 152.
100 Originally *Il était une fois...la vie*, created by Albert Barillé, which aired in 1987 on Canal+.
101 See Latour, "Third Lecture: Gaia, a (Finally Secular) Figure for Nature."
102 Ibid., 93.

become the work of algae, and mountains the dead organisms that have fallen to the seafloor. Latour describes an affective dizziness induced by this material merry-go-round: Gaia is "dizzying. And our vertigo is much more pronounced than the one set off by Galileo when he described the Earth orbiting around the Sun." Latour argues this is because we can feel, sense, even smell the agents integral to Lovelock's model.[103] With Lovelock, the earth suddenly ceases to be the ball orbiting the sun on which we conduct our business. This business is revealed to be so entirely dependent upon and permeated by other intentionalities, other actors, that it is no longer possible to speak of the environment as occupied by inert matter, let alone as inert background itself. In the Gifford lectures, importantly, Latour also draws a connection to Uexküll, arguing that, despite Gaia being thinkable as an organism, it is not possible to think of it as a "general *Umwelt.*"[104] It is, rather, the amalgamation of countless *Umwelten* and their interaction. Wonder, as the experience of other *Umwelten,* acquires special significance here; it is, as we shall see in the next section, the way in which the human attends to the background that can no longer be conceived as such.

4.3.2 Human unexceptionalism?

In this topsy-turvy world, suffused with life, enzymes, and bountiful nonhuman agency, the question of the role of the human looms large. This broadening of the concept of agency and acknowledgment that we are far from the only global actors means that "we now find ourselves fully embodied and embedded within a nature that has its own wild intelligence, and our subjectivity seems no longer entirely ours."[105] Gaia, as we shall see in this section, can be described as essentially indifferent to the human, but Lovelock, ever the optimist, also carves out a special (but not privileged) place for the species.[106] It is, however,

---

103 Ibid., 93, 94.
104 Latour, "The Puzzling Face of a Secular Gaia."
105 Abram, "In the Depths of a Breathing Planet," 222.
106 He distinguishes, in fact, his human interest in the perpetuity of the species from that which is strictly Gaian, stating that, "Gaia philosophy is not

not strictly on the material level that the human has something to contribute to Gaia (although all inhabitants of Gaia contribute something on the material level). The human contribution to Gaia is affective, dealing more with our relation to the global system than our capacity to influence it.

Gaia deals many blows to anthropocentric human hubris, but the two largest surround our status as organisms and the impression that we operate separately or in opposition to what is "natural." This first attack on anthropocentrism might be best understood by looking at Lovelock's claim that, ever since anaerobic bacteria were driven from the surface of the earth roughly two eons ago by the rapid oxygenation of the atmosphere, "large animals including ourselves serve mainly to provide them with their anaerobic environment." He continues, "They are now back again on the surface in the most comfortable and secure of environments, enjoying a truly pampered existence and optimum status, while continuously supplied with food. These minute organisms now inhabit the gut of all animals from insects to elephants."[107] This goes above and beyond the nineteenth-century injuries of evolutionary theory. It is not just that we are descended from apes, thinkable as animals, and therefore robbed of some our divinity. Our status as homes and apparent wonderlands for anaerobic bacteria robs us, at least in part, of our humanity. It implies we have survived not by dint of our ingenuity and willful climbing of the tree of life — not, in other words, by "excelling" as organisms — but because, just like other large mammals, we provide a habitat for microflora that isn't half bad. In this light, we become something like biochemical mules, and the ceaseless drive to reproduce becomes less about passing on genes and more about carrying out the metabolic work of Gaia. The second blow dealt to the human in Gaia involves our insistence, also referred to in the previous section on disenchantment, that we are tampering with the "natu-

humanist. But being a grandfather with eight grandchildren I need to be optimistic" (Lovelock, "The Earth as Living Organism," 488).
107 Lovelock, *Gaia: A New Look at Life on Earth,* 109.

ral" order of things. Lovelock writes quite pointedly that "The very concept of pollution is anthropocentric and it may even be irrelevant in the Gaian context.[108] He uses the example of fluorocarbons, which were just coming under fire at the time Lovelock was writing *Gaia* for their role in damaging the ozone layer:

> The man-made gases such as the fluorocarbons, which have their sources mainly in the chemical industry and were never in the air before industrial man appeared, are very indicative of life at work. A visitor viewing the Earth from outer space and discovering aerosol-propellant gases in our atmosphere would have no doubt whatever that our planet bore life, and probably intelligence of a kind as well. In our persistent self-imposed alienation from nature, we tend to think that our industrial products are not "natural." In fact, they are just as natural as all the other chemicals of the Earth, for they have been made by us, who are surely living creatures. They may of course be aggressive and dangerous, like nerve gases, but no more so than the toxin manufactured by the botulinus baccilus.[109]

Here, industrial products are emissions no different than those from bacteria or insects. Pollution, Lovelock consistently assures us, is merely life at work, and while there can be consequences from it that we consider deleterious, there is nothing inherently bad about the substances themselves. The structure of the chemical compounds might mark pollutants as having been produced by factories rather than organisms directly, but they are "just as natural as all the other chemicals of the Earth." And Lovelock reminds us, cheekily, that sometimes our "fouling of the nest" has accidental benefits, noting that "roses still bloom better in London than in remote country areas, a consequence of the destruction by the pollutant sulfur dioxide of

108 Ibid., 110.
109 Ibid., 80.

the fungi which attack them."[110] The point is that it is hubris to view our own activity on Gaia as somehow outside of the global metabolism; it forms an integral part of it: "In other words, like it or not, and whatever we may do to the total system, we shall continue to be drawn, albeit unawares, into the Gaian process of regulation."[111] This is not, of course, to imply that our con-tribution to the global metabolism will ultimately serve us as a species. Lovelock is very careful to warn of Gaia's indifference to anything but life: "Her unconscious goal is a planet fit for life. If humans stand in the way of this, we shall be eliminated with as little pity as would be shown the micro-brain of an interconti-nental ballistic nuclear missile in full flight to its target."[112]

If we stand out neither as organisms nor for the chemicals we produce, what can we make of the strange bipeds that have so altered Gaia's surface? Lovelock, we might observe, wants to as-sign a special role to the human, but he is hesitant to, once again, elevate "technological man" to the status of mind for Gaia's body. He asks, for instance, "To what extent is our collective intelli-gence also a part of Gaia? Do we as a species constitute a Gaian nervous system and a brain which can consciously anticipate environmental changes?"[113] He never properly answers these questions, perhaps because he realizes that framing the human as "the brain" of Gaia represents, ultimately, a very strong form of anthropocentrism. Other advocates of Gaia are savvier in this regard. Volk, for instance, frames the formation and prolifera-tion of the idea of Gaia itself as the earth acquiring awareness:

By our mental models we become conscious of our own ac-tivities and those of the whole Earth and beyond. We do not have to wait for the slow meandering of evolution to adapt us to the altered climate and atmospheric chemistry our guild

110 Ibid., 110.
111 Ibid., 128.
112 Lovelock, *The Ages of Gaia*, 212.
113 Ibid., 147.

[the human and domesticated flora and fauna] is now cre-ating.[114]

While, in one way, this presents the same old story of the cul-tural gaining the upper hand over the biological ("the slow me-andering of evolution"), it is also more generous than that; this new consciousness or awareness involves attuning to the myriad ways in which culture is nature. It also means that, always prior to altering the manner in which one engages in the global me-tabolism, awareness of one's participation in this metabolism is necessary. Lovelock refers to this as "keep[ing] in touch with Gaia,"[115] and although this has a distinctively new age ring, it is not the worst phrase for describing the most basic of affective engagements with Gaia. Merely by existing, of course, we keep in touch with Gaia, "just like a cell does in the body," but we also "interact individually in a spiritual manner through a sense of wonder about the natural world and from feeling a part of it."[116] He goes on to state, "In some ways this interaction is not unlike the tight coupling between the state of the mind and body."[117] It is this wording, as opposed to the question posed earlier about whether the human species might serve as a brain or nervous system, that bears closer examination. He does not state that the human has exclusive province over the "mind" of Gaia (to the extent that we can even speak that way), or even that mind is a discrete phenomenon. Affective engagement with Gaia, and with it wonder, is still rooted strictly in the material: Mind and body co-create Gaia. And as a significant part of the very mate-rial mind of Gaia, we must wonder if we are to remain a part of Gaia for any significant length of time. Survival in a dynamic world demands the constant expansion of the *Umwelt* and a constant attunement to new affects. Wonder may be an end in itself, but it is also, in the long term, a survival strategy.

114 Volk, *Gaia's Body*, 250.
115 Lovelock, *The Ages of Gaia*, 211.
116 Ibid.
117 Ibid.

Curiously, Latour claims that Gaia has created a crisis in our relation to the earth as small creatures that wonder at its immensity, stating, "Only galaxies and the Milky way might still be available for the old humbling game of wonder, because they are beyond the Earth (and thus beyond our reach)."[118] Gaia, for Latour, means a return to finitude; "the closed and limited cosmos" of the earth overshadows the "infinite universe" and becomes all-important.[119] Such a reading of Lovelock's prose is ungenerous and ignores the extent to which he goes to establish Gaia as infinite in its vitality. If anything, it is the lifelessness of all we know beyond the earth, in dull chemical equilibrium, that extinguishes wonder. Gaia, in so fiercely defending life and, moreover, in perpetually swapping out its parts, virtually guarantees the experience of new affects.

4.4
An Indifferent Eden

The existence of infinitely variable life and the possibility of experiencing it are not, however, the only reasons to wonder at (and in) Gaia. The living earth, as depicted by Lovelock, teeters between hospitality and precarity. As Wilson also points out, the very existence of such plentiful life against such odds is a cause for wonder. What is so unique to Gaia, however, is that precarity and fragility are two very different characteristics. Life on earth is precarious insofar as it could easily not have come about and, at least if one looks to deep time, will come to an end. But fragile it is not; life on Gaia may be, for the moment, Edenic, but its robustness also means that, at least as far as the individual organism is concerned, it is capable of great cruelty. Gaia is an indifferent Eden, a fickle paradise, and this becomes, in Lovelock's work, all the more reason to wonder at her current state, which creates so many possibilities for affiliation.

118 Latour, "Waiting for Gaia," 3.
119 Latour, "Third Lecture: Gaia, a (Finally Secular) Figure for Nature," 80.

4.4.1 Home, precarious home

There is an exploration of the genesis of life on earth near the beginning of *Gaia* that is quite the ride. This is not because it is an especially gripping account of the manner in which some primordial soup spontaneously arranged itself into a proto-amoeba, but because it presents the reader with an irresistible cosmic "will they or won't they?" that ends in a strange twist. Lovelock begins with a look at the chemical building blocks of life, stating, "It seems almost as if our galaxy were a giant ware-house containing the spare parts needed for life." He continues: "If we can imagine a planet made of nothing but the component parts of watches, we may reasonably assume that in the fullness of time — perhaps 1,000 million years — gravitational forces and the restless motion of the wind would assemble at least one working watch."[120] In a galaxy containing the right chemicals, on a planet containing the right compounds, it is implied, life will, most probably, arise. Lovelock elaborates:

> The odds against such a sequence of encounters leading to the first living entity are enormous. On the other hand, the number of random encounters between the component molecules of the Earth's primaeval substance must have been incalculable. Life was thus an almost utterly improbable event with almost infinite opportunities of happening. So it did.[121]

Wilson and Sagan go on at length about this same improbability of life, but only Lovelock insists on the near certainty of it arising somewhere. In a universe that for all intents and purposes may be described as infinite, we are the rarest of inevitabilities. In *The Ages of Gaia*, Lovelock writes that life "is characterized by an omnipresence of improbability that would make winning a sweepstake every day for a year seem trivial by comparison."[122]

120 Lovelock, *Gaia: A New Look at Life on Earth,* 14.
121 Ibid.
122 Lovelock, *The Ages of Gaia,* 23.

But it is not only the genesis of life that could have easily not occurred at all. The idea that a series of unlikely developments has produced Gaia as we know it comes back in many guises. Lovelock devotes a great deal of attention to the earth's atmosphere, which he notes was blown away when "the sun was settling down" and left the "planet...for a while as bare as the moon."[123] It is life, of course, that would transform and stabilize earth's atmosphere. Lovelock makes guesses as to how it may have happened that the earth did not turn out like the moon, or Mars, or Venus, but the manner in which this lifeless fate was escaped is shrouded in mystery. He likens the development of life on earth to the improbability of finding a sandcastle that had randomly assembled itself on an empty beach, claiming, furthermore: "If her partners in life were not there, continually repairing and creating, as children build fresh castles on the beach, all Gaia's traces would soon vanish."[124] That the atmosphere developed in a way that allowed life to flourish was one improbable eventuality; that it evolved to maintain life is another. Lovelock also comes back again and again to the amount of oxygen in the earth's atmosphere, which is high enough to sustain life and enable humans to light fires, but just low enough to not "bring the world into danger of conflagration."[125] He continues by describing what would happen should the amount of oxygen in the earth's atmosphere increase by only four percent:

> At 25 per cent oxygen level even camp vegetation will continue to burn once combustion has started, so that a forest fire started by lightning flash would burn fiercely until all combustible material was consumed. Those science fiction stories of other worlds with bracing atmospheres due to the richer oxygen content are fiction indeed. A landing of the heroes' spaceship would have destroyed the planet.[126]

123 Lovelock, *Gaia: A New Look at Life on Earth*, 77.
124 Ibid., 31.
125 Ibid., 38.
126 Ibid.

Earth, in other words, could have easily developed as a kind of fiery inferno, a hell. There is a strange power in the negative hypothetical in Lovelock's writing — what could have happened but did not — that perpetually asks the reader to reevaluate the present moment. The implication is not only that we could have easily not been here at all, but, even more profoundly, all the affective richness that characterizes the living earth was nothing like inevitable.

With these negative hypotheticals, Lovelock also connects to the readerly *Umwelt*. He muses:

> It is an intriguing thought that without the assistance of those anaerobic micro-flora living in the stinking muds of the seabeds, lakes, and ponds, there might be no writing or reading of books. Without the methane they produce, oxygen would rise inexorably in concentration to a level at which any fire would be a holocaust and land life, apart from micro-flora in damp places, would be impossible.[127]

Contingent life is, for Lovelock, the most decisive factor in our ability to contemplate life now. Life on Earth has given rise to "nature" as we know it, but also culture. What Lovelock does not allow us to forget is that it could have so easily gone wrong. Life has given us something to wonder at; without it, there would be no *Umwelten*, no affective richness to the world.

Indeed, one day, it will go wrong. Lovelock harbors no illusions regarding Gaia's immortality. The sun will, at some point aeons in the future, burn too bright for even life to manage, but "[c]ompared with the lifetime of our species, let alone that of an individual human being, this time span is no tragic brief spell, but offers almost an infinity of opportunities to terrestrial life."[128] Gaia's occurrence may be infinitely improbable, but, as long as life remains, it also offers unthinkable affective abundance.

127 Ibid., 74.
128 Ibid., 125.

4.4.2 Too robust for us: earth's strange hospitality
At the same time that Gaia presents us with a world seen in the light of what very well might not have been, it presents the earth as a kind of pleasure garden. There is no need to get back to the garden, Lovelock implies, because we already occupy it. The conditions that frame our lives are, against all odds, ideal. To a certain extent, of course, we are bound to the environment in which sentient life evolved as an Eden, "because if there were any evolutionary lineages for which that world were a Hell, they would not persist long enough to develop intelligent life forms."[129] But Lovelock also frames the earth as an ideal habitat, if we dare use such a term, in deep time. Even the ice ages, he proclaims, were not all bad, affecting only the most extreme latitudes. He writes:

> Because of the unbroken record of life, we also know that the oceans can never have either frozen or boiled. Indeed, subtle evidence from the ration of the different forms of oxygen atoms laid down in the rocks over the course of time strongly suggests that the climate has always been much as it is now, except during glacial periods or near the beginning of life when it was somewhat warmer.[130]

These conditions, Lovelock informs us, are not easy to maintain. The earth, by all accounts, "would have been in a frozen state during the first one and a half aeons of life's existence" because of fluctuations in the sun's activity.[131] It was not, and Lovelock points to the fossil record to support this. And life does not merely serve as Gaia's thermostat, but also maintains the chemical balances that allow for it to continue:

> Some essential elements are required in bulk, others in trace quantities, and all may need rapid redeployment at times;

129 Kirchner, "The Gaia Hypothesis," 392.
130 Lovelock, *Gaia: A New Look at Life on Earth,* 19.
131 Ibid.

poisonous wastes and litter must be dealt with and, if possible, put to good use; acidity must be kept in check and a neutral to alkaline overall environment maintained; the seas should stay salt, but not too salt; and so on. These are the main criteria, but there are many others involved.[132]

We are only beginning to realize what unbelievable complexity is involved in the maintenance of what, for much of human history, many cultures have considered the backdrop for their own activities. With the articulation of Gaia and the realization of the enormity of what it accomplishes then, the earth as it is now is returned to us as the real garden.

It is a garden, Lovelock makes clear, we have not been expelled from yet. Large mammals, let alone humans, hardly form an essential part of the global metabolism:

Life on this planet is a very tough, robust, and adaptable entity and we are but a small part of it. The most essential part is probably that which dwells on the floors of the continental shelves and in the soil below the surface. Large plants and animals are relatively unimportant. They are comparable rather to those elegant salesmen and glamorous models used to display a firm's products, desirable perhaps, but not essential.[133]

If anything, Lovelock implies, we are Gaia's poster children: attractive, but not essential to the real operations. Thus as soon as earth is revealed as a paradise to us, as soon as the concept of Gaia reenchants terrestrial existence, it is revealed that no one cares if we eat the forbidden fruit. Expulsion from Gaia is not possible, but extinction is. Because Lovelock's interest in Gaia is not predominantly human, he does not dwell on apocalypse scenarios, but he does issue some quietly ominous warnings: "Perhaps our continuing orderly existence over so long a period can be attributed to yet another Gaian regulatory process,

132 Ibid., 25.
133 Ibid., 40.

–178–

which makes sure that cheats can never become dominant."[134] Within a Gaian framework, much rests on the human ability to acknowledge the earth as an indifferent Eden. The next and last section turns to the more concrete problem of global warming, sketching the outlines of an affective ecology for a miraculous, uncaring planet.

4.5
An Affective Ecology for an Indifferent Planet

This last section turns to one of the trickier questions Lovelock poses: "How then should we live with Gaia?" As with Wilson, Lovelock never offers us a concrete, point-by-point program. Nevertheless, there is an affective, or Gaian, ecology that may be gleaned from Lovelock's work. Four characteristics distinguish it:

First of all, it asks for the abandonment of technological pessimism. In one of the only passages in which Lovelock does explicitly acknowledge Gaia's significance with regard to ecological thought, he is careful to distinguish himself both from thinkers who hold a "concept of man as the steward of life on Earth" and from those who would insist "that our only means of escape is to renounce most of our technology, especially nuclear energy."[135] Given that Lovelock, at his most radical, makes no distinction between the technological and biological, there is no reason to assume he would oppose it in principle. What he offers is a technological middle way.

This is evident, first of all, in his focus on agricultural reform. He accuses greens of focusing on "the bloody consequences of the hunter's gun or the foxhound's teeth" rather than "the piecemeal death and dispossession wrought by the bulldozer, the plough, and the flame thrower." He continues:

134 Ibid., 47.
135 Ibid., 123.

> So normal among us all is the acceptance of genocide whilst rejecting murder, the straining at gnats while swallowing camels, that we may well ask ourselves whether this double standard of behavior is, as altruism is said to be, paradoxically an evolved characteristic favoring the survival of our own kind.[136]

That we would attend to one kind of suffering while ignoring the larger scale devastation wrought by the business of day-to-day life is, for Lovelock, part of the cheat that has enabled the human to proliferate. He asks us to wise up to ways in which "bad farming is also disturbing the atmosphere on a global scale and to an extent at least comparable with the effects of urban industrial activity."[137] The *Umwelt* circumscribed by human activities, it is implied, is much larger and intersects with the *Umwelten* of others in more ways than most acknowledge. For him, the solution is not a "reactionary 'back to nature' campaign," but the modification and economization of existing technologies.[138]

This rejection of technological pessimism also permeates Lovelock's highly controversial support for nuclear power. Here he takes a slightly different tack, insisting that "it is easy to forget that nuclear fission is a natural process."[139] Later, in *The Ages of Gaia,* he goes on to state:

> It is easy to ignore the fact that we are the anomalous ones. The natural energy of the Universe, the power that lights the stars in the sky, is nuclear. Chemical energy, wind, and water wheels: such sources of energy are, from the viewpoint of a manager of the Universe, almost as rare as a coal-burning star. If this is so, and if God's universe is nuclear-powered, why then are so many of us prepared to march in protest against its use to provide us with electricity?[140]

136 Ibid., 59.
137 Ibid., 120.
138 Ibid., 117.
139 Ibid., 16.
140 Lovelock, *The Ages of Gaia,* 171.

Nuclear power is framed here not as the human acquiring ever more destructive power, but as one of the main forces powering the universe that we, too, may harvest. Of the concerns relating to nuclear power's safety, Lovelock claims, "The present dangers are real but tend to be exaggerated."[141] Besides, he reminds, nuclear radiation may be lethal or toxic for people, but it does not at all spell the death of ecosystems; Bikini Atoll, despite its nuclear bombardment, is a lush green paradise.[142] A Gaian ecology thus asks for the abandonment of prejudices surrounding what is and is not "green." The perceived naturalness of the activity, moreover, says nothing about what kind of contribution it makes to Gaia. Technologies are necessary to sustain us but must be developed in a kind of dialogue with the earth.

Secondly, the goal of a Gaian ecology is not stewardship, but the prevention of activity that might limit Gaia's own mechanisms for recovery. The most productive greenbelts of the earth, "the tropics and the seas close to the continental shores," are, for this reason, most in need of preservation:

> It is in these regions, where few do watch, that harmful practices may be pursued to the point of no-return before their dangers are recognized; and so it is from these regions that unpleasant surprises are most likely to emerge. Here man may sap the vitality of Gaia by reducing productivity and by deleting key species in her life-support system; and he may then exacerbate the situation by releasing into the air or the sea abnormal quantities of compounds which are potentially dangerous on a global scale[143]

Not all human interference in the global metabolism is created equal. What is interesting about this stance is that it involves ascertaining at least approximately what Gaia's "life support system" is and adopting a selective hands-off approach. It does not

141 Lovelock, *Gaia: A New Look at Life on Earth*, 17.
142 Ibid., 40–41.
143 Ibid., 121.

argue that human activities on Gaia are inherently antagonistic, but that they should be pursued in a way that recognizes Gaian agency. We do not "fix" Gaia, but modify our own activities so that she may fix herself.

The worst-case scenario for Lovelock is that the human would have to serve as steward and take more control of the global metabolism:

> This could happen if, at some intolerable population density, man had encroached upon Gaia's functional power to such an extent that he disabled her. He would wake up one day to find that he had the permanent lifelong job of planetary maintenance engineer. Gaia would have retreated into the muds, and the ceaseless intricate tasks of keeping all of the global cycles in balance would be ours. Then at last we should be riding that strange contraption, the "spaceship Earth", and whatever tamed and domesticated biosphere remained would indeed be our "life support system."[144]

If we do not recognize the enormity of what Gaia provides us with, we run the risk of undermining her characteristic robustness. While Lovelock mostly maintains that Gaia would exact revenge on the human before being reduced to Spaceship Earth, a mere shell for life, at times he does indulge in this kind of nightmare scenario. Even worse than Gaia getting rid of us is assuming the gargantuan task of "planetary maintenance engineer" and having to ourselves become responsible for the affects of the earth.

At the same time that Lovelock warns against irreparably damaging Gaia's life support systems, he is careful not to indict all human "dabbling." The English countryside, at least prior to the heavy industrialization following World War II, becomes in his prose a garden within the garden that is Gaia:

144 Ibid., 132.

The England I knew as a child and a young man was breath-takingly beautiful, hedgerows and small copses were abundant, and small streams and rivers teemed with fish and fed the otters. It inspired generations of poets to make coherent the feelings we could not ourselves express. Yet that landscape of England was no natural ecosystem; it was a nation-sized garden, wonderfully and carefully tended.[145]

It is not only Gaia minus the human that occasions wonder, then, but the often sizable human contributions to Gaia. What marks the English countryside as "a living example of how one small group of humans, for a brief spell, did it right"[146] is the degree to which it acknowledged overlapping *Umwelten* and added to, rather than subtracted from, the affective richness of Gaia.

Thirdly, feeling and perceiving may be key to a Gaian ecology, but that ecology simultaneously urges the practice of a rigorous non-sentimentality. Central to Gaia is the acknowledgment of a vitality present in material we formerly assumed was inert (i.e. rocks) and on scales we did not think were possible, not merely the identification with creatures like us. A Gaian ecology concerns itself less with the polar bear afloat on a small island of diminishing ice and more with the outgassing of methane occasioned by the thawing of the arctic tundra. Lovelock explains his own strategy for refusing sentimentalizing:

Sometimes, when confronted with the excesses of sentiment about life on Earth I follow Lynn's [Margulis's] lead and take the role of shop steward, the trade union representative of microorganisms and the lesser under-represented forms of life. They have worked to keep this planet fit for life for 3.5 billion years. The cuddly animals, the wildflowers, and the people are to be revered, but they would be as nothing were it not for the vast infrastructure of the microbes.[147]

145 Lovelock, *The Ages of Gaia*, 233.
146 Ibid., 232.
147 Ibid., xvi.

This fits in well with the idea that life operates in biochemical guilds to sustain Gaia. The organism, in this case, is the enemy, because focusing only on it entails a blindness to the *Umwelten* that make life for that organism possible. Notice here, too, that Lovelock speaks of taking the role of "shop steward," which is distinct from earth or environmental steward. Indeed, it represents a less hubristic view of our ecological task. Rather than stepping in as manager, the metaphor of shop steward implies merely that we act in a way that protects the interest of those we represent.

Moreover, Lovelock refuses to dwell on the tragedy of extinction events. He cites the example of the great North American land mammals, such as the mammoth and megatherium:

> Migration of humans from the Bering strait was responsible for the extinction of the larger mammals on the continent using fire-drive hunting. By any reckoning this was at that time an ecologically disastrous application of new technology, and yet, as Eugene Odum [the pioneering systems ecologist] has reminded us, its application led to the development and evolution of the great grassland ecosystems.[148]

There is nothing obvious, we are reminded, about the ecological status quo. To insist on its absolute maintenance means, at least partially, to foreclose the possibility of new landscapes, new organisms, and new affects. With Gaia, there are only consequences. While one can certainly decide certain constellations of affects are worth preserving, as long as life and the possibility for it continue unabated, Gaia remains indifferent. This is not to imply that there is no place for sentimentality in ecology, only that Gaia shows us how to temper it.

Finally, a Gaian ecology implies that, if we wish to inhabit Gaia for any length of time, we must become more sensitive to changes, particularly anthropogenic ones like "the Carbon

---

148 Lovelock, *Gaia: A New Look at Life on Earth,* 133.

Dioxide Fever."[149] Climate, "the historical result of reciprocal connections, which interfere with one another, among all creatures as they grow,"[150] as perhaps the most far-reaching and omnipresent of Gaia's regulatory processes, must come to occupy center stage. The task is a more difficult one than many green politicians allow because, as David Abram phrases it, "we seem unable to master this curious flux in which we're immersed, unable even to glean a clear comprehension of this mostly invisible field of turbulence and tranquil eddies so fundamental to our existence."[151] This is compounded by the fact that, due to increasing population, we play an ever greater role in Gaia's metabolism; there is no simple cause and effect, but a series of dizzying feedback loops. This is the strange Moebius strip with the human on one side and Gaia on the other to which Latour alludes[152]: The global metabolism leads seamlessly into the human industrial and vice versa.[153]

Given the degree to which the human has come to be tangled up with global processes like climate regulation, it becomes all the more necessary to attend to the affective earth, to wonder at the global metabolism. Abram continues:

The resulting torsions within the planetary climate are at last forcing humankind out of its self-enclosed oblivion…. Only through the extremity of the weather are we brought to notice the uncanny power and presence of the unseen medium, and so compelled to remember our thorough immersion within the life of this breathing planet.[154]

---

149 Lovelock, *The Ages of Gaia*, 156.
150 Latour, "Third Lecture: Gaia, a (Finally Secular) Figure for Nature," 106.
151 Abram, "In the Depths of a Breathing Planet," 229.
152 Latour, "Waiting for Gaia," 10.
153 For Latour, this is the condition that characterizes the Anthropocene, the age of the human, in which we have acquired unthinkable influence at precisely the time that we realize just how small the world is and how unpredictable the consequences of our own activities are. We will return to the concept of the Anthropocene in Chapter 6.
154 Abram, "In the Depths of a Breathing Planet," 241.

Because of, and not despite, our new prominence on Gaia, we must now begin to pay attention. That Abram refers to the ignorance of climate as a state of self-enclosed oblivion is more than apt. Not attending to global warming now implies nothing less than a refusal to acknowledge the manner in which every *Umwelt* now overlaps with our own.

On the other hand, should Gaia succeed in acquiring awareness, it becomes possible to not only ensure the continuation of Gaia's effective richness, made possible only by life, but also to help her reproduce. In the most optimistic of visions of the "Gaia-in-us or us-in-Gaia,"[155] "we may be able to aid in the flowering of earth life into the astronomically voluminous reaches of space."[156] Seeking to preserve the infinity of affects on earth may, in this way, represent the real inauguration of the space age — dominated not by miniature Spaceship Earths, but by neighboring bodies saved from the affectively dull fate of lifelessness.

Gaia presents us with an especially compelling affective ecology because it does not rely on the fantasy of futurity, acknowledging from the beginning that life, let alone human life, will enjoy limited tenure on the earth. What it asks for instead is that we begin to acknowledge our participation in the global metabolism now. Buying into Gaia means letting go of the notion that cultural and industrial activities perpetrated by humans are somehow unnatural or separate from the living earth; it involves letting go of the technological pessimism that, for so many years, was a fixture of green movements. However, this does not encourage planetary engineering solutions to "fix" Gaia. Planetary stewardship, for Lovelock, is a worst-case scenario, and the best we can do is prevent activities that would impinge on Gaia's own living mechanisms for recovery. Furthermore, a Gaian ecology insists that affiliation is not merely sentimental. The charismatic megafauna that currently form much of the bread and butter of environmentalist discourse are upstaged on Gaia

155 Latour, "Waiting for Gaia," 10.
156 Margulis and Sagan, "God, Gaia, and Biophilia," 357.

by the microbes that do the real heavy lifting in the maintenance of the global metabolism. And finally, a Gaian ecology insists that any organism wishing to inhabit Gaia for any length of time must learn to become sensitive to changes in the living earth and adapt accordingly. An affective engagement with the earth becomes, in this way, a kind of survival strategy.

Paradoxically, the only way for the species to cope with Gaia's indifference to us is to become less indifferent to the *Umwelten* that surround us, to, like Craven in the next section, survey the sometimes hopeless mire of anthropocentric politics from the hillside. This chapter has sought not only to explain Gaia as a concept with a great deal of affective potential but also to investigate what about it tempts us away from conventional understandings of greenness and even science. In assigning agency and vitality to the biosphere and its constituent parts, Gaia is a concept that, however small, radically reenchants. And when the human is no longer seen as the only actor on Gaia, the landscape begins to look quite different. If there is anything exceptional about us as bipeds, it is in our ability to wonder, to attend to other *Umwelten,* and, ultimately, to compose concepts like Gaia.

4.6
Postscript:
The Edge of Darkness—Who Is a Gaian?

The six-part 1985 BBC mini-series *Edge of Darkness,* written by Troy Kennedy Martin and directed by Martin Campbell, approaches Gaia at first only obliquely, and even at times misrepresents it, but its main protagonist, detective Ronald Craven (played by Bob Peck), is so thoroughly Gaian by the end that one cannot dismiss it out of hand. "I am on the side of the planet!" Craven says near the end in a drunken, radiation-soaked stupor, and we cannot doubt him.

It helps to know that the show begins as a much more standard-issue detective series, with the mysterious gunning down of Craven's beloved daughter, Emma, on the front steps of their

Yorkshire home. We are led, like Craven, to believe that the gunman was really after him, and didn't intend to shoot Emma, a young physicist who we know at least dabbles in radical politics. But this belief soon unravels, as does the pretense that this is a standard whodunit; Craven discovers a gun in his daughter's room, along with a mysterious box, complete with maps and a Geiger counter, labeled "Gaia." Gaia, we learn in time, is an organization of scientists (referred to by the CIA and British secret service as a terrorist cell) opposing British nuclear policy. They have discovered a Plutonium processing facility deep in Yorkshire's Northmoor mines, where, legally, it should not be, and are now either dead or being picked off one by one.

Craven spends the majority of the series pretending to cooperate with various British agencies in London, then pretending to cooperate with a CIA agent, in order to simply find out what Gaia is. In the end, his search will lead him through Northmoor mines, along the same path that the Gaians took just weeks prior to his daughter's death, to a pile of dead Gaians and then a "live cell" that will soon mean his own death. Nothing surprises him, and he does not become suddenly politicized by the amount of corruption and secrecy that was required for the secret nuclear facility to be built and then shielded by the death of the Gaians from public scrutiny. He does not, in short, become a member of Gaia as organization in the course of the film. He simply marches on, an unwavering, watery-eyed Yorkshireman, indifferent to everything but the knowledge that will satisfyingly explain his own daughter's death. Even when exposed to lethal amounts of radiation, he does not, as the Gaians do, necessarily oppose the nuclear (as weapon or form of power).

What he does oppose, in his own indifference and refusal in the end to pick sides, is the intricate web of politics and profit surrounding the whole sordid affair. "I am not on your side!" he screams to a British intelligence officer in the last episode, after they have shot his irradiated American companion Darius Jedburgh and the British officer has informed his underlings, "It's okay; he's on our side." Nor does he presume, like his daughter, to be a kind of eco-warrior, although he does tell Jedburgh that he is on the side of the planet. In the last scene of the series, Craven, very close to death, is simply a figure on a *hillside,* screaming words no one can hear as they retrieve the plutonium Jedburgh stole from the mines and threw in a Scottish loch.

In the next shot, Craven has disappeared from his perch in the landscape, and black flowers have sprouted where he stood before. Their significance has already been revealed to the viewer in a previous scene, when Emma shows up as one of Craven's hallucinations and explains:

> Millions of years ago when the Earth was cold, it looked like life on the planet would cease to exist. But black flowers began to grow, multiplying across the landscape until the entire surface was covered in blooms. Slowly, the blackness of the flowers sucked in the heat of the sun and life began to evolve again. That is the power of Gaia. The planet will protect itself. If man is the enemy, it will destroy him.[157]

This is a dark ecology[158] if there ever was one. Lovelock, in his earlier books, ascribes a similar role to a dark marsh grass that, long ago, proliferated and increased the earth's albedo dramatically, making it warmer and therefore suitable for life.[159] And while Lovelock has not prophesied the return of this grass, he repeats over and over again in his work that it is not Gaia that

---

157 *Edge of Darkness,* Ep. 6: "Fusion."

158 A term coined by Timothy Morton in *The Ecological Thought* (Cambridge: Harvard University Press, 2012): "The ecological thought, the thinking of interconnectedness, has a dark side embodied not in a hippie aesthetic of life over death, or a sadistic-sentimental Bambification of sentient beings, but in a 'goth' assertion of the contingent and necessarily queer idea that we want to stay with a dying world: dark ecology" (184–85). Dark ecology appears as part of the relatively recent wave of environmental pessimism. See also the Dark Mountain Project, which emphasizes the precarity of life on earth, but also insists, "Precarious as this moment may be, however, an awareness of the fragility of what we call civilisation is nothing new": Paul Kingsnorth and Dougald Hine, "Uncivilization: The Dark Mountain Manifesto," The Dark Mountain Project, 2009, http://dark-mountain.net/about/manifesto/.

159 Cf. Lovelock, *Gaia: A New Look at Life on Earth,* 24–25.

is at stake when we speak of anthropogenic climate change and environmental devastation, but human civilization itself. Gaia is not an earth mother that watches over us benevolently, but an entity that will stop at nothing to maintain conditions suitable for life in general, even if that means ousting the human population in a feverish haze brought on by global warming or, as *Edge of Darkness* has it, black flowers.

It is this profoundly indifferent Gaia that Craven sides with in the end, a choice that becomes clear in a memorable scene in which he bids adieu to another member of Gaia, the closest thing the series gives us to a love interest. She knows he will die within three days, and asks to travel with him so that he will not die alone, but he refuses her, caressing her cheek with a black flower. With his daughter's death, the sentimental has been drained from him, and there is no longer a place in the series for love. This strange caress is the ultimate refusal of sides; he is not with the British, he is not with the Americans, and he is most certainly not with a woman. Afterwards, he speeds off to Scotland, spending three strange, hellish days in the landscape, first chasing Jedburgh and his stock of plutonium, then drinking with the man as the radiation kills them, and finally, after the Texan force of nature is shot, wandering alone among the grass and the stones and the wind. That the man moves — from his cramped quarters in the city to the seemingly endless tunnels of the mine to, finally, the highlands — is significant. The *Umwelt* of the detective is ripped open by the death of his daughter, and, in order to get to the heart of the matter, he must himself become more expansive. What is clear at the end, as the man yells in the twilight and there is no one close enough to hear him, is that he feels there is something to which he is not indifferent. By this time, however, there is no one to take up his call. The following shot is of the same cliff, now in daylight. It is unclear how much time has passed, but it is now home only to the black flowers.

I want to propose here that Craven, despite spending the series attempting to find out who the Gaians are, is the real Gaian. Wracked by grief from the death of his daughter, with his professional defenses pried from him bit by bit, he lives, in the end, in an affective present. On the hillside, he is fully subject to (and of) the elements. His final action is to take part in the deterritorializing action of the earth, to give himself up. Kennedy Martin initially envisioned Craven literally metamorphosing at the end of the series, telling a number of people, "I am writing this story about a detective that turns into a tree."[160] The idea was rejected by Bob Peck, the actor playing Craven, and director Martin Campbell, "but not before some of its spirit had rubbed off on Craven's character."[161] That Craven does not, in the end, turn into a tree makes little difference; he is at the center of a detective story that self-destructs, a curious narrative that evaporates in Gaia's presence, supplanted by invisible radiation, rocks tumbling down hillsides, a loch swirling below the protagonist, and black flowers waving in the wind — the affects of the earth.

Craven as Gaian, screaming on the hillside, begs the question: What does it mean to be on the side of the planet when, increasingly, the planet is not on our side? One option, certainly, is to embrace extinction, or, as Edelman would have it with regard to Leonard in South by Southwest, the death drive. One might recall here the Voluntary Human Extinction Movement referred to in Chapter 1 in this volume. But Craven gives us another way; childless and wifeless, he does not embody a narrative of futurity. He does not choose the woman, but goes straight for the radioactive depths of the live cell and then the unsheltered hillside. "I'm not on your side!" becomes a kind of "I'd prefer not to," a stubborn insistence that the choices with which he is confronted — to side with the corrupt industrialists, the British secret service, or a CIA operative gone AWOL — are not choices at all.

We might view Craven as an embodiment of the anthropos trying to come to terms with Gaia's radical non-anthropocentrism. Cast by Lovelock as technologically-advanced apes, we represent a modest, yet thorny part of Gaia:

---

160 Troy Kennedy Martin, "Introduction," in *Edge of Darkness* (London: Faber and Faber, 1990), vii–xv at x–xi.
161 Ibid., x–xi.

Contemporary ecology may be deeply embedded in human affairs, but this book [and I would claim Gaia] is about the whole of life on Earth within the older and more general framework of geology. Still, the nettle, a most unecological vegetable, bristling with poison barbs, must now be grasped. How then should we live within Gaia? What difference does her presence make to our own relationships with the world and with one another?[162]

Craven, always bristling, anchored, by the end, firmly in the ground above a Scottish loch, is nothing if not a nettle. But, if we are to listen to Lovelock's pleas that we acknowledge and make sense of our own problematic proliferation, so are we. Gaia does more, however, than allow us to recognize ourselves as continuous with the world around us, as "most unecological vegetables." At the very moment it allows us to give way to the indifference of the elements, it offers the concept itself as a bridge to a new kind of subjectivity. As Deleuze and Guattari maintain in *What Is Philosophy?*, while the earth exerts a deterritorializing action, the concept reterritorializes, summoning forth a new earth and a corresponding new people.[163] This, perhaps, is the best way of explaining how, with Gaia, indifference gives way to wonder. Gaia asks us to take part in the deterritorializing action of the earth, to view our activities not as personal or human but as part of the global metabolism. At the same time, the mere knowledge of the concept inaugurates us all as Gaians and insists that the human *Umwelt* and our activities in it, like it or not, are far more extensive than the Earthlings of the past may have realized.

162 Lovelock, *Gaia: A New Look at Life on Earth*, 124.
163 Deleuze and Guattari, *What Is Philosophy?*, 109–10.

5

Cosmos

'THE SUBTLE MACHINERY OF
AWE'

"We are made of star stuff," Sagan reminds us again and again in
Cosmos, and this revelation becomes the one that paves the way
for countless others. Much more than constituting a reason to
affiliate with the cosmos, like Lovelock's Gaia, it is a proclamation that we affiliate, whether we like it or not. That we share a
great deal with the stars forms the seed around which the cosmic perspective, the subject of *Cosmos* and this chapter, crys-
tallizes. As described by Sagan, the cosmic perspective involves
an embrace of the "subtle machinery of awe"[1] with which the
universe confronts us; it is an orientation towards wonder. Although *Cosmos* shares a great deal with *Gaia* and *Biophilia* in
celebrating the infinity and excess of life on earth, it is also fundamentally about the potential for reenchantment in an age in
which we are just beginning to realize the vastness of that which
we have not yet experienced in the universe.

Framing *Cosmos* both temporally and conceptually are the
Voyager spacecraft, which also begin and end this chapter.
Though they were initially conceived of as mere probes, Sagan
was responsible in the late 1970s for outfitting each of the spacecraft with a Golden Record — a greeting to the stars and pos-

1   Carl Sagan, *Cosmos* (New York: Random House, 1980), 2.

sible extraterrestrial intelligences — and also a fragmentary and highly affective portrait of the human species. This, I argue in 5.1, crucially informs the way Sagan portrays the relationship between the human and the universe in *Cosmos*. Section 5.2 moves on to the series and book itself, describing both their unprecedented success as works of popular science and also explaining why it makes sense to treat them as ecological. The following sections move on to the so-called cosmic perspective in *Cosmos*. Section 5.3 looks at what Richard Dawkins has derided as Sagan's "cosmic sentimentality": the notion that our connection with the stars is not merely material and energetic, but also affective. Section 5.4, entitled "Precious worlds/Precarious Life," in turn, focuses on another leitmotiv in *Cosmos*: the idea that life, let alone intelligent life, is so rare and so fleeting that the very realization of this fact must produce an ethic of care. Stepping back slightly from the series, section 5.5 takes a broader look at the scholarship on and criticism of *Cosmos* in the '80s, addressing what has become the elephant in the room: the series' religious undertones. The final section returns to Voyager, now cruising through interstellar space with a collection of affects that will outlast the planet earth and potentially the human species.

5.1
The Golden Record: Terrestrial Murmurs in the Cosmic Ocean

In 1977, a mere three years before *Cosmos* would air, the two Voyager spacecraft were launched by NASA.[2] At the time of their launch, the planets, aligned just so, would enable the vehicles to travel remarkably fast via gravity-assisted trajectories[3] that flung them through the solar system, flying by Jupiter, Saturn,

---

2   Carl Sagan, F.D. Drake, Ann Druyan, Timothy Ferris, Jon Lomberg, and Linda Salzman Sagan, "Preface," in *Murmurs of the Earth: The Voyager Interstellar Record* (New York: Random House, 1978), 222.
3   Ibid.

and, in the case of Voyager 2, Uranus and Neptune.[4] Though they ceased relaying images to the earth in 1990,[5] they have managed to capture some of the most iconic images of the outer planets and are still traveling. In 2013, scientists confirmed that Voyager 1 had entered interstellar space in 2012, thirty-five years after its launch.[6]

But it is no empty vessel outfitted only with a few rudimentary instruments that has left the solar system. Carl Sagan campaigned, successfully, to furnish each craft with an identical golden record (really gold-plated copper) and record player, serving as a kind of deep time and deep space capsule. A committee, organized and chaired by Sagan, was made responsible for what was to appear on the record. In the end, it would carry:

> 118 photographs of our planet, ourselves, and our civilization; almost 90 minutes of the world's greatest music; an evolutionary audio essay on "The Sounds of the Earth"; and greetings in almost sixty human languages (and one whale language), including salutations from the President of the United States and the Secretary General of the United Nations.[7]

The effort, documented by the committee members themselves in *Murmurs of the Earth: The Voyager Interstellar Record* (1978), was a monumental one. Although Sagan held out hope that the Record would serve "as a message to possible extraterrestrial civilizations that might encounter the spacecraft in some distant space and time," he was not naïve about the endeavor. Given the likelihood that the Record would be swept up by intelligent

---

4   Tony Greicius, "NASA Spacecraft Embarks on Historic Journey into Interstellar Space," *NASA*, August 7, 2017, www.nasa.gov/mission_pages/voyager/voyager20130912.html#.Vlqf8zGjOSo.
5   Brooks Barnes, "In a Breathtaking First, NASA's Voyager 1 Exits the Solar System," *New York Times*, September 13, 2013, http://www.nytimes.com/2013/09/13/science/in-a-breathtaking-first-nasa-craft-exits-the-solar-system.html.
6   Greicius, "NASA Spacecraft Embarks on Historic Journey."
7   Sagan et al., "Preface," 222.

life cruising through space, Sagan admitted that, ultimately, the Record was for us on earth.[8]

And what does the Golden Record, hurtling away from home at roughly two billion kilometers per year,[9] do for us? As far as the human is concerned, Sagan's writing implies that it served two purposes. It allowed the committee, first of all, to frame human beings not just as "perceiving and thinking" but as "feeling creatures."[10] The Record emphasized the affective dimensions of the human: a multiple-exposure shot showing how a gymnast moves on the beam,[11] the "harbor-filling bray of an ocean liner's foghorn,"[12] a Navajo night chant in which "one can almost see the dance by listening to the recording."[13] Ann Druyan's audio essay, "The Sounds of the Earth," attempted even to place these human affects on a deep time scale: Beginning with a series of tones arranged in time like the orbit of the planets in the solar system, it then progressed to sounds of volcanoes erupting, earthquakes, and thunder — the elemental earth. This gives way to a series of animal sounds, out of which emerges the biological and then the technological human.[14] Machines quite literally occupy the same plane as animals on the Record, and the human appears alongside the geological. At the end, there is a recording of "Life Signs," a minute-long compression of Druyan's own brain waves produced by an hour of thinking, followed by the sound of a pulsar.[15] Druyan offered the following explanation for this particular part of the sequence: "My recorded life signs sound a little like recorded radio static from the depths of space. The electrical signatures of a human being and a star seem, in such recordings, not so different, and symbolize our relatedness

8   Ibid. 11.
9   Greicius, "NASA Spacecraft."
10 Sagan et al., "Preface," 13.
11 Jon Lomberg, "Pictures of Earth," in *Murmurs of the Earth,* 71–121, at 106.
12 Ann Druyan, "The Sounds of Earth," in *Murmurs of the Earth,* 149–60, at 150.
13 Timothy Ferris, "Voyager's Music," in *Murmurs of the Earth,* 161–209, at 188.
14 Druyan, "Sounds of Earth," 160.
15 Ibid., 157.

and indebtedness to the cosmos."[16] With this gesture, the feeling of a human is related to the radiation emanating from a star; this is the celestial human. The Golden Record emphasizes, in this way, that we are feeling creatures in a cosmos that not only gave birth to that feeling but that also potentially has other elements that feel (although certainly not as we do).

The second purpose of the Golden Record is to emphasize the contingency of contemporary Western culture and, in so doing, affirm the openness of the present to other ways of living:

> Our modern technical civilization is one ten-thousandth as old as mankind. What we know well has lasted no longer than the blink of an eyelash in the enterprise of cosmic time. Our epoch is not the first or the best. Events are occurring at a breathless pace and no one knows what tomorrow will bring — whether our present civilization will survive the perils that face us and be transformed, or whether in the next century or two we will destroy our technological society. But in either case it will not end the human species.
>
> There will be other people and other civilizations, and they will be different from us.[17]

The Golden Record makes no claims to portray the apotheosis of evolution on earth. Even now, not even half a century later, it seems very much a product of its time. But this is also precisely what it aspired to be, a reminder of "life's ever-branching and beautiful ramifications" destined, perhaps, for a place with "murmurs…very unlike our own," but also a record of all the terrestrial voices "silenced forever by carelessness or merely by time."[18] The Golden Record acknowledges the certainty that the conditions it presents will change (and they already have). Simultaneously, however, it casts a new light on the present. Contemplating it, we inevitably position ourselves as the intelligent

16 Ibid., 160.
17 Sagan, "Preface," 4.
18 Druyan, "Sounds of Earth," 150 (quoting Darwin), 160.

extraterrestrials who have snapped it up, experiencing a small part of earthly existence during a narrow window of time, and we can wonder anew at it.[19]

I have begun with Voyager and the Golden Record because I want to suggest that it is an important philosophical precursor to the series and the book that appear in 1980. *Cosmos* will return, time and time again, to the affective connection we have to that beyond the earth, to the way feeling cannot possibly be separated from the stars. And despite the neat historico-scientific genealogy that it offers, *Cosmos* also insists that there are other ways of living and that stubbornly maintaining otherwise is not only a recipe for disenchantment but also endangers the only intelligent life we know.

5.2
Bathed in Strange Light: An Introduction to Cosmos

Cosmos began as a television series for the American Public Broadcasting System (PBS), with Carl Sagan as the nearly constant awe-struck science-god star.[20] As the most widely watched American public television series during all of the 1980s, it is estimated to have been seen by 600 million people worldwide over the years.[21] It was this show that would catapult an already media-friendly Sagan to fame and earn him the title of the "prince

---

19 Lomberg, who led the effort to select the images for the record, even writes, "I found myself increasingly playing the role of extraterrestrial, a mental exercise I had done in fun for many years (while playing Frisbee, for example, I'd ask myself, 'What would ETI make of this?'). Only now it was in earnest. I would look at the pictures and try to imagine that I'd never seen the subject before" (Lomberg, "Pictures of Earth," 77).

20 Carl Sagan, Ann Druyan, and Steven Soter, *Comos: A Personal Voyage*, DVD (1980; Los Angeles: PBS, 2010).

21 See "Cosmos: A Personal Voyage," *Cosmolearning*, http://www.cosmolearning.com/documentaries/cosmos/.

of popularizers."[22] A few weeks after the debut of the series, he would grace the cover of *Time* magazine. Frederic Golden, who wrote the feature in *Time,* proclaimed: "In the casualness of tur-tleneck jersey and chino pants, his butcher-boy haircut tousled by the wind, Sagan sends out an exuberant message: science is not only vital for humanity's future well-being, but it is rousing good fun as well."[23] Although Sagan would be mocked for this exuberance, most famously by Johnny Carson on *The Tonight Show, Cosmos* is not thinkable without it. Riding, perhaps, on the series' success, the book also became a bestseller. Until Stephen Hawking's *A Brief History of Time* (for which Sagan also wrote the introduction) was published in 1988,[24] it was the best-selling science book ever written, staying on the bestseller list for over a hundred weeks.[25]

Both the book and the series were immensely successful, re-taining enough of a cult following today to merit a sequel fi-nanced by a major (notably non-public) network.[26] Sagan him-self writes at the beginning of the book that, although the book and the series are organized in a similar fashion, the book "goes more deeply into many topics than does the television series."[27] And, indeed, the script is lifted overwhelmingly from pages of the book. For this reason, I understand the book and the series as part of the same project and differentiate between them only when they deviate from one another. For practical purposes, this chapter draws on quotations from the book rather than the script, although the occasional reference to Sagan's behavior in

22 See Keay Davidson, *Carl Sagan: A Life* (New York: Wiley & Sons, 2000), 330.

23 Davidson, *Carl Sagan,* 330.

24 See Stephen Hawking, *A Brief History of Time* (New York: Bantam Books, 1988).

25 See Michael B. Shermer, "Stephen Jay Gould as Historian of Science and Scientific Historian, Popular Scientist and Scientific Popularizer," in *Social Studies of Science* 32, no. 4 (2002): 489–524, at 490

26 For how produced a sequel with astrophysicist Neil deGrasse Tyson in the lead role. See Ann Druyan and Steven Soter, *Cosmos: A Spacetime Odyssey,* DVD (Los Angeles: Twentieth Century Fox, 2014).

27 Sagan, *Cosmos,* xvii.

the series is illuminating. Indeed, given that Sagan spends half of his time in the televised version bathed in strange light, face directed towards the heavens, marveling, one cannot but make reference to these undeniably affectively-charged images.[28] The televised series also includes a "Ship of the Imagination," shaped like a dandelion seed, which allows Sagan to play galactic tour guide. The ship, for obvious reasons, is left out of the book, which means that much of the language relating to traveling and exploration is as well. In episode 1, for instance, when introducing the Ship, Sagan proclaims, "Our travels allow us to see the Earth anew, as if we came from somewhere else."[29] The Ship of the Imagination, like Wilson's motion picture projector of magical versatility, should be a familiar fiction by now: a kind of ultimate scientific tool, which, like any revolutionary tool in science, shows us just how small our *Umwelten,* our own small sectors of nature, are.

The associations one has with *Cosmos,* especially for those who may have grown up with the series, may not be immediately ecological. At first glance, *Cosmos* appears to be a glorified history of astronomy and its antecedents that is simply heavy

28 These images were, in fact, a source of contention; Sagan thought they were too much, and they have certainly contributed to the impression that the series represents the height of 1980s popular science kitsch. Keay Davidson, Sagan's biographer, remarks: "Indeed, of all the things that people remember most vividly about the *Cosmos* series, the most annoying are the long, tedious close-ups of Sagan's face. 'Most of the criticism of Cosmos centered on Carl's shit-eating grin in the spacecraft,' says Don Goldsmith [an author of popular science and a consultant for the series] — a grin that he gleefully imitates. Stanley Miller [chemist and good friend of Sagan's] claims that Sagan blamed the shots on [director] Malone, who (Sagan told Miller) kept shooting Sagan in close-up 'to screw him.' (Soter [co-producer along with Sagan and Druyan] and Goldsmith doubt this.). In Soter's view, the spaceship shots were 'the major flaw of the series. Those were all Adrian [Malone]'s idea…Carl went along with Adrian's judgment and it turned out to be a bad call,' Soter said. But Sagan certainly deserves at least some of the blame: after all, he had driven the Cosmos staff half-crazy by trying to run everything" (*Carl Sagan,* 333).

29 *Cosmos: A Personal Voyage,* Episode 1, "The Shores of the Cosmic Ocean," written by Carl Sagan and Ann Druyan, aired September 28, 1980, PBS.

on the editorial. At heart, however, *Cosmos* is about the relation of the human species with the universe — historically, scientifically, and prospectively. Near the beginning of the work, Sagan justifies the title he has chosen: "*Cosmos* is a Greek word for the order of the universe. It is, in a way, the opposite of *Chaos*. It implies the deep interconnectedness of all things. It conveys awe for the intricate and subtle way which the universe is put together."[30] For Sagan, *cosmos* is the ecological condition — these "exquisite interrelationships" — and this constitutes for him, again and again, a cause for celebration and wonder. This is the "subtle machinery of awe."[31] Sagan's book is ecological literature understood in the most fundamental sense (few secular authors, at least, attempt to tackle our relation with the universe). He tells us, "Every aspect of Nature reveals a deep mystery and touches our sense of wonder and awe,"[32] and by "every aspect," he means supernovae as much as steam engines.

But the ecological bent of *Cosmos* is just as dependent upon what Sagan will mysteriously refer to as the "cosmic perspective." Though the term sounds suspiciously like a scientist's none-too-cloaked universalizing move, a way to make a certain code of ethics and practices obvious by reference to their supposed groundedness in the universe and scientific fact, the cosmic perspective is more subtle and tentative than that. In *Dragons of Eden*, published just a few years before *Cosmos*, Sagan makes his first references to the term:

The current resurgence of interest in the ecology of the planet Earth is also connected with this longing for a cosmic perspective. Many of the leaders of the ecological movement in the United States were originally stimulated to action by photographs of Earth taken from space, pictures revealing

---

30 Sagan, *Cosmos*, 10–11.
31 Ibid., 2.
32 Ibid., 275.

a tiny, delicate, and fragile world, exquisitely sensitive to the depredations of man — a meadow in the middle of the sky.[33]

The cosmic perspective, rather than merely insisting that the image of the earth from afar automatically provides solutions to local problems, points to a more tentative ethic of care fueled by wonder. It is from space, Sagan argues, that life finally appears as something in need of nurturing. And it is by caring for and regarding the living world with awe, in turn, that we can fully inhabit our role in the cosmos as "matter grown to consciousness."[34] The following sections examine this cosmic perspective in more detail, first by examining the alleged "sentimentality" involved in Sagan's view of the relation between the human and the cosmos (5.3), and then by looking more closely at Sagan's insistence that life's rarity in the universe demands we develop a different orientation towards it (5.4).

5.3
Cosmic Sentimentality?

If there is something about the phrase "subtle machinery of awe" that does not sit quite right, it is because it contains a paradox central to *Cosmos* and the cosmic perspective it embodies and presents. Awe is there for the taking — spinning, exploding, and flying through space — but is also engineered by Sagan himself. Indeed, it would be foolhardy to suggest that *Cosmos* grants us unmediated access to the affects of the universe. And yet, what I want to suggest here is that the series and the book are not merely cosmic kitsch. They choose, in most instances, sensation over sentiment. Thus the cosmic perspective, although it is a mediated view of the universe, does not sentimentalize it.

---

33 Carl Sagan, *Dragons of Eden* (London: Holder and Stoughton Limited, 1977), 49.
34 "Shores of the Cosmic Ocean."

Many reactions to *Cosmos,* however, involve scientists in particular taking objection to just that — the supposed surfeit of emotions Sagan invests in space. In the preface to his own book on wonder and science, Richard Dawkins insists that "the debunking of cosmic sentimentality," by which he means the various ways "we tie our life's hope to the ultimate fate of the cosmos…must not be confused with a loss of personal hope." Instead, and in apparent direct opposition to this "cosmic sentimentality," he appeals to the "feeling of awed wonder that science can give us," which he claims is "one of the things that the late Carl Sagan did so well."[35] As much as I agree with the assessment of Sagan as an ambassador of scientific wonder, my argument here is that the cosmic perspective must not be confused with cosmic sentimentality. *Cosmos* revolves around not the feeling the universe has for us, but the profound connections between the human earth-bound and the cosmos. Life's hope is indeed bound up with the fate of the cosmos, but so is everything else. This can hardly be termed sentimental in the sense alluded to in Chapter 1.

The cosmic perspective, as explored here, is a mode of seeing the ways in which the everyday is situated in and reliant upon the cosmic — for instance, how one's bus-ride to work is, through the magic of fossil fuel, powered by the light of a younger sun. From the cosmic perspective, nothing is trivial, and it consists of constantly recasting that which we thought we knew as part of a much larger network of relations. This is what, in Sagan's words, "stirs us"; our own relations, perceived within an Umwelt that is literally and figuratively expanding, acquire a newness and occasion wonder.

At the beginning of *Cosmos,* Sagan proclaims directly that our own destinies are intimately tied up with the universe. He writes:

We have grown distant from the *Cosmos.* It has seemed remote and irrelevant to everyday concerns. But science has

---

35 Richard Dawkins, *Unweaving the Rainbow* (New York: First Mariner Books, 2000), ix.

found not only that the universe has reeling and ecstatic grandeur, not only that it is accessible to human understanding, but also that we are, in a very real and profound sense, a part of that *Cosmos*, born from it, our fate deeply connected with it. The most basic human events and the most trivial trace back to the universe and its origins. This book is devoted to the exploration of that cosmic perspective.[36]

Here Sagan repeats the short version of the disenchantment tale, only to state that science can repair the damage we think has been done (the universe has, after all, only "seemed remote and irrelevant"). Science, rather than serving to further alienate the human from the universe, in a dramatic reversal, is precisely that which will return us to an exalted place among the stars. It is here, in the very beginning, that Sagan ties the trivial and earth-bound to the vastness of the cosmos and begins to lay the groundwork for the cosmic perspective.

Sagan does not attempt, at first, to close the distance between his readers and the cosmos, but appeals directly to their immediate reactions to the attempt to think vastness in space and time: "*The Cosmos is all that is or ever was or ever will be.* Our feeblest contemplations of the *Cosmos* stir us — there is a tingling in the spine, a catch in the voice, a faint sensation, as if a distant memory, of falling from a height. We know we are approaching the greatest of mysteries."[37] Sagan tries to *evoke* an affective relation to the cosmos here, and we experience its unthinkable dimensions as sensation. A mere reminder of the size to which the twentieth, not to mention twenty-first, century human *Umwelt* has grown, inducing a kind of wonder. Significantly, it is not necessarily the experience of new affects that produces wonder in this case, but the notion that, given the sheer size of the tracts of space and time at stake in the "contemplation of the cosmos," one cannot possibly say what new affects await. But that they

36 Sagan, *Cosmos,* xvi.
37 Ibid., 1, emphasis mine.

are there for the taking (or, rather, to take one up) cannot be disputed; the infinity of the cosmos promises this, at least.

Within this cosmic perspective, the earth, far from being reduced to a meaningless speck, acquires a new significance. "The surface of the Earth," he announces, "is the shore of the cosmic ocean."[38] In the television series, he stands on a rock outcropping of an actual beach in his trademark turtleneck, hair blowing in a wind one realizes is not entirely terrestrial in origin, as he says this.[39] But what does it really mean for the earth to be "the shore of the cosmic ocean"? Such a statement smacks of the cosmic sentimentality derided by Dawkins, yet it proves not quite as naïve as it seems on first examination. Rather than constituting the solid ground that the rest of the universe, known and unknown, laps against, the earth here is the vantage point from which one receives information from the cosmos (even if we send out "scouts," the information must be relayed back). Sagan writes:

> We inhabit a universe where atoms are made in the centers of stars, where each second a thousand suns are born; where life is sparked by sunlight and lightning in the airs and waters of youthful planets; where the raw material for biological evolution is sometimes made by the explosion of a star halfway across the Milky Way; where a thing as beautiful as a galaxy is formed a hundred billion times — a *Cosmos* of quasars and quarks, snowflakes and fireflies, where there may be black holes and other universes and extraterrestrial civilizations whose radio messages are at this moment reaching the Earth.[40]

---

38 Ibid., 2.

39 Sagan's novel, *Contact,* also features a beach, along which the scientist-as-tronauts, after traveling in an alien spacecraft through several wormholes, finally are able to converse with the extraterrestrial hosts. See Carl Sagan, *Contact* (New York: Pocket Books, 1985), 344–72.

40 Sagan, *Cosmos,* 275.

One could speak of other kinds of messages at other wavelengths, as well, but Sagan is, after all, a radio astronomer. Any special significance one might associate with the earth becomes the result of a cosmic awakening, a willingness to contemplate extraterrestrial affects. Wondering at and in the cosmos is, for Sagan, eminently human. And the space age presents unparalleled opportunities for further expanding this sense of wonder:

> We embarked on our cosmic voyage with a question first framed in the childhood of our species and in each generation asked anew with undiminished wonder: What are the stars? Exploration is in our nature. We began as wanderers, and we are wanderers still. We have lingered long enough on the shores of the cosmic ocean. We are ready at last to set sail for the stars.[41]

This is a call to explore and experience radically new *Umwelten* (and they are *Umwelten;* the possibility of encountering alien life is upheld on countless occasions) — the ones only glimpsed and imagined in the so-called "childhood of our species." It constitutes, on the one hand, an enthusiastic declaration of support for NASA and other organizations involved in space exploration, but it is also a call to the reader. Sagan pleads constantly for an awareness that we are on a planet orbiting a sun, in one of the arms of the Milky Way, spinning through the universe.

For most of his readers, this is doubtless not a radical thought, but he reminds us that it constitutes a departure from both classical and Christian traditions: "The Platonists and their Christian successors held the peculiar notion that the Earth was tainted and somehow nasty, while the heavens were perfect and divine. The fundamental idea that the Earth is a planet, that we are citizens of the Universe, was rejected and forgotten."[42] Sagan argues for a possibly unfamiliar kind of ecological embeddedness. He rejects the idea of heaven and earth, surface and sky, in

41 Ibid., 155.
42 Ibid.

favor of a dizzyingly post-Copernican view of the universe and our place in it. The analogy to earthly ecological concerns becomes more apparent when one considers the Ship of the Imagination, shaped like a dandelion seed, ostensibly launched by the dandelion shown in the intro and credits at the end. As a dandelion seed is to the earth, we are to the cosmos. The resurrection of the idea that we are in and of the heavens, "that we are citizens of the universe," moreover, forms an uncanny echo of Clebsch's claim, referred to in Chapter 1, for a uniquely American brand of spirituality (section 5.5 will return to this). It is also a powerful response to contemporary narratives of disenchantment.

But Sagan's claim about cosmic citizenship goes further than the recognition that we inhabit a planet of the universe; it is also a claim about the human. Again and again, he reminds us: "The nitrogen in our DNA, the calcium in our teeth, the iron in our blood, the carbon in our apple pies were made in the interiors of collapsing stars. We are made of starstuff."[43] Materially and energetically, human destinies are indeed deeply intertwined with the cosmos. Our atoms have been smelted in cosmic ovens, and, as Sagan also tells us on a number of occasions, we are made of atoms, as is everything we have ever known or ever will know. Even the baking of the humble apple pie, he famously tells us, first requires the invention of the universe.[44]

But he goes even farther than this, arguing that neither our subsistence nor our current biological form would have been possible without the awesome power of the sun. "We are, almost all of us, solar-powered," he claims, highlighting the role of plants as "grudging intermediaries." He goes on to state that

---

43 Ibid., 190. It should be noted that this is in one sense only a more elaborate, and more scientifically informed, illustration of some of the vaguely ecosophical/cosmological declarations of the 1960s. The chorus from Joni Mitchell's "Woodstock" (from *Ladies of the Canyon,* Reprise, 1969, LP), for instance, goes: "We are stardust. / We are golden. / And we've got to get ourselves back to the garden." Sagan's work contains none of the nostalgia, retrogressivism, or Luddism to be found in what one might term "hippy cosmologies" (one would be hard pressed to find "the garden"), but certainly contains some of the same leitmotifs.

44 Sagan, *Cosmos,* 180, 179.

the mutations so essential to evolution "are produced in part by cosmic rays — high-energy particles ejected almost at the speed of light in supernova explosions," concluding, "The evolution of life on Earth is driven in part by the spectacular deaths of distant, massive suns."[45] That we exist at all and have continued to flourish can thus be viewed as the result of a strange amalgam of interstellar accidents.

What is significant about this view of the human, as a creature of the stars as much as the earth, is that these connections to the universe manifest at the affective level before they become the object of scientific inquiry. Sagan explains:

> We are, in the most profound sense, children of the *Cosmos*. Think of the Sun's heat on your upturned face on a cloudless summer's day; think how dangerous it is to gaze at the Sun directly. From 150 million kilometers away, we recognize its power. What would we feel on its seething self-luminous surface, or immersed in its heart of nuclear fire? The Sun warms us and feeds us and permits us to see. It fecundated the Earth. It is powerful beyond human experience. Birds greet the sunrise with an audible ecstasy. Even some one-celled organisms are known to swim to the light. Our ancestors worshiped the Sun, and they were far from foolish. And yet the Sun is an ordinary, even a mediocre star. If we must worship a power greater than ourselves, does it not make sense to revere the Sun and stars? Hidden within every astronomical investigation, sometimes so deeply buried that the researcher himself is unaware of its presence, lies a kernel of awe.[46]

This primordial fascination with the cosmos, unleashed by sensation — the heat on one's "upturned face," or even the racket birds make at sunrise — is the original cosmic wonder. The recognition of an entity like the sun (or the stars, or the moon) also entails the recognition that something lies beyond one's

45 Ibid., 191.
46 Ibid., 189–90.

own "soap bubble."[47] What that is exactly can only be revealed or approximated with a kind of science, but the first taste of the cosmic unknown is undeniably affective. Only later might the extent of our absolute reliance on that which lies beyond the earth become known. But even after a place is carved out in the cogito for the sun, for instance, it in no way precludes an affective engagement with it. One may know exactly what kinds of rays are striking one's upturned face and still wonder at the sun. This most fundamental kinship with the universe, the idea that extraterrestrial affects have somehow brought us into being, is the cosmic perspective. Sagan grandly declares: "We have bravely tested the waters and have found the ocean to our liking, resonant with our nature. Something in us recognizes the *Cosmos* as home. We are made of stellar ash. Our origin and evolution have been tied to distant cosmic events."[48]

This awakening to the scope of the human *Umwelt,* both in material terms and in terms of the realm of inquiry, is not only eminently human for Sagan, but also an occasion for unparalleled wonder. He continues, "In the last few millennia we have made the most astonishing and unexpected discoveries about the *Cosmos* and our place within it, explorations that are exhilarating to consider. They remind us that humans have evolved to wonder, that understanding is a joy, that knowledge is a prerequisite to survival."[49] The take-home point for Sagan is that "our future depends on how well we know this *Cosmos* in which we float like a mote of dust in the morning sky."[50] And lest our cosmic origins and ability to contemplate them lead to any kind of human hubris, Sagan constantly reminds us of our smallness.

47 See Jakob von Uexküll, "A Stroll Through the Worlds of Animals and Men: A Picture Book of Invisible Worlds," trans. Claire Schiller, *Semiotica* 89, no. 4 (1992): 319–91, at 338. Uexküll also writes: "Sun, moon and stars wander without any difference in depth on the same distant plane, which surrounds all visible things," but "[t]he location of the farthest plane is not rigidly fixed" (336). The distant plane, for Uexküll, is a horizon rather than a boundary.
48 Sagan, *Cosmos,* 264.
49 Ibid., 1.
50 Ibid., 1–2.

Our destinies may have been set in motion by nothing smaller than the Big Bang, but we still only "a mote of dust in the morning sky."

Despite the fact that our own mote of dust, our own abundant planet, not to mention our own star, so overshadows that which might lie beyond it, Sagan assures us that there is a whole universe with which to become acquainted:

Each star system is an island in space, quarantined from its neighbors by the light-years. I can imagine creatures evolving into glimmerings of knowledge on innumerable worlds, every one of them assuming at first their puny planet and paltry few suns to be all that is. We grow up in isolation. Only slowly do we teach ourselves the *Cosmos.*[51]

This is another lesson in interrelation: The notion of any kind of solitude is a preposterous one for Sagan. Partially this is because he nourished the hope, up until the end of his life, that other intelligences might be encountered.[52] But not all of his argument hinges upon the existence of alien beings. He insists, as well, that the contemplation, not to mention exploration, of the extraterrestrial brings us closer to it, or at least extends our own imaginary *Umwelt* to such bounds that solitude simply no longer computes.

Learning the cosmos, moreover, which Sagan claims we are slowly doing as a species, is as much a matter of contemplation as of action. In a particularly evocative passage, Sagan compares the 3.6-million-year-old footprint of an early hominid found by Mary Leakey in Tanzania to a footprint left by astronauts in the Sea of Tranquility on the moon: "We have come far in 3.6 million years," he asserts, "and in 4.6 billion and in 15 billion,"

---

51 Ibid., 4.
52 The SETI (Search For Extraterrestrial Intelligence) Institute, in fact, has a Carl Sagan Center for the Study of Life in the Universe. See "Carl Sagan Center," SETI Institute Online, http://www.seti.org/carlsagancenter.

the approximate ages of the earth and the universe respectively. Further, he writes,

> For we are the local embodiment of a Cosmos grown to self-awareness. We have begun to contemplate our origins: star-stuff pondering the stars; organized assemblages of ten billion billion billion atoms considering the evolution of atoms; tracing the long journey by which, here at last, consciousness arose. Our loyalties are to the species and the planet. *We* speak for Earth. Our obligation to survive is owed not just to ourselves but also to that Cosmos, ancient and vast, from which we spring.[53]

The core of Sagan's cosmic perspective consists much more of a belief in the wondering human than in any distinct vision of the cosmos. Sagan asks for nothing less than the ceaseless expansion of the human *Umwelt,* whether with telescopes, microscopes, or moon-shoes. Thus, although the stars may be marvelous, of primary importance is the ability to contemplate and wonder at them, and, prior even to this, the people that are able to contemplate and wonder. This star-fed wonder, as we will see in the next section, far from producing an indifference to the terrestrial, seeks to honor and protect the earth as cosmic exception.

5.4
Precious Worlds / Precarious Life

The commitment to the earth and the human would not come as readily if Sagan did not also contend that life, not to mention intelligent life, constituted a relative rarity. But in space (given the sheer amount of emptiness one is likely to encounter) and time (given our own short life spans and the relatively short time the species has been in existence), just as with Wilson and Lovelock, Sagan repeatedly insists on the sheer luck involved in

---

53 Sagan, *Cosmos,* 286.

an intelligent life form existing here and now. Sagan concludes, multiple times, that our existence is both extremely fortunate and extremely precarious, marveling constantly throughout *Cosmos* at the richness of this precarious life and that of which it is capable. This constitutes the seeds of an ethics to accompany his cosmic perspective. Sagan writes of our impermanence:

> Compared to a star, we are like mayflies, fleeting ephemeral creatures who live out their whole lives in the course of a single day. From the point of view of a mayfly, human beings are solid, boring, almost entirely immovable, offering hardly a hint that they ever do anything. From the point of a view of a star, a human being is a tiny flash, one of billions of brief lives flickering tenuously on the surface of a strangely cold, anomalously solid, exotically remote sphere of silicate and iron.[54]

In deep cosmic time, even more so than in deep ecological time, the duration of the human is hardly worth remarking upon. Like Wilson, Sagan insists on the importance of scale in our understanding of the species. But in contrast to Wilson's profound anthropocentrism, where the human acquires a significance disproportionate to its time in existence as a life form, Sagan's message is more humbling, and more in line with Lovelock's: "We are like butterflies who flutter for a day and think it is forever."[55]

In space, as well, our existence is a relative anomaly. As obvious as it may be to the reader, Sagan points to countless permutations of the fact that that which extends beyond the earth exceeds, in size and quantity, anything to be found on it. He goes back to the beach for one comparison:

> A handful of sand contains about 10,000 grains, more than the number of stars we can see with the naked eye on a clear night. But the number of stars we can see is only the tiniest fraction of the number of stars that *are*. What we see at night

54 Ibid., 177–78.
55 Ibid., 20.

is the merest smattering of the nearest stars. Meanwhile the *Cosmos* is rich beyond measure: the total number of stars in the universe is greater than all the grains of sand on all the beaches of the planet Earth.[56]

As nearly infinitely numerous as these points of light might be, itself an overwhelming and wondrous fact, most of the cosmos is in fact empty. Simply locating a planet, however hostile and lifeless, is a challenging exercise. Sagan states this already at the beginning of *Cosmos* with one of his first dizzying statistics: "If we were randomly inserted into the Cosmos, the chance that we would find ourselves on or near a planet would be less than one in a billion trillion trillion (10^{33}, a one followed by 33 zeroes). In everyday life such odds are compelling. Worlds are precious."[57] The universe is simultaneously "rich beyond measure" and desert-like in *Cosmos* — rich because scientists are just beginning to conceive of the number and variety of entities that populate it, and desert-like because those entities are so few and far between. Though Sagan holds out hope that earth does not harbor the only life, he insists that it is exceptional in the vast reaches of space and time:

There are some hundred billion (10^{11}) galaxies, each with, on the average, a hundred billion stars. In all the galaxies, there are perhaps as many planets as stars, $10^{11} \times 10^{11} = 10^{22}$, ten billion trillion. In the face of such overpowering numbers, what is the likelihood that only one ordinary star, the Sun, is accompanied by an inhabited planet? Why should we, tucked away in some forgotten corner of the Cosmos, be so fortunate? To me, it seems far more likely that the universe is brimming over with life. But we humans do not yet know. We are just beginning our explorations. From eight billion light-years away we are hard pressed to find even the cluster in which our Milky Way Galaxy is imbedded, much less the

56 Ibid., 161.
57 Ibid., 2.

Sun or the Earth. The only planet we are sure is inhabited is a tiny speck of rock and metal, shining feebly by reflected sunlight, and at this distance utterly lost.[58]

Sagan contends that we exist here and now against exceptional odds. If there is extraterrestrial life, he informs us, it will be far away, farther than we can easily imagine, and easily long dead or yet to come into existence. Life forms, like worlds, are precious for this astronomer with an astrobiological bent — precious because they are precarious, because they could so easily be overlooked in space and time.

This is a slightly different spin on Butler's precariousness, based not necessarily on "an understanding of how easily life is annulled,"[59] but how difficult it is to encounter in the first place. Butler has alluded to the idea that this precariousness might also "link human and nonhuman life in ethically significant ways,"[60] claiming, "If humans actually share a condition of precariousness, not only just with one another, but also with animals, and with the environment, then this constitutive feature of who we 'are' undoes the very conceit of anthropocentrism." She goes on to propose "'precarious life' as a non-anthropocentric framework for considering what makes life valuable."[61]

This shared precariousness-in-the-universe also links life "in ethically significant ways" for Sagan, although he is far from espousing any kind of elaborate anti-anthropocentrism.[62] With all other creatures of the earth, Sagan claims, we share the indifference of the universe, neither "benign nor hostile": "That

58 Ibid., 3.
59 Judith Butler, *Precarious Life: The Powers of Mourning and Violence* (London: Verso, 2004), xvii.
60 Judith Butler, "Antigone's Claim: A Conversation with Judith Butler," interview by Pierpaolo Antonello and Roberto Farneti, *Theory and Event* 12, no. 1 (2009).
61 Butler, "Antigone's Claim."
62 It can more accurately be called a kind of casual or instrumental anti-anthropocentrism. Sagan states: "If we are to survive, our loyalties must be broadened further, to include the whole human community, the entire planet Earth" (*Cosmos*, 283).

we live in a universe which permits life is remarkable," Sagan proclaims, "That we live in one which destroys galaxies and stars and worlds is also remarkable."[63] One might draw parallels here to Gaia's indifference, which also, paradoxically, becomes the basis of an ethic of care. The indifference of the cosmos, however, can be seen as even more profound, as it is not framed in any way as geared towards the preservation of life.

What this precariousness-in-the-universe entails, in the end, is a plea for non-violence with regard to the earth as much as with regard to fellow humans. Sagan states, "The Earth is a tiny and fragile world. It needs to be cherished."[64] As far as the human is concerned, even given the possibility that alien life may be encountered, Sagan states the following:

> The Cosmos may be densely populated with intelligent beings. But the Darwinian lesson is clear: There will be no humans elsewhere. Only here. Only on this small planet. We are a rare as well as an endangered species. Every one of us is, in the cosmic perspective, precious. If a human disagrees with you, let him live. In a hundred billion galaxies, you will not find another.[65]

Sagan asks us to wonder at the precariousness of life, to contemplate the extinguishing of *Umwelt*en and the affects that characterize them.[66] That we exist at all, any of us, he reminds us, is also something at which to wonder. And his argument for pacifism, although it may sound hopelessly naïve, is statistically sound. Death, in the end, entails a loss of complexity and reduction in the range of affective registers for which the most breathtaking nebulae can likely not compensate.

63 Ibid., 205.
64 Ibid., 84.
65 Ibid., 283.
66 See also Sagan's description of the death of the Sun and "the last perfect day on Earth," followed merely by "an eerie radiance, the ghost of the Sun" (*Cosmos*, 188–89).

In *Cosmos,* which is remembered, oddly, for its optimism, Sagan provides us with a precursor to the dark ecologies emerging more recently in the twenty-first century, most notably from within the object-oriented ontology movement.[67] Like the ecologies that will come later, the cosmic perspective "presents an image of the universe that is indifferent to our existence, without design, teleology, or built-in equilibrating mechanisms that will ineluctably save us from catastrophe."[68] This indifference, rather than merely allowing us to give up and give in to the indifference of the universe, "is intended to spur us to action."[69] As Levi Bryant, himself an avowed dark ecologist states, "black ecology reveals just how precious, rare, and precarious life is, reminding us that we have to fight hard to preserve it."[70] Sagan makes precisely the same claims, at least 30 years earlier, but does not explicitly offer them as a counterweight to the more optimistic ecosophies of the time. Still, in its emphasis on the vast emptiness of space and the miracle that there is something rather than nothing, let alone life, Sagan's ecology is without question a dark one.

When Sagan is not concerned with the precariousness of life in the universe, however, he extolls the richness and potential of the forms of life we know. Although he does not mention Gaia

---

67 Graham Harman and Timothy Morton, whose work is briefly discussed in Chapter 3.4 in this volume, are prominent members of the movement. See, in particular, Timothy Morton, *Hyperobjects: Philosophy and Ecology after the End of the World* (Minneapolis: University of Minnesota Press, 2013).

68 See Levi R. Bryant, "Black," in *Prismatic Ecology: Ecotheory beyond Green,* ed. Jeffrey Jerome Cohen (Minneapolis: University of Minnesota Press, 2013), 290–310, at 292.

69 Bryant, "Black," 292. That one should strive precisely because of the universe's indifference is also not a new idea, but was articulated extensively by existentialists. Camus writes at the end of *The Myth of Sisyphus*: "This universe henceforth without a master seems to him neither sterile nor futile. Each atom of that stone, each mineral flake of that night filled mountain, in itself forms a world. The struggle itself toward the heights is enough to fill a man's heart." See Albert Camus, *The Myth of Sisyphus and Other Essays,* trans. Justin O'Brien (New York: Vintage International, 1991), 78.

70 Bryant, "Black," 302.

explicitly, he appears deeply impressed by the manner in which life regulates planetary systems, noting, for instance, that "99% of the Earth's atmosphere is of biological origin. The sky is made of life."[71] The earth is constituted by the sum activities of its living inhabitants; small affects beget much, much larger ones. The terms he uses to describe macrobiological processes are much more vivid than a reader of more sober scientific literature on the subject may be accustomed to, and are on par, in their vitalist ring, with Lovelock's own. Sagan writes, "What a marvelous cooperative arrangement — plants and animals each inhaling the other's exhalations, a kind of planet-wide mutual mouth-to-stoma resuscitation, the entire elegant cycle powered by a star 150 million kilometers away."[72] It is evident from this description of the manner in which the earth's gasses are maintained that he grants life an immensely powerful role. Although often threatened by the extraterrestrial, life is also in league with it. It is foolish to think that only the human enjoys an affective relation with the cosmos. The real difference between the human and the nonhuman is that the human may be fully cognizant of this relation — hence the unique capacity for wonder.

Despite Sagan's baby steps towards a kind of anti-anthropocentrism, towards embracing the whole earth community, he devotes a large amount of energy to admiring the human and its potential. Here, he does not point to poetry or the achievements of the humanities but seems to examine the much more fundamental question, the Spinozan question raised in the first chapter, of what a body can do. And in the end, despite the fact of precariousness, the human, for Sagan, is more or less infinitely capable. The nature and ends to which this capability may be put, aside from, perhaps, "a fundamental redesign of economic, political, social and religious institutions,"[73] remain largely mysterious, but one might point to three areas of inexhaustible human potential he explores.

71 Sagan, *Cosmos*, 22.
72 Ibid., 24.
73 Ibid., 272.

The first is the genetic reservoir granted to us by the universe. Sagan observes the following:

[T]he number of useful ways of putting nucleic acids together is stupefyingly large — probably far greater than the total number of electrons and protons in the universe. Accordingly, the number of possible individual human beings is vastly greater than the number that have ever lived: the untapped potential of the human species is immense.[74]

Here Sagan presents us with a truly wonder-inducing biological non-essentialism: Who really knows what is possible with biology?[75] We can never really know the limits of the human, because the permutations of the species are inexhaustible. Certainly, this could constitute a rallying cry for any species, but, as far as we know, only the human is capable of thinking this thought. Because we cannot know the limit of the human, we also have no way of ascertaining the boundaries of the human *Umwelt,* nor of ascertaining which affects are proper to us, if one can even speak of "proper affects" in the first place. As with many references to the infinite, this constitutes a kind of higher order of wonder, not geared toward the realization of any novel affects in particular, but toward the realization of their inexhaustibility.

The second area of human potential lies with the ability to contemplate the infinite and nearly infinite. Sagan notes when discussing the googolplex (ten to the power of one hundred, or effectively infinity): "A piece of paper large enough to have all the zeroes in a googolplex written out explicitly could not be stuffed into the known universe."[76] Mathematics, if nothing else, pushes

74 Ibid., 25.
75 This quintessentially human non-essentialism is also to be found in early twentieth-century philosophical anthropology, for instance in Plessner's notion of the eccentricity of the human. See Jos de Mul, "Artificial by Nature: An Introduction to Plessner's Philosophical Anthropology" in *Plessner's Philosophical Anthropology: Perspectives and Prospects,* ed. Jos de Mul (Amsterdam: Amsterdam University Press, 2014), 11–40, at 17.
76 Sagan, *Cosmos,* 181.

the boundaries of the imaginary *Umwelt*; the ability to conceive of the infinite means, at some level, that one is no longer bound by Uexküll's soap bubble. One should not, of course, confuse an infinitely large imaginary *Umwelt* with an ability to conceive of the *Umwelt*en of other creatures. Sagan is not exactly firm on this point, often preferring to gesture towards a dizzying expansiveness and our united precariousness in it than the various ways in which the inhabitants of the earth endanger one another.

Finally, Sagan alludes time and time again to the unplumbed depths of human curiosity and insatiable drive to explore. This is something that far exceeds our more familiar capacities as organisms:

> [A] fertilized egg takes as long to wander from the fallopian tubes and implant itself in the uterus as Apollo 11 took to journey to the Moon; and as long to develop into a full-term infant as Viking took on its trip to Mars. The normal human lifetime is longer than Voyager will take to venture beyond the orbit of Pluto.[77]

If space exploration is not "going beyond the organism," in the sense referred to by Buchanan and Deleuze and Guattari, then nothing is. 'This is how far we've come," Sagan seems to say again and again, and he consistently advocates going further. As a NASA romantic, he is an advocate of the ceaseless expansion of the human *Umwelt*. Every new landing, every stride made beyond the tiny fraction of space known intimately, involves a renewal of wonder and becomes renewed proof of the capacity of the human.

Whether or not Sagan intends it, this involves a much more enterprising view of the human than Wilson and Lovelock put forth. For Lovelock, humans are just another organism on Gaia, albeit with the capacity to marvel at her. Wilson, in turn, advocates a kind of conservationism to nourish the human capacity for wonder at life and the life-like. Sagan alludes only obliquely

---

77 Ibid., 113 (asterisked note).

to such earthly concerns. *Cosmos* is not so much about the exploration of nonhuman *Umwelten,* but the relentless, both wonderful and terrifying, expansion of our own. Put more reductively, Wilson gives us a species nourished by affective relations with nonhuman life, Lovelock endows the earth with affects in which we cannot help but take part, and Sagan gives us a species nourished by affective relations with the stars (although he, too, held out for the possibility of life there).

5.5
Numinous Science: Cosmos and the Sacred

It is difficult, particularly when confronted with shots of Sagan grinning, eyes closed but directed towards the heavens, to resist associating the cosmic perspective with a certain religiosity. The Ship of the Imagination resembles not a cockpit crowded with instruments, but a cathedral, with a console where the pulpit should be. Sagan is positioned as priest or minister, and the entire television audience as congregation.[78] Among the cliffs on the California coast, one cannot help but hear *The Cosmos is all that is or ever was or will be* and the subsequent description of the "tingling in the spine, a catch in the voice, a faint sensation, as if a distant memory, of falling from a height" when "approaching the greatest of mysteries"[79] as the beginning of a sermon. These scenes, as well as some very incisive contemporary criticism (which I will turn to shortly), beg the question: Does *Cosmos* present us with a vision of an exalted or an immanent science? Does its capacity to reenchant lie merely in aping the structure and rhetoric of religion, or does it indeed offer a kind of secular reenchantment?

---

78 The 2014 remake of the series featured a redesigned Ship of the Imagination, in which one looks down, rather than up, into the universe with guide Neil deGrasse Tyson, as if into a well.

79 Sagan, *Cosmos,* 1.

Sagan was himself not at all clear about when wonder slips into worship. In *Pale Blue Dot,* for instance, written near the end of his life, his criticism of religion is not that it posits the existence of a transcendental realm, but that the transcendental it posits is too small:

> In some respects, science has far surpassed religion in delivering awe. How is it that hardly any major religion has looked at science and concluded, "This is better than we thought! The Universe is much bigger than our prophets said, grander, more subtle, more elegant. God must be even greater than we dreamed"? Instead they say, "No, no, no! My god is a little god, and I want him to stay that way." A religion, old or new, that stressed the magnificence of the Universe as revealed by modern science might be able to draw forth reserves of reverence and awe hardly tapped by the conventional faiths. Sooner or later, such a religion will emerge.[80]

It is tempting to conceptualize the cosmic perspective as precisely "such a religion," but here I will argue against it. Although scholars and critics from the 1980s were eager to frame *Cosmos* as "an attempt to ground science in a higher order, to place science within the realm of the sacred, and consequently remove it from the banalities of profane existence,"[81] this ignores the extent to which Sagan uses science to rob profane existence of its banality, to place the earth in the heavens.

This does not mean, however, that there are no holy or sacred dimensions to the cosmic perspective. By insisting that everything is of the heavens, Sagan, in fact, banishes profane existence altogether. It is helpful here to consult Rudolf Otto's formulation of the holy or the sacred (*das Heilige*) to understand the way in which a scientific perspective is even compatible with the sa-

---

80 Carl Sagan, *Pale Blue Dot* (New York: Ballantine Books,1997), 35.
81 Thomas M. Lessl, "Science and the Sacred Cosmos: The Ideological Rhetoric of Carl Sagan," *Quarterly Journal of Speech* 71, no. 2 (1985): 175–87, at 183.

cred.[82] For Otto, the sacred does not merely designate that which is morally good, but also includes a "clear overplus of meaning," which he identifies as the "numinous": that which "cannot, strictly speaking, be taught, it can only be evoked, awakened in the mind."[83] He continues, "the nature of the numinous can only be suggested by means of the special way in which it is reflected in the mind in terms of feeling. Its nature is such that it grips or stirs the human mind with this and that determinate affective state."[84] The numinous as Otto understands it is akin to the virtual, or the infinity of becomings that are possible. There cannot, then, be any one relation to the numinous or a way of knowing it objectively; it is perceivable in one's own relation to it. And one's relation to it, as Otto frames it, is very similar to wonder: "creature-feeling" describes one aspect, in which the creature is "overwhelmed by its own nothingness."[85] "Mysterium Tremendum" describes another, which "may at times come sweeping like a gentle tide [...] the hushed, trembling, and speechless humility in the presence of — whom or what? In the presence of that which is a *Mystery* inexpressible above all creatures."[86] If one tallies up the number of references to the effectively infinite and the unlikelihood or smallness of life on earth, not to mention invocations of mystery in *Cosmos,* there is a lot of creature-feeling and mysterium tremendum. One cannot deny that *Cosmos* speaks not merely to the finite and knowable, but just as, if not more, to the numinous. From this perspective, the cosmos is indeed sacred.

But does the prominence of the numinous in *Cosmos* imply that the cosmic perspective is a kind of religion, albeit a scientific one? Perhaps the most sustained criticism of *Cosmos*'s supposed religious bent has come from communications scholar Thomas Lessl. In a 1985 article entitled "Science and the Sacred

82 Rudolf Otto, *The Idea of the Holy,* trans. John W. Harvey (London: Oxford University Press, 1936).
83 Ibid., 5, 7.
84 Ibid., 12.
85 Ibid.
86 Ibid., 13.

Cosmos: The Ideological Rhetoric of Carl Sagan," he distinguishes between Sagan the scientist, who adheres to the "dominant
mechanistic model of nature" and Sagan the cosmologist:

> When Sagan the cosmologist speaks, a different set of epis-
> temic principles seems to be in force. Suddenly, through the
> subtle suggestiveness of metaphor, Sagan breathes life into
> the formerly dead machine universe, transforming it into a
> self-determining, purposive cosmos. The fact that this vital-
> ism is given to nature through deliberate metaphor is im-
> portant. The ambiguity of figurative speech allows Sagan the
> capacity to transgress the more rigid forms of scientific de-
> scription.[87]

Lessl neglects to explain why the mechanistic model of nature
is the only appropriate model for science, as well as what exactly about Sagan's cosmos is purposive. That Sagan's cosmos
is to a large extent self-determining and populated with living
bodies is, however, consistent with my own reading. As evidence of Sagan's vitalism, Lessl points to his discussion of the
lifecycle of a star, which includes an "adolescence," and the use
of oceanic metaphors for the universe.[88] But we are never told
by Lessl how this vitalism renders the cosmos purposive or
transcendental. I would argue that this light vitalism actually
allows the cosmos to seem more accessible to the reader. When
Sagan declares that "The Earth is a place. It is by no means the
only place,"[89] he announces the cosmos as no more elusive than
our terrestrial reality.

Four years later, in 1989, Lessl published another article
examining *Cosmos* as religious testament or artifact — "The
Priestly Voice."[90] Here, Lessl distinguishes between the bardic
and priestly voices, explaining, "Whereas we think of the bard

87 Lessl, "Science and the Sacred Cosmos," 181.
88 Ibid
89 Sagan, *Cosmos*, 2.
90 Thomas M. Lessl, "The Priestly Voice," *Quarterly Journal of Speech* 5 (1989):
    183–97.

as one submerged in the culture of his or her audience, the priest mediates a configuration of symbols and a conception of reality that for the most general audience is at once both near and remote."[91] He goes on to describe the priesthood as "given an elite status as well as a formative role in creating a particular society's existential consciousness."[92] The priestly voices stand apart from everyday experience, while Bardic communication takes ordinary experience as its subject. And while "the bard's communication is lateral, extending across the well-traveled highways of a cultural milieu," speaking "to the profane dimension of human experience," the priestly voice is "largely vertical, descending from above as an epiphanic Word, filled with mystery and empowered with extra-human authority."[93] In which voice, then, does Sagan speak?

Unsurprisingly, Lessl makes the case for Sagan as priest: "By virtue of his ability to give audiences the perception — some would call it the illusion — that they can understand science, Sagan is a master of priestly communication."[94] Spun this way, Sagan speaks on high from the pulpit of the techno-scientific elite. In a 1980 review of the series, David Paul Rebovich also points to Sagan's exalted status: "The answer to the question 'Who Speaks for the Earth?' [posed by Sagan in the series] is the scientist. The scientist is the exalted pursuer of knowledge and the witness for the paramount values and aspirations of mankind and, for that matter, any rational species."[95] He continues, "Sagan wants to explain how man is ultimately connected to the universe, and it is science that teaches man this special knowledge."[96] Science here is at least part sacred order, and Sagan is one of the initiates generous enough to impart to us some of its knowledge.

91 Ibid., 183–84.
92 Ibid., 185.
93 Ibid.
94 Ibid., 189.
95 David Paul Rebovich, "Sagan's Metaphysical Parable," *Society* 18, no. 5 (1981): 91–95, at 93.
96 Ibid., 94.

Yet, Sagan also speaks from the televisions in our living rooms as he wanders the northern California coast; there is something of the bard in him.[97] I acknowledge that there is a priestly aspect to Sagan, but, particularly in the more affective parts of *Cosmos,* there is more at work. In his capacity as "prince of popularizers," Sagan does not merely administer science like so many sermons. Science serves, rather, to expand the boundaries of our own world and draw attention to the degree to which we are of the universe. When Sagan tells us that we are made of star stuff, it may have a theological ring, but in practice, he places the human and the stellar on the same plane and establishes a relation between them. With regard to the universe, there is nothing like the obedience, discipline, or piousness traditionally associated with religion.[98]

At the end of his essay, Lessl begins to move to an understanding of popular science as a hybrid discourse:

> To popularize is not merely to make science suitable for the people; it is also to make the people suitable for science. Rather than conceiving of public science as the popularization of technical knowledge, we might better conceive of it as the scientization of popular consciousness. Popular treatments of science do as much to bring people to the scientific domain as they do to bring science to the people.[99]

This, finally, begins to do Sagan and his immense popularity justice. It is not merely that he as a privileged actor was able to impart (the impression of) privileged information. *Cosmos* does as much to teach us about our place in the universe as it prepares us to occupy this place — not just describing Earthlings, but invoking them. To do this, Sagan must be both priest and

---

97 Lessl even points to Fiske and Hartley's characterization of television as "the modern bard" ("The Priestley Voice," 184).

98 See *Oxford English Dictionary Online,* s.v, "religion," https://en.oxforddictionaries.com/definition/religion.

99 Lessl, "The Priestly Voice," 196.

bard, bounded by an electronic nutshell and simultaneously a king of infinite space.

Perhaps in the discussion of the sacred and profane, the priest and the scientist, it is wise to return to the concept of the cosmos itself. Sagan describes it as "the deep interconnectedness of all things,"[100] but Latour also points to its less neutral, Platonic meaning: "the well-formed collective."[101] For Latour, the composition or becoming of the cosmos is an unending task in which science plays a crucial role.[102] Why not, then, view Sagan's *Cosmos* as a particularly bold attempt to invoke a people and a collective? The wonder that *Cosmos* transmits and instigates is no reverence for a higher celestial plane, but the recognition, again and again, of the infinite forms collectivity can take.

5.6
The Effects of the Earth after the Death of the Sun

The Ship of the Imagination assists Sagan in composing a cosmos, in positioning the human in a community far bigger than ever thought possible, but so, too, do the very real Voyager spacecraft. For the short time that the spacecraft did operate as probes, they revealed more effectively than anything before and perhaps since just how tiny our sector of nature was and is. One series of photographs, in particular, stands out in this regard, taken in 1990 when Sagan requested that Voyager take "one last glance homeward" just after flying past Saturn.[103] Sagan would write an entire book towards the end of his life named after the resulting composite photograph — Pale Blue Dot.[104]

100 Sagan, *Cosmos*, 10.
101 Bruno Latour, *Politics of Nature: How to Bring the Sciences into Democracy*, trans. Catherine Porter (Cambridge: Harvard University Press, 2004), 183.
102 Ibid., 102.
103 Sagan, *Pale Blue Dot*, 10.
104 Image accessible on NASA's *Visible Earth Catalog*, http://visibleearth.nasa.gov/view.php?id=52392.

Pale Blue Dot is the counterpoint to the Blue Marble photograph,[105] with the earth visible only as "lonely pixel," indistinguishable from "the luminous dots"[106] that are the other planets and distant stars. They are two planetary selfies, taken eighteen years apart. Pale Blue Dot is, however, less self-obsessed — a luminous point taking more of a family portrait. Only an accident of light, the sun reflecting off one of Voyager's surfaces, marks the earth — it "seems to be sitting in a beam of light, as if there were some special significance to this small world." Sagan is quick to sternly remind us that "it's just an accident of geometry and optics."[107] He continues:

Our posturings, our imagined self-importance, the delusion that we have some privileged position in the Universe, are challenged by this point of pale light. Our planet is a lonely speck in the great enveloping cosmic dark. In our obscurity, in all this vastness, there is no hint that help will come from elsewhere to save us from ourselves.

The Earth is the only world known so far to harbor life. There is nowhere else, at least in the near future, to which our species could migrate. Visit, yes. Settle, not yet. Like it or not, for the moment the Earth is where we make our stand.

It has been said that astronomy is a humbling and character-building experience. There is perhaps no better demonstration of the folly of human conceits than this distant image of our tiny world. To me, it underscores our responsibility to deal more kindly with one another, and to preserve and cherish the pale blue dot, the only home we've ever known.[108]

The Pale Blue Dot photograph humbles and reveals definitively that what we know and experience is comparably little. But it also makes a better case, arguably, for the ecological than the

105 Image accessible on NASA's *Visible Earth Catalog,* http://visibleearth.nasa.
    gov/view.php?id=55418.
106 Sagan, *Pale Blue Dot,* 12.
107 Ibid., 12.
108 Ibid., 13.

Blue Marble image. With earth as a "mote of dust suspended on a sunbeam,"[109] one is not overwhelmed by the greenness and swirling clouds that have come to mean life to us; there is no sublime beauty that provides an aesthetic impulse to protect life. Pale Blue Dot reveals our tinyness, our precariousness in time and space, and makes it clear that "the Earth is where we make our stand." Sagan writes, "Look again at that dot. That's here. That's home. That's us,"[110] and it would not be out of place if he added, "That's it." It is a powerful antidote to the disenchantment narratives that claim an exaggerated power and place for the human.

The Voyager spacecraft are strange vehicles now. They carry no one, no longer relay back pictures, and by roughly 2025 will no longer relay back anything at all.[111] Hurtling through space towards nowhere in particular, the spacecraft, carrying the Golden Records which play the sights and sounds of the earth, will outlast not only all of us but also our small planet:

> Billions of years from now our sun, then a distended red giant star, will have reduced Earth to a charred cinder. But the Voyager record will still largely be intact, in some other remote region of the Milky Way galaxy, preserving a murmur of an ancient civilization that once flourished — perhaps before moving on to greater deeds and other worlds — on the distant planet Earth.[112]

The Voyager spacecraft are the affects of the earth set loose. This is their legacy in deep time and deep space — not to conquer and humanize the extraterrestrial, but to bring human sentiment to the vacuum of space.

109 Ibid., 12.
110 Ibid.
111 See Dan Vergano, "Voyager 1 Leaves Solar System, NASA Confirms," *National Geographic Online,* September 12, 2013, http://news.nationalgeographic.com/news/2013/13/130911-voyager-interstellar-solar-system-nasa-science-space/.
112 Sagan, "Preface," 42.

The Voyager spacecraft are the cosmic perspective in action. They fly on, at once proclaiming the universe's vastness and indifference and the richness and precariousness of earthly life. Here, I have explained how the probes and the Golden Record themselves embody the cosmic perspective and sentimentality that Sagan will go on to describe more fully in *Cosmos*. The focus on the cosmic within the series does not mean an automatic orientation towards the global, as one might assume, but rather focuses on local, affective connections to the stars. At times, Sagan's proclamations about the individual relation to the cosmos seem like those of a privileged initiate to followers of a religious order, but what *Cosmos* offers, like *Gaia* and *Biophilia,* is a vision of an immanent science. It asks for a recognition of the human *Umwelt* as precisely that, a subjective world, and attempts to reveal the pleasure of exposing our own "small sector of nature" to the elements. *Cosmos* is an affective ecology for deep time and deep space.

6

CONCLUSION:
ENCHANTED POPULAR SCIENCE
AND ITS AFTERLIVES

With *Biophilia* (1984), *Gaia* (1979), and *Cosmos* (1980),[1] we have moved from the inexhaustibility of a handful of dirt, to a planet that will stop at nothing, including dispensing of us in a fever, to maintain life, to a cosmos that "is rich beyond measure."[2] The affective ecologies with which these works present us operate at vastly different scales, but these become more reconcilable with the march of time. This final chapter looks at the findings of the last three chapters in a more condensed fashion, and in particular at what these works of reenchantment hold in common. It does not shy away, however, from the subtle ways in which they differentiate themselves. These are all works that reenchant science and modern life by mobilizing affective wonder, by drawing attention to modes of interrelation in the present, but no two attempt this in precisely the same way. There are other vectors of comparison, moreover, that allow us to see these works more meaningfully in relation to one another: In addition to how they

1   Edward O. Wilson, *Biophilia* (Cambridge: Harvard University Press, 1984); James Lovelock, *Gaia: A New Look at Life on Earth* (Oxford: Oxford University Press, 1979); Carl Sagan, *Cosmos* (New York: Ballantine Books, 1980).
2   Sagan, *Cosmos*, 161.

reenchant and what role they assign to wonder, one may look more directly at their relation to the ecological. Here, this will mean examining which role each affective ecology assigns to the human, as well as the unique vision each work provides for an anti-sentimental ecology that is, nevertheless, keenly felt.

The claims and recommendations made by these works, as well as the attitudes that they assume, are more relevant now that we have entered the so-called Anthropocene: the age of the human. The second section here moves beyond the 1980s to the future of popular science: "The Poet-in-Scientist Now" (6.2) looks at how we can understand our current ecological quandary and how the role of popular science may be evolving because of it. In a world that is increasingly influenced by the human, the task of the poet-in-scientist is, more than ever, to show the ways in which background is nothing of the sort. A new generation of poet-in-scientists currently writes not about how a potential ecological crisis will limit the horizons of and opportunities to wonder, as Wilson, Lovelock, and Sagan did, but how we are currently shaping the contours of what, thirty years ago, we were calling the crisis that must be averted. The human seen in these vastly inflated, arguably geological, dimensions might be a cause for wonder anew, although not necessarily the type of wonder we associate with pleasure.

Finally, we turn to "Paths Unfollowed" (6.3), threads that I may have taken up briefly within this work, but which cry out for further investigation. Popular science enjoys more public attention now than ever before, and my plea at the end is that scholars in the cultural studies, in particular, begin to acknowledge the unique position of popular science and the pop cultural production surrounding it in the Anthropocene. In an era in which the cultural has revealed itself to be a coextensive and constitutive subset of the natural, as well as one in which the truth claims made by scientists are fought over as never before, the figure of the poet-in-scientist cries out for further investigation.

6.1
Affective Ecologies: Back to the Present

It should be clear by now why, in the pursuit of affective ecologies that operate in the present, I have turned to these works of popular science. They are far, far more than tools that allow a scientific elite to explain the foundations of their disciplines to a lay audience. There is, indeed, very little of the ivory tower to be found in them; the poet-in-scientist authors consistently explore how they are in and of the world, and how intrinsic this is to their science. There is also less hard science in them than one might expect. Instead, one is confronted with a proliferation of what Jeanne Fahnestock refers to as the "epideictic" — appeals to wonder and, less often, application.[3] I have focused here on wonder, the affect which directs us to the experience of countless others, and which is, I argue, reenchantment in action.

These works discuss, explore, and push the bounds of their and our own "tiny sector of nature"[4] as we read them. They operate in and insist upon the contingency of the present. Unlike in the more traditional green environmentalisms referred to in the introduction, hope is not invested in the figure of the child, and as the children inevitably grow up, endlessly deferred. Like in Morton's dark ecology or the Dark Mountain Project today,[5]

---

3 Jeanne Fahnestock, "Accomodating Science: The Rhetorical Life of Scientific Facts," in *The Literature of Science: Perspectives on Popular Scientific Writing*, ed. Murdo William McRae (Athens: The University of Georgia Press, 1993), 17–36.

4 Jakob von Uexküll, "A Stroll through the Worlds of Animals and Men: A Picture Book of Invisible Worlds," trans. Claire Schiller, *Semiotica* 89, no. 4 (1992): 319–91, at 389.

5 The Dark Mountain Manifesto begins: "Those who witness extreme social collapse at first hand seldom describe any deep revelation about the truths of human existence. What they do mention, if asked, is their surprise at how easy it is to die. The pattern of ordinary life, in which so much stays the same from one day to the next, disguises the fragility of its fabric." See Paul Kingsnorth and Dougald Hine, "Uncivilization: The Dark Mountain Manifesto," *The Dark Mountain Project*, 2009, http://dark-mountain.net/about/manifesto/.

hope is rather beside the point. *Biophilia, Gaia,* and *Cosmos,* as Morton would have it, "ooze…through despair"[6] rather than attempting to sidestep it altogether. They point us in a direction very different from that pursued by so many mainstream environmentalist groups today. Not only is there no child to speak of within these texts, but there is also no charismatic megafauna, as in Greenpeace's polar bear stranded in an increasingly warm ocean or the World Wildlife Fund's panda, staring plaintively at the viewer. They direct us, instead, to the task of placing the human back in a milieu from which, in any case, we were never really absent. The polar bear and panda give way to more complex and ambiguous figures: Craven, for instance, in *The Edge of Darkness,* screaming from the hillside at the men who think only in terms of their own petty affairs, in terms of *bios,* and never in terms of the planet, in terms of *zoē.* Or Björk perhaps, who in "Crystalline" listens to "crystals grow[ing] like plants" in order to conquer her claustrophobia. There is no "saving the planet" here, because the logic of this simply doesn't compute. These figures and the attendant concepts of biophilia and Gaia demand a more fundamental reconsideration of the bounds of the human Umwelt and the way we interact within it. They call for and articulate, at least fragmentarily, a new kind of ethics — not a series of prohibitions or guidelines, but "a composition of fast and slow speeds, of capacities for affecting and being affected on this plane of immanence."[7] They are explorations of what is possible with regard to the human relation to the ecosphere, as well as how things, referring broadly to this constellation of relations, could become *otherwise.*

6.1.1 Wonder-machines: comparing cogs and gears
It is therefore possibility, rather than hope, that permeates *Biophilia, Gaia,* and *Cosmos.* We will not, at some point in the fu-

6 Timothy Morton, *The Ecological Thought* (Cambridge: Harvard University Press, 2012), 95.
7 Gilles Deleuze, *Spinoza: Practical Philosophy,* trans. Robert Hurley (San Francisco: City Light Books, 1988), 125.

ture, get ourselves "back to the Garden." Wilson, Lovelock, and Sagan insist that we already inhabit a garden and, if anything, run the risk of expelling ourselves from it if we do not acknowledge and wonder at the fact now.

The works thus powerfully oppose, in a number of ways, the disenchantment narrative discussed in Chapter 2. They do so first of all by taking science out of the lab and embedding it within and relating it to the world of the reader. Their sheer accessibility runs counter to the alienated science supposedly ushered in by the industrial revolution. Secondly, they reject with varying degrees of explicitness the validity of the disenchantment narrative itself. Lovelock does so when he critically discusses the casualness with which we imply that "early man was in total harmony with the rest of Gaia,"[8] but Sagan's "we are made of star stuff" and Wilson's insistence that our humanity is a result of our affiliation with the nonhuman are variations on the same theme. Thirdly, Wilson, Lovelock, and Sagan suggest that, if anything, affective investments in the world are enriched and deepened by scientific world-views. The process of investigation becomes catalytic rather than exhaustive. And, finally, even if one does not accept the idea that science allows us to realize (in both senses of the term) our own immanence, there are plenty of leaks, of "recalcitrant fugitives from rationalization,"[9] to be found within the works. The authors here allude to the mysterious and infinite as often as they provide explanation. This is how the works discussed refuse to pander to notions that we have lost touch with "nature," the world, and the cosmos, and that science is wholly or mostly responsible for it.

But they also actively reenchant, and this is where wonder comes into play. Affective wonder, as *the realization that the affects one is undergoing are new,* is the recognition of novel relations — something entirely precluded by a supposedly disenchanted world. Wonder allows the poet-in-scientists here, and

8   Lovelock, *Gaia: A New Look at Life on Earth,* 107.
9   Jane Bennett, *The Enchantment of Modern Life: Attachments, Crossings, Ethics* (Princeton: Princeton University Press, 2001), 57.

the reader along with them, to attend to the fullness, even the excess, of the world and the universe and one's own participation in it. Each work examined here, however, mobilizes wonder and reenchants slightly differently.

Biophilia, in its more progressive, non-evolutionarily driven forms, focuses on the inexhaustibility of life and the notion that, more than any other creature, we are formed from and informed by this infinite vitality. This does not mean, of course, that we present no concrete danger to the biodiversity of life, only that, as much as we explore and affiliate, there will always be something more to experience and possibly disentangle. There are thus sources of wonder to be found everywhere, and the "brain is prone to weave the mind from the evidence of life, not merely the minimal contact required to exist, but a luxuriance and excess spilling into virtually everything we do."[10] Wilson speaks here of the virtual dimension of life as much as the mathematical. He returns constantly to the idea that being human means encountering other *Umwelten* and their attendant affects, and that there are more of these than we can ever know. Try as we might, we only ever experience "a tiny sector of nature" because "[m]ore organization and complexity exist in a handful of soil than on the surface of all the other planets combined."[11] Wilson's affective wonder draws our attention to the virtual dimension of earthly life and the degree to which we are caught up in it.

Gaia, on the other hand, focuses not on life in the plural, but what it is capable of accomplishing in concert. Lovelock grants agency (albeit of an impersonal sort) to a planet formerly regarded as inert, and in so doing endows everything on it (whether organic, inorganic, or something in between) a metabolic function. As Latour writes, "it reacts, feels, and might get rid of us, without being ontologically unified."[12] The reen-

10 Wilson, *Biophilia,* 7.
11 Edward Wilson, "Biophilia and the Conservation Ethic," in *The Biophlia Hypothesis,* eds. Edward Wilson and Stephen Kellert (Washington, DC and Covelo: Island Press/Shearwater Books, 1993), 31–41, at 39.
12 Bruno Latour, "Waiting for Gaia: Composing the Common World Through Arts and Politics," lecture, French Institute, London, November

chanting genius of Gaia is that the very contemplation of the entity, the very discussion of the concept, implicates the reader in its processes. It does not merely describe a process of reenchantment, but performatively enacts this process. Whenever our sensations are revealed as affects of the earth, every affect becomes novel. In this way, human processes are endowed immediately with renewed wonder as part of the larger Gaian metabolism, rather than merely being seen as "fouling the nest."[13] Science, too, acquires another, more wonderful dimension as seen through Gaia. David Abram points to a Gaian science in which experimentation, as in the alchemical tradition, becomes "a form of participation, a technique of communication or communion which, when successful, effected a transformation not just in the structure of the material experimented upon, but in the structure of the experimenter himself."[14] The Gaian scientist, in the pursuit of wonder via the expansion of the human *Umwelt*, is often, like Lovelock, an instrument maker.

Lastly, and perhaps most ambitiously, *Cosmos* informs us that every aspect of experience, and every affect, has its origins in a stellar furnace. "We are made of star stuff" is a reenchantment rallying cry for the ages. This is the cosmic perspective in a nutshell, and it works to immediately banish anything trivial, mundane, or terrestrial from experience. Life, more than anything, becomes something at which to wonder because of the sheer unlikelihood of such entities emerging in the violence, volatility, and comparative emptiness of space. As with *Gaia*, every sensation becomes something at which to wonder, but this time because it testifies to our relation with the universe. Thus, something as simple as the "heat on your upturned face

2011, http://www.bruno-latour.fr/sites/default/files/124-GAIA-LONDON-SPEAP_0.pdf, 23.

13 Lovelock, *Gaia: A New Look at Life on Earth*, 107.

14 David Abram, "The Mechanical and the Organic: On the Impact of Metaphor in Science," in *Scientists on Gaia*, eds. Stephen Schneider and Penelope Boston (Cambridge: MIT Press, 1991), 66–74, at 67.

on a cloudless summer's day"[15] is endowed by the cosmic perspective with wonder.

6.1.2 Not all anthropocentrisms are created equal

These slightly divergent modes of wondering correspond to dramatically different visions of the ecological role of the human. All three works do embrace and wonder at the sheer unlikelihood and precariousness of life, and intelligent life most of all. They are, moreover, all careful not to view the development of intelligent life as as a departure from the rest of the kingdom of life. But this, really, is where the common ground ends. There is nothing inherently ecocentric or anthropocentric about an affective ecology, and these works demonstrate that an affective ecology may be anything from wholly indifferent to the human species, as in Lovelock's *Gaia,* to revolving entirely around it.

Wilson's biophilia, certainly, appeals to the latter. It has earned the appellation bestowed on it in Chapter 3: the most anthropocentric conservation ethic of them all. The human in Wilson's writing is nourished literally and figuratively by life, and exists as a kind of affective composite of it: "Humanity is exalted not because we are so far above other living creatures, but because knowing them well elevates the very concept of life."[16] If we are to continue this exalted existence, Wilson implies, we must have the luxuriance and excess of the rest of life with which to affiliate. Survival is entirely secondary here. As Margulis and Sagan note, a biophilic ethic involves rather "the preservation of a certain quality of human life."[17] Biophilia is thus anthropocentric to its very core, but its emphasis on the human affiliation with life rather than mere survival moves us to ask more interesting and relevant questions about the way conservation is done. In Chapter 3, I discussed Project Isabela, the largest ecosystem restoration project to date, involving the extermination of the bounti-

15 Sagan, *Cosmos,* 13.
16 Wilson, *Biophilia,* 22.
17 Lynn Margulis and Dorion Sagan, "God, Gaia, and Biophilia," in *The Biophlia Hypothesis,* eds. E.O. Wilson and Stephen Kellert (Washington, DC: Island Press, 1993), 345–64, at 358.

ful goat populations on several islands in the Galapagos in order to restore them to the state in which Darwin first encountered them. The project was highly controversial, both because of the number of animals killed (over 100,000) and because an idea of ecological Eden took precedence over many concerns held by the native human population. A biophilic orientation would have required the abandonment of this ecological ideal, calling for questions about what human actors really desired from life on the islands. This may not have done anything to simplify matters, but it does show that biophilia's deep anthropocentrism is one that calls for something other than conservation for conservation's sake. Within *Biophilia,* conservation is for fueling human wonder.

Sagan's concerns in *Cosmos* are less geared towards conservation practice, but offer a compelling dual vision of the human: Our connection to the stars simultaneously enlarges and humbles us. *Cosmos,* on the one hand, asks for the relentless, both wonderful and terrifying, expansion of the human *Umwelt* via the exploration of space. The probing of the universe also becomes an act of self-discovery. If we are intelligent starstuff, with the "nitrogen in our DNA, the calcium in our teeth, the iron in our blood, the carbon in our apple pies…made in the interiors of collapsing stars," it is clear, in any case, that we occupy an *Umwelt* far larger than we may have assumed. Much of *Cosmos* extolls the human as "the Cosmos grown to self-awareness," bounded as such by few constraints, and this vision is indeed anthropocentric. On the other hand, Sagan is quick at other times to remind us that, seen from space, our entire planet is but "a mote of dust in the morning sky."[18] We may be the only known instance of intelligent life in the universe, but the earth is also the only planet known to harbor life and is, seen even from the comparatively short distances of neighboring planets, very small indeed. Sagan's plea at the end of *Cosmos* is for the protection of not only human life, but also life in general. He contends that the earth is very probably all we've got, and very possibly all

18   Sagan, *Cosmos,* 190, 286, 1–2.

there is. Seen from this perspective, Sagan's glorification of the human becomes more tempered.

Gaia adopts a different tack entirely. As entity and ecosophy, Gaia is refreshingly indifferent to the human but constitutes a cautionary tale for us nevertheless. On Gaia, we are but another metabolic function. We cannot separate ourselves from the affects of the earth, and the very attempt to conceive of ourselves in this manner is a kind of anthropocentrism. Lovelock describes even the notion of pollution as anthropocentric,[19] preferring to speak of waste products that, incidentally, we share with all other forms of life. That we seem to be producing a lot of waste products is cause for only short-term concern. We may drastically limit the life-span of the human species with our activities and carry whole ecosystems with us, but life and the living assemblage known as Gaia will go on. Gaia is radically geocentric, eschewing not just an attachment to the human, but also to life as we know it, although its more general commitment to life is unwavering. If humankind wishes to make a stand on Gaia, it must do so from a human place, while at the same time internalizing that we are an organ of Gaia that is fully expendable. With Gaia, we have neither the luxury of viewing the human as the apotheosis of all life, as in Wilson's biophilia, nor the time, as in Cosmos, to contemplate our affiliation with the stars. We are instead Gaians who must come to terms with the fact that we share the affects of the earth.

6.1.3 Anti-sentimental environmentalism

The adjectives "anti-sentimental" or "non-sentimental" have cropped up far more than I anticipated when beginning this work. As I understand it now, this focus on feeling and sensation, on affective ethics rather than a sentimental morality, is responsible for the unique and lasting contributions *Biophilia,* *Gaia,* and *Cosmos* are able to make to ecological thought. These books refuse to pander to ideas of harmony with "nature" or pretend that we have been alienated from it, whatever it is, or

19 Lovelock, *Gaia: A New Look at Life on Earth,* 110.

its inhabitants. What they ask is that we become more sensitive to our own embeddedness and interaction in the world. I would identify four uniquely non-sentimental aspects of these works, which render them invaluable contributions to ecological literature:

1. The first is their rejection of the recognition of kinship as a driving force in ecological thought. In none of these accounts are we told to protect life because we recognize ourselves in it. Life here is valuable in the plural, in its nearly infinite manifestations and as a forceful collective with which we may affiliate and be drawn out of ourselves — with which we may, in other words, become. The so-called charismatic megafauna (i.e. tigers, elephants, bears, and, arguably, our children) are entirely left out of the works.[20] They seek instead to persuade the reader of the virtues of encountering the "strange stranger," living forms and *Umwelten* of which we cannot even conceive. Thus Wilson's ants, with which he has no illusion of becoming friends, are at the root of biophilia as an affective ecology; it is necessary that we experience and learn to embrace their very alienness. Similarly, Lovelock advocates focusing on biochemical guilds and serving as a kind of shop steward for microorganisms, rather than proclaiming stewardship merely with regard to megafauna. Notably, he points to theories that all large mammals, ourselves included, are merely hosts for countless anaerobic bacteria, forced to retreat as the composition of the earth's atmosphere changed. Affective ecologies recognize the full depth and breadth of affiliation that is possible, decrying the notion that we only relate to creatures like us.

2. Secondly, these works highlight how "keep[ing] in touch"[21] need not mean pretending that we ever lost it. They firmly

20 In their essay on Gaia and Biophilia, Sagan and Margulis directly criticize ecological orientations in which these large mammals are somehow "more equal" than other ecological actors ("God, Gaia, and Biophilia," 357).

21 James Lovelock, *The Ages of Gaia: A Biography of Our Living Earth* (Oxford: Oxford University Press, 1988), 211.

insist on the human as, like every other life, immanent. What they do encourage is that we attend more fully to that in which we are implicated. For Wilson, this means acknowledging the extent to which our humanity has been and continues to be formed by the nonhuman. For Lovelock, this means becoming sensitive to affects larger than ourselves of which we are nevertheless a part. He encourages us to view our interaction with Gaia as "not unlike the tight coupling between the state of the mind and the body,"[22] where, in Lovelock's world, we are neither fully mind nor body. Latour, too, takes this up, describing this process as the "slow operation that consists in being enveloped in sensor circuits in the form of loops."[23] In a kind of planetary attachment therapy, "After each passage through a loop we become *more sensitive* and *more responsive* to the fragile envelopes that we inhabit."[24] Sagan, for his part, puts forward surprisingly concrete ideas for how we might get a better sense of the human in the vastness of the cosmos. His Golden Record, carried by the Voyager probes and launched just prior to *Cosmos* in the late '70s, is a message to the stars as much as it is an invitation to consider and wonder at our place among them. The ecological crisis, these works suggest, is one of inattention or purposeful blindness rather than alienation.

3. Thirdly, perhaps because these works were penned by scientists who were heavily reliant on technology in their professions, *Biophilia, Gaia,* and *Cosmos* urge the abandonment of technological pessimism. Real instruments, such as the Hubble space telescope and the electron capture detector, and imagined instruments, such as the "motion picture projector of magical versatility" and the "Ship of the Imagination," operate in these accounts to encourage affiliation and help us cali-

---

22 Ibid.

23 Bruno Latour, "Fourth Lecture: The Anthropocene and the Destruction of (the Image of) the Globe," in *Facing Gaia: Eight Lectures on the New Climatic Regime,* trans. Catherine Porter (Cambridge: Polity Press, 2017), 111–45, at 139.

24 Ibid., 140.

brate and question the ways in which it happens. Machines in these accounts have the potential to serve as instruments of wonder, allowing for the expansion of the Umwelt rather than the continuation of business as usual. Technology exists for these authors as "a kind of creative mediation between nature and humanity."[25]

4. Finally, these works refuse sentimentality by confronting the contingency and precarity of life head-on. Life, and the development of intelligent life, in particular, is neither taken for granted nor presented as a phenomenon that will necessarily continue; Sagan reminds us that "[w]e are like butterflies who flutter for a day and think it is forever."[26] Life, the human included, will rearrange itself into different shapes and then dissolve into chemical equilibrium. From this perspective, too, conservation for its own sake becomes a ridiculous notion: Just what is this Eden we seek to resurrect, and for exactly how long? Conservation is not nearly as simple as the name implies. In many cases, it is an incredible feat of resurrection and continued meddling. Keeping in mind the scarcity of life in space and time, we must increasingly ask which affects we want to preserve. At their most eloquent, the arguments *Biophilia, Gaia,* and *Cosmos* make for the contingency of life also bleed into those that argue for the contingency of culture. Life was and will be otherwise, and so could our relation to it. This is the ultimate feat accomplished by their non-sentimentality. Rather than making the case on terms more recognizable to us for why, for instance, we must save the rain forest, they ask us to change. Popular science, like any form of literature, is capable of invoking a people to come. Refusing to assure us of our humanity, but still speaking in the first person plural, these works ask us to become biophiliacs, Gaians, and Earthlings.

25 Félix Guattari, *Chaosmosis: An Ethico-Aesthetic Paradigm,* trans. Paul Bains and Julian Pefanis (Bloomington: Indiana University Press, 1995), 33.
26 Sagan, *Cosmos,* 20.

6.2
The Poet-in-Scientist in the Anthropocene

Affective ecologies and their attendant non-sentimentality become more important in an age that is all too human. Although this work never confined itself strictly to the period in which the works in the corpus were written, we will move fully into the present day, referred to increasingly often as the Anthropocene. The Anthropocene, more than the Holocene that in theory precedes it, demands an immanent popular science and the figure of the poet-in-scientist to write and embody it. There are good reasons, in other words, why biophilia and Gaia are still terms that crop up remarkably often in popular culture, ecological circles, and why *Cosmos* was remade in 2014. But here we will also begin to move beyond these works, to the future of a genre that must grapple with conditions that appear at a far remove from those described by the disenchantment narrative.

But first, how can we understand the Anthropocene? It is, in many ways, more of a dream come true than a nightmare scenario for humanities scholars. This is a postmodernism, if one dares to articulate it in this way, that has come to pass — "what you have when," as Fredric Jameson tells us, "the modernization process is complete and nature gone for good."[27] At least at first glance, the Anthropocene appears to be the golden ticket that finally allows us to talk to scientists about the end of nature, or, at the very least, non-essentialist concepts of the so-called natural world. There is no escaping culture in the Anthropocene; the study of the human becomes the study of the earth, and vice versa. Described by the scientific architects of the term as a "quantitative shift in the relationship between humans and the global environment" and, more specifically, "our own species" becoming "so large and active that it now rivals some of

---

27 Fredric Jameson, *Postmodernism: Or, the Cultural Logic of Late Capitalism* (Durham, NC: Duke University Press, 1991), ix. Jameson continues, "It is a more fully human world than the older one, but one in which 'culture' has become a veritable 'second nature.'" Latour will pick up on the term "second nature" in his own work on Gaia and the Anthropocene.

the great forces of Nature in its impact on the functioning of the Earth System,"[28] the term was in fact coined by Eugene Stoermer in the 1980s. Paul Crutzen, atmospheric chemist and Nobel laureate, made famous for calling attention to the hole in the ozone layer, popularized the term in the early 2000s.[29] It largely stayed out of non-scientific mass media until the Royal Stratigraphy Commission decided to establish the Anthropocene Working Group in 2009 to evaluate whether or not to amend earth history to accommodate a new geological epoch.[30] Whether the idea of the human as geological force appealed to the human sense of self-importance, or simply provided an interesting spin on apocalyptic rhetoric surrounding global warming and ecological crisis, it began appearing more and more often in popular science journalism. In 2011, *The Economist* dedicated an entire issue[31] to the notion. The term has gradually trickled into the humanities as well. Historian Dipesh Chakrabarty was already articulating the implications of the new epoch for his own discipline in 2009.[32] Bruno Latour took up the term in "Waiting for Gaia," a 2011 lecture already referenced many times in this work, casting the nature-culture relation as a Moebius strip, and also dedicating one of his 2013 Gifford Lectures to the topic.

There are two characteristics of the Anthropocene that cast a new light on the subjects with which this book deals. Firstly, the Anthropocene corresponds neatly to events that are often connected with disenchantment but is simultaneously at odds with the disenchantment narrative. The great volume of Anthropocene literature offers several options for when the period began, although a consensus has yet to be established: the dawn of

28 Will Steffen et al., "The Anthropocene: Conceptual and Historical Perspectives," *Philosophical Transactions of the Royal Society A: Mathematical, Physical, and Engineering Sciences* 369, no. 1938 (2011): 842–67, at 843.
29 Paul Crutzen, "Geology of Mankind," *Nature* 415, no. 3, art. 23 (January 2002).
30 Steffen et al., "The Anthropocene," 843.
31 See The Economist, "Welcome to the Anthropocene," May 26, 2011, https://www.economist.com/leaders/2011/05/26/welcome-to-the-anthropocene.
32 Dipesh Chakrabarty, "The Climate of History: Four Theses," *Critical Inquiry* 35, no. 2 (Winter 2009): 197–222.

wide-spread agriculture, at roughly 10,000 BCE, the beginning of the Industrial Revolution in the nineteenth century, and the start of the nuclear era in the twentieth century — all of which have left their mark in the soil. For those in disenchantment camps, these dates are also meaningful. The beginning of agriculture marks our supposed alienation from the cycles of nature since it meant we were no longer as dependent on circumstance for food, the beginning of the Industrial Revolution marks the union of science and technology that would go on to produce moderns that were simultaneously insatiably materialist and alienated from the authentically material, and the nuclear era presents the ultimate victory of "man" over the most elemental forces of nature. From this perspective, the Anthropocene is disenchantment come to pass: We are now as gods. However, in the Anthropocene we are also gods that are consistently outwitted by the very forces we are supposed to have mastered. This is because the Anthropocene offers us no vantage point from the heavens with which to view that which we bring upon ourselves. In the Anthropocene, the human has its fingers in everything, but cannot possibly know the nature of all that it is *affecting*. The human is omnipresent, and very powerful indeed, but that power is always undermined by our embeddedness and inability to fully predict the dynamics of complex systems. Seen this way, the idea of the Anthropocene powerfully contradicts the disenchantment narrative. We might wish for a state in which we were more alienated — i.e. independent — from the earth. Along with Latour, Ben Dibley insists, in opposition to the narrative of alienation, on a narrative of "attachment" to go along with the Anthropocene that "posits that science, technology, markets and so on"[33] have increased the number and intensity of human connections with so-called "nature." The Anthropocene allows us to see that we have never lost touch; we have simply

---

33 Ben Dibley, "'The Shape of Things to Come': Seven Theses on the Anthropocene and Attachment," *Australian Humanities Review* 52 (May 2012): 139–53, at 144, http://australianhumanitiesreview.org/2012/05/01/the-shape-of-things-to-come-seven-theses-on-the-anthropocene-and-attachment/.

not adequately attended to our affective and material engagements with the world.

Secondly, the Anthropocene, as geological time unfolding now, directs us to a new kind of temporality. Dibley has referred to the Anthropocene as the *"crease of time"*[34] and indeed it seems to present the collision of many extra-human scales with human time. For Dibley, a Marxist, the Anthropocene is the collision of "the deep time of geology and a rather shorter history of capital," while for Chakrabarty, as a historian, it presents the more general "collapse of the age old humanist distinction between natural history and human history."[35] Latour, too, picks up on this, noting, "The formula 'geological time' is now used for an event that has come and gone more quickly than the Soviet Union! As though the distinction between history and geostory had suddenly disappeared."[36] Chakrabarty, moreover, states that, although we have always been able to conceive of ourselves as biological agents, the idea of geological agency "scale[s] up our imagination of the human"; we are no longer merely *bios* and *zoē*, but also *geos*.[37] And in the Anthropocene, as never before, the present matters because it is conceivable in deep time.

It is for the Anthropocene's strange entwining with and rejection of the disenchantment narrative, as well as its inauguration of a new kind of temporality, that the period calls for the kind of poet-in-scientist and attendant immanent popular science upon which this work has focused. The popular scientist as mere explicator will not suffice in the Anthropocene. From which place is it even possible any longer to explicate? Instead, the poet-in-scientist, I wish to suggest, must be able to illuminate the ways in which we are already tangled up, with which we, according to Barad, "intra-act," and gesture, with the help of an embedded science, to the significance of the present. That the poet-in-scientists in this project have accomplished these tasks

34 Ibid., 140.
35 Ibid. Chakrabarty, "The Climate of History," 201.
36 Latour, "Fourth Lecture: The Anthropocene and the Destruction of the Image of) the Globe," 116.
37 Chakrabarty, "The Climate of History," 206.

by becoming wonder-machines does not necessarily mean that the only way to approach popular science in the Anthropocene is through wonder. At the same time, there are indications that the Anthropocene offers new opportunities for exploring our relation to this particular affect.

Two more recent works of popular science point to new strategies the poet-in-scientist might pursue in the Anthropocene. The first is *The Earth after Us*,[38] written by Jan Zalesiewicz, a geologist who also happens to be the head of the commission deciding upon the bureaucratic fate of the Anthropocene. Zalesiewicz's prose is decidedly more detached than that explored in this work, and this is part of the conceit that drives the book: to examine "*Homo Sapiens* from the standpoint of a future paleoecologist."[39] We have, in other words, all died out, and an extraterrestrial has come to Earth to exhume our civilization from the sediment filled with our building material and plastic, which have by now been compressed into a layer in the rock. Zalesiewicz is quick to point out that geological strata that already exist have been formed by life in the past, and that "[l]ife has not been passive in this regard," but he also muses that "if we make enough of a mess of the world, we might compete with the Yucatan meteorite, or with the mysterious forces that, almost exactly a quarter of a billion years ago, suffocated most of the Earth's oceans and killed off an estimated 95 per cent of the world's species, bringing the Paleozoic Era to a dead halt."[40] The bottom line is that, while we are not very special with regard to our general ability to leave traces, we are likely the first single biological entity to leave a trace this pronounced, and certainly the first that is cognizant of the fact. After many diverting discussions of the spirit in which these future paleoecologists might unearth us (Zalesiewicz suggests that they might regard us in much the way that we do the dinosaurs), and the chances

---

38 Jan Zalesiewicz, *The Earth after Us: What Legacy Will Humans Leave in the Rocks?* (Oxford: Oxford University Press, 2008).

39 Ibid., 5.

40 Ibid., 23, 156–57.

of finding fossilized human remains,[41] Zalesiewicz makes the following proclamation about the impact of the human at the end of the work:

[W]hatever we as a species do from now, we have already left a record that is now indelible, even while the scale of this fossilization event is still in question, and within our power to determine. Humankind has, through its various activities, done enough to preserve its relics into the far future. The 'environmental' changes that we have set in train will, without a shadow of a doubt, be translated into the solid rock of the Earth. The Urban Stratum is now, in substantial part, effectively eternal. More: our actions now will literally be raising mountain belts higher, or lowering them, or setting off volcanoes (or stifling them), or triggering new biological diversity (or suppressing it) for many millions of years to come. The knock-on effects of our geochemical experiments are unpredictable in detail, but will be substantial and likely surprising. We have left our mark. However we are interpreted in some distant future, there will be little doubt that we will be associated with — and responsible for — some of the most extraordinary geology of this, or any other, planet.[42]

That "we have left our mark" in so ostentatious a manner allows us to wonder at the scope of what we currently refer to as the ecological crisis. The present in which we affiliate is now, we are told, guaranteed to last in deep time. What is so fascinating about Zalesiewicz's account is that the entire earth becomes, like the Golden Record, a kind of deep time capsule for the human. The difference here, of course, is that it is time itself, and not Carl Sagan and his team that will choose the contents. Zalesiewicz refuses to issue recommendations based on the fact that what we do now will be raising mountains long after our ancestors are dead, and, indeed, there is little that can be done. It

41 Ibid., 191, 159.
42 Ibid., 240–41.

becomes clear in the course of the work that our plastics and our building materials, what we leave as traces and ends up, coincidentally, as effectively eternal, is not necessarily what we value. The punch that *The Earth after Us* pulls is that it directs us with its focus on our relatively impoverished existence in the strata of deep time to the richness of what we experience and make now.

The second work of popular science one might point to is Elizabeth Kolbert's *The Sixth Extinction: An Unnatural History* (2014).[43] Kolbert, strictly speaking, is not a poet-in-scientist, but a scientist-in-poet, a journalist and writer who has become well known for covering popular scientific topics. *The Sixth Extinction,* like *The Earth after Us,* catalogs a deed that has already been done, or at least embarked upon with such earnestness that it may as well be: the massive loss of biodiversity caused by humans. In Kolbert's book, as in Zalesiewicz's, however, we may wonder at the enormity of the deed. Kolbert makes it known that we can never really know precisely what we have lost and how much potential has been exhausted. The work is a study in the way in which background extinctions, which biologists speak of as happening constantly,[44] become, in various regions around the world, nothing of the sort; background becomes foreground, as in so much of the material examined here, and background extinction moves rapidly into anthropogenic mass extinction. For Kolbert, as well, the Anthropocene is not another code word for describing our alienation from the natural world, but a kind of shorthand for the now explosive way in which we meddle with it:

One of the striking characteristics of the Anthropocene is the hash it's made of the principles of geographic distribution. If high-ways, clear-cuts, and soybeans plantations create islands where none before existed, global trade and global travel do the reverse: they deny even the remotest is-

43 Elizabeth Kolbert, *The Sixth Extinction: An Unnatural History* (London: Bloomsbury, 2014).
44 Ibid., 15–16.

lands their remoteness. The process of remixing the world's flora and fauna, which began slowly, along the routes of early human migration, has, in recent decades accelerated to the point where in some parts of the world, non-native plants now outnumber native ones. During any given twenty-four-hour period, it is estimated that ten thousand different species are moved around the world just in ballast water. Thus a single supertanker (or, for that matter, a jet passenger) can undo millions of years of geographic separation.[45]

Kolbert highlights unusually well the manner in which we have created, unbeknownst to us until recently, a garden of our own making. It may not be a garden we find very appealing or which will sustain us for any length of time, which she is not reluctant to point out. Nevertheless, this work adopts much of the same strategy as Zalesiewicz's, leaving us to puzzle out why and how we ought to care about that with which the Anthropocene presents us.

These are works that follow in the footsteps of *Biophilia, Gaia,* and *Cosmos.* They direct us to an ecology of the present and insist that how we engage with the world right now does and will matter. Zalesiewicz's paleoecologist of the future is no different from Sagan's Ship of the Imagination or Wilson's "motion picture projector of magical versatility" — only now the deep time lens has been turned back on us. Kolbert's work, too, is an effort to situate the human in deep time, to explain concretely how our impact may be on par with that of an asteroid. These works, like their predecessors, embody a science that does not merely explain our contemporary reality, but exists in the midst of it and helps us negotiate positions of objectivity from which we might begin to systematically articulate what we already feel as the staggering influence of our species. Increasingly in these accounts, the world is the subject of an experiment that has no control.

45 Ibid., 198.

Biophilia, Gaia, and *Cosmos* have certainly prepared the ground for works like Zalesiewicz's and Kolbert's, but the more recent works also react to the conditions we are now beginning to realize characterize the Anthropocene. As I alluded to before, they do not, like Rachel Carson's *Silent Spring* or Wilson's *Biophilia,* read as cautionary tales; much of the deed has already been done. As such, they do not expound at length on the infinite varieties of life and the wonder that arises when confronted with it. They are works, rather, that insist that an awful lot has been lost. If they offer a kind of wonder, it is characteristic of a new, bleaker kind of reenchantment centering around the human. There is wonder, possibly of a terrible sort, surrounding the realization that we have, unbeknownst to ourselves, left virtually nothing untouched. We have created a series of new Umwelten in our image, although we are far from knowing them well at all.

6.3
Paths Unfollowed: The Poet-in-Scientist Lives On

This project has opened my eyes to the wealth of work, and particularly cultural studies work, on popular science that has not been done. Aside from Lessl's work in the 1980s,[46] two volumes of essays from the '80s and '90s,[47] and Sarah Perrault's recent *Communicating Popular Science*[48] (none of which are strictly cultural studies), popular science has received shockingly little

---

46 See Section 5.5 in this volume.
47 Terry Shin and Richard Whitley, eds., *Expository Science: Forms and Functions of Popularization* (Dordecht: D. Reidel Publishing Company, 1985) and Murdo William McRae, ed., *The Literature of Science: Perspectives on Popular Scientific Writing* (Athens: The University of Georgia Press, 1993).
48 As the full title, *Communicating Popular Science: From Deficit to Democracy,* suggests, the work takes a pragmatic look at popular science, examining its potential to democratize the institutions of techno-science (New York: Palgrave Macmillan, 2013).

academic attention. Despite the fact that it continues to gar-
ner high ratings on television, to produce best-sellers, and to
launch new popular science stars like Neil deGrasse Tyson, it
seems, like many other popular genres (at least until very recently), to have been largely neglected by cultural studies. It is
possible that scholars in the humanities consider works of popular science insufficiently literary, or naïve in their treatment of
subjectivity. I hope to have demonstrated here, however, that
neither is the case. The genre is a particularly important one,
even among other popular genres, because it is not merely dedicated to describing how things work. It is capable of mediating
the reader's or viewer's relation to the scientific establishment,
the planet, and the reaches of outer space, and all the more effectively because it does so under the banner of science. I would
like to suggest, moreover, that the figure of the poet-in-scientist
has only gained more traction since Sagan's time, and that there
are two aspects of this figure outside the scope of this work that
deserve further investigation.

The first is the enormous amount of pop cultural production surrounding the figure of the poet-in-scientist. Ever since
Cosmos first aired in 1980, there has been a dizzying variety of
it, and the internet age is only accelerating the rate at which it
is produced. Whether one looks at popular YouTube remixes
of Sagan's own work combined with Stephen Hawking's,[49] the

49 See "A Still More Glorious Dawn Awaits," which is not only a quote from
the first episode of *Cosmos,* but also the chorus from a 2009 YouTube video with nearly ten million views. A three-and-a-half minute musical remix
of the show nearly thirty years after the fact, Sagan's imitation of a whale
provides the beat and auto-tuned lines from the series form the lyrics. "If
you wish to make an apple pie from scratch," a cyborg Sagan intones, "you
must first invent the universe." Stephen Hawking (who we are much more
accustomed to hearing mediated by the digital), featured in the bridge,
delivers a few lines from *Stephen Hawking's Universe,* his own PBS series
from the 1990s. Shots of Sagan, wondering in awe, alternate with those of
the untrammeled terrestrial and simulations of the Milky Way. melodysheep, "Carl Sagan – 'A Glorious Dawn' ft Stephen Hawking (Symphony
of Science)," *YouTube,* September 17, 2009, https://www.youtube.com/
watch?v=zSgiXGELjbc. The video is the work of video artist John Boswell;

numerous documentaries dedicated to the lives of the scientists, Johnny Carson's brilliant parodying of Sagan in the 1980s, or the sudden emergence of internet memes featuring gifs and images of poet-in-scientists like Sagan, Hawking, and deGrasse Tyson with captions like "smoke weed everyday,"[50] it is clear that the poet-in-scientist is alive and well in the popular imaginary. A proper study of this pop cultural production would certainly also broaden the temporal scope of the investigation to include figures like Stephen Hawking, whose *Brief History of Time* would, upon its publication in 1988, not only outsell *Cosmos* and spawn its own PBS series, but give rise to several bio-pics dedicated to the man, and Neil deGrasse Tyson, whose public profile looms even larger than his poet-in-scientist predecessors. As the star of the 2014 remake of Carl Sagan's *Cosmos* — *Cosmos: A Spacetime Odyssey*[51] — he explicitly frames himself as Sagan's successor, recounting his visit to Sagan's Ithaca home as a teenager and Sagan's kindness to him. And as with Sagan, the masses have officially dubbed him a meme,[52] and the corresponding images and gifs, often used completely out of context, are widely available for use and re-appropriation. This is only the tip of an iceberg that testifies to the fact that, although these figures are certainly emissaries for the scientific academy, they are celebrities in their own right who have been lent some of the luminosity of the heavenly bodies that they study, and whose own star quality doubtless now informs the relation to the sky enjoyed by many of us.

Secondly, further work might investigate the unique way in which the poet-in-scientist, particularly those with back-

see also *Know Your Meme,* s.v. "Symphony of Science," http://knowyourmeme.com/memes/symphony-of-science.

50 The image, as far as I can trace it, originally appeared on Carl Sagan Rocks!'s *Tumblr* page, April 30, 2013, http://carlsaganrocks.tumblr.com/post/49310250368.

51 Ann Druyan and Steven Soter, *Cosmos: A Spacetime Odyssey,* Twentieth Century Fox, 2014.

52 See *Know Your Meme,* s.v. "Neil deGrasse Tyson," http://knowyourmeme.com/memes/people/neil-degrasse-tyson.

grounds in astronomy and astrophysics, is able to play out and often upend tensions between sincerity and authentic admiration, on the one hand, and irony and kitsch on the other. If the books and series authored by the popular scientists feature awe-filled moments that initially produce "a tingling in the spine,"[53] in their afterlives online and in parody, the effect of these moments metamorphoses, almost too easily, into a cringe. This cringe, however, does not undermine the tingling, but coexists unproblematically with it. The sincerity of the scientist-priest communicated in the excess of sentiment or affect involved in the popularizing effort is only reconfirmed by attempts to inject it with irony. Perhaps because of their association with the scientific academy, the figure of the scientist-priest stands as one of the few bastions of sincerity in a cynical era. In the pop-cultural production surrounding the figure, the celebrations of wonder and the numinous can simultaneously be embraced as an alternative form of spirituality and treated as a kind of reenchantment kitsch. Gifs of Carl Sagan overlaid with text, extracted from Cosmos, proclaiming that the "total number of stars in the universe is larger than all the grains of sand on all the beaches of the planet earth"[54] can thus exist side-by-side with images of Sagan in his signature turtleneck promoting the consumption of marijuana. In speaking about the infinite and numinous as often as the rational and knowable, these figures influence, in fascinating and complex ways, our relation with the scientific establishment and the world. The ambiguity of these poet-in-scientists and their attendant reenchanting tactics today, moreover, points to the fact that our willingness to embrace even this first of affects, wonder, may fluctuate according to historical moment and milieu.

53 *Cosmos: A Personal Voyage*, Episode 1, "The Shores of the Cosmic Ocean," written by Carl Sagan and Ann Druyan, September 28, 1980, PBS. See also *Cosmos: A Spacetime Odyssey*, Episode 1, "Standing Up in the Milky Way," starring Neil deGrasse Tyson, March 9, 2014, Fox.
54 See *Know Your Meme*, s.v. "Carl Sagan," http://knowyourmeme.com/memes/people/carl-sagan.

This work, however, has stuck to a set of works and artifacts inspired by them that are, for the most part, perfectly sincere. *Biophilia, Gaia,* and *Cosmos,* all published within five years of one another, are important records of attempts from within the modern scientific academy to construct and explore enchanted materialisms. And they are not merely titles, but concepts that have served and continue to serve as the basis for affective ecologies with wonder at their core. They are popular science, but they are also hot philosophy, and they continue to weave us into a world from which we were never really separate, to animate the organic and the inorganic, and to make the world dance.

Bibliography

Abram, David. "In the Depths of a Breathing Planet: Gaia and the Transformation of Experience." In *Gaia in Turmoil: Climate Change, Biodepletion and Earth Ethics in an Age of Crisis,* edited by Eileen Crist and H. Bruce Rinker, 66–74. Cambridge: MIT Press, 2010.

———. "The Mechanical and the Organic: On the Impact of Metaphor in Science." In *Scientists on Gaia,* edited by Stephen Schneider and Penelope Boston, 66–74. Cambridge: MIT Press, 1991.

Abumrad, Jad, and Robert Krulwich. "Galapagos." *Radiolab,* WNYC, July 16, 2014. https://www.radiolab.org/story/galapagos.

Academy of Achievement. "E.O. Wilson Biography." 2013. http://www.achievement.org/achiever/edward-o-wilson-ph-d/.

Agamben, Giorgio. *Homo Sacer: Sovereign Power and Bare Life.* Translated by Daniel Heller-Roazen. Stanford: Stanford University Press, 1998.

———. *The Open: Man and Animal.* Translated by Kevin Attel. Stanford: Stanford University Press, 2004.

Ansell-Pearson, Keith. *Germinal Life: The Difference and Repetition of Deleuze.* London: Routledge, 1999.

Barad, Karen. *Meeting the Universe Halfway: Quantum Physics and the Entanglement of Matter and Meaning.* Durham: Duke University Press, 2007.

Barbiero, Giuseppe. "Affective Ecology for Sustainability." *Visions for Sustainability* 1, no. 3 (2014): 20–30. https://doi.org/10.13135/2384–8677/1419.

Barnes, Brooks. "In a Breathtaking First, NASA's Voyager 1 Exits the Solar System." *New York Times,* September 13, 2013. http://www.nytimes.com/2013/09/13/science/in-a-breathtaking-first-nasa-craft-exits-the-solar-system.html.

Barthes, Roland. *Camera Lucida: Reflections on Photography.* Translated by Richard Howard. New York: Hill and Wang, 1981.

Bennett, Jane. *The Enchantment of Modern Life.* Princeton: Princeton University Press, 2001.

Bennett, Jane. "The Force of Materiality: A Vitalist Stopover on the Way to a New Materialism." In *New Materialisms: Ontology, Agency, and Politics,* edited by Diana Coole and Samantha Frost, 47–69. Durham: Duke University Press, 2010.

———. *Vibrant Matter: A Political Ecology of Things.* Durham: Duke University Press, 2010.

Berman, Morris. *The Reenchantment of the World.* Ithaca: Cornell University Press, 1981.

Blackman, Lisa. "Habit and Affect: Revitalizing a Forgotten History." *Body & Society* 19, no. 186 (2013): 186–216. https://doi.org/10.1177/1357034X12472546.

Bryant, Levi R. "Black." In *Prismatic Ecology: Ecotheory beyond Green,* edited by Jeffrey Jerome Cohen, 290–310. Minneapolis: University of Minnesota Press, 2013.

Buchanan, Brett. *Onto-Ethologies: The Animal Environments of Uexküll, Heidegger, Merleau-Ponty, and Deleuze.* Albany: State University of New York Press, 2008.

Buell, Lawrence. "Foreword." In *Prismatic Ecology: Ecotheory Beyond Green,* edited by Jeffrey Jerome Cohen, ix–xii. Minneapolis: University of Minnesota Press, 2013.

Butler, Judith. "Antigone's Claim: A Conversation with Judith Butler." Interview by Pierpaolo Antonello and Roberto

Farneti. *Theory and Event* 12, no. 1 (2009). https://doi.org/
doi:10.1353/tae.0.0048.

———. *Precarious Life: The Powers of Mourning and Violence.*
London: Verso, 2004.

Camus, Albert. *The Myth of Sisyphus and Other Essays.* Translated by Justin O'Brien. New York: Vintage International,
1991.

Carl Sagan Rocks!, "Smoke Weed Everyday." *Tumblr*, April 30,
2013. http://carlsaganrocks.tumblr.com/post/49310250368.

Carson, Rachel. *The Sense of Wonder.* New York: Harper &
Row, 1998.

Chakrabarty, Dipesh. "The Climate of History: Four Theses."
Critical Inquiry 35 (Winter 2009): 197–222. https://doi.
org/10.1086/596640.

Chambers, Neil. "How Biophilia Can Improve Our Lives – Part
I." *Treehugger,* March 27, 2012. https://www.treehugger.com/
green-architecture/biophilia-can-improve-lives.html.

———. "How Biophilia Can Improve Our Lives – Part IV."
Treehugger, April 2. 2012, https://www.treehugger.com/
green-architecture/how-biophilia-can-improve-our-lives-
part-iv.html.

Chisholm, Dianne. "Biophilia, Creative Involution, and the
Ecological Future of Queer Desire." In *Queer Ecologies: Sex,
Nature, Politics, Desire,* edited by Catriona Mortimer-Sand-
ilands and Bruce Erickson, 359–381. Bloomington: Indiana
University Press, 2010.

Clebsch, William. *American Religious Thought.* Chicago: University of Chicago Press, 1973.

Cosmolearning. "Cosmos: A Personal Voyage." http://www.
cosmolearning.com/documentaries/cosmos/.

Crutzen, Paul. "Geology of Mankind." *Nature* 415, no.
3, art. 23 (January 2002). https://doi.org/https://doi.
org/10.1038/415023a.

Davidson, Keay. *Carl Sagan: A Life.* New York: Wiley & Sons,
2000.

Dawkins, Richard. *The Extended Phenotype: The Long Reach of
the Gene.* Oxford: Oxford University Press, 1989.

———. *Unweaving the Rainbow: Science, Delusion, and the Appetite for Wonder.* New York: Mariner Books, 1998.

Daston, Lorraine, and Kathrine Park. *Wonders and the Order of Nature, 1150–1750.* New York: Zone Books, 2001.

Deleuze, Gilles. *Bergsonism.* Translated by Hugh Tomlinson and Barbara Habberjam. Cambridge: Zone Books, 1988.

———. "Immanence: A Life." In *Pure Immanence: Essays on A Life,* translated by Anne Boyman, 25–34. New York: Zone Books, 2001.

———. "Literature and Life." In *Essays Critical and Clinical,* translated by Daniel W. Smith and Michael A. Greco, 1–6. Minneapolis: University of Minnesota Press, 1997.

———. *Spinoza: Practical Philosophy.* Translated by Robert Hurley. San Francisco: City Light Books (1988).

——— and Claire Parnet. "The Actual and the Virtual." In *Dialogues II,* translated by Eliot Ross Albert, 148–59. New York: Columbia University Press, 2002.

Deleuze, Gilles, and Félix Guattari. *Anti-Oedipus: Capitalism and Schizophrenia.* Translated by Robert Hurley, Mark Seem, and Helen Lane. London: Continuum, 2004.

———. *A Thousand Plateaus.* Translated by Brian Massumi. 1987; rpt. London: Continuum, 2004.

———. *What Is Philosophy?* Translated by Hugh Tomlinson and Graham Burchell. New York: Columbia University Press, 1994.

Dibley, Ben. "'The Shape of Things to Come': Seven Theses on the Anthropocene and Attachment." *Australian Humanities Review* 52 (May 2012): 139–153. http://australianhumanities-review.org/2012/05/01/the-shape-of-things-to-come-seven-theses-on-the-anthropocene-and-attachment/.

Dillard, Annie. "The Present." In *Pilgrim at Tinker Creek,* 77–103. New York: Harper & Row, 1974.

———. "Total Eclipse." In *Teaching a Stone to Talk,* 9–28. New York: Harper Collins, 1982.

Doolittle, W. Ford. "Is Nature Really Motherly?" *CoEvolution Quarterly* 29 (1981): 58–63.

Dove, Alan. "Microbiomics: The Germ Theory of Everything."
Science 340, no. 6133 (2013): 763–65. https://doi.org/10.1126/
science.340.6133.763.

The Earth Charter Initiative. "Download the Charter." *The
Earth Charter.* http://www.earthcharterinaction.org/con-
tent/pages/read-the-charter.html.

The Economist. "Welcome to the Anthropocene." May 26, 2011.
https://www.economist.com/leaders/2011/05/26/welcome-
to-the-anthropocene.

Edelman, Lee. *No Future: Queer Theory and the Death Drive.*
Durham: Duke University Press, 2004.

Ensor, Sarah. "Spinster Ecology: Rachel Carson, Sarah Orne
Jewett, and Nonreproductive Futurity." *American Literature* 84, no. 2 (June 2012): 409–35, at 419, https://doi.
org/10.1215/00029831–1587395.

E.O. Wilson Biophilia Center. "About Us." http://www.eowil-
soncenter.org/#!-about-us/c20r9.

Felski, Rita. *Uses of Literature.* Oxford: Blackwell Publishing,
2008.

Fisher, Philip. *Wonder, the Rainbow, and the Aesthetics of Rare
Experiences.* Cambridge: Harvard University Press, 1998.

Fromm, Erich. *The Anatomy of Human Destructiveness.* New
York: Holt and Company, 1971; repr. New York: Holt and
Company, 1992.

Fuller, Buckminster. "Chapter 4: Spaceship Earth." In *Operating
Manual for Spaceship Earth.* Buckminster Fuller Institute,
March 8, 2010 (first published 1969). https://web.archive.
org/web/20100823120750/http://www.bfi.org:80/about-
bucky/resources/books/operating-manual-spaceship-earth/
chapter-4-spaceship-earth.

Fuller, Robert. *Wonder: From Emotion to Spirituality.* Chapel
Hill: The University of North Carolina Press, 2006.

Galapagos Conservancy. "Project Isabela." https://www.galapa-
gos.org/conservation/project-isabela.

Geppert, Alexander C.T. "Rethinking the Space Age: Astroculture and Technoscience." *History and Technology* 28, no. 3
(2012): 219–23. https://doi.org/10.1080/07341512.2012.722789.

Gibson, William. *A Reenchanted World: The Quest for a New Kinship with Nature*. New York: Holt Paperbacks, 2009.

Greicius, Tony. "NASA Spacecraft Embarks on Historic Journey into Interstellar Space." NASA, August 7, 2017. www.nasa.gov/mission_pages/voyager/voyager20130912.html#.Vlqf8zG-jOSo.

Griffin, David Ray. "Introduction: The Reenchantment of Science." In *The Reenchantment of Science*, edited by David Ray Griffin, 1–46. Albany: State University of New York Press, 1988.

Grossberg, Lawrence. "Affect's Future: Rediscovering the Virtual in the Actual." In *The Affect Theory Reader*, edited by Gregory J. Seigworth and Melissa Gregg, 309–38. Durham: Duke University Press, 2010.

Grosz, Elizabeth. "Thinking the New: Of Futures Yet Unthought." In *Becomings: Explorations in Time, Memory, and Futures*, edited by Elizabeth Grosz, 15–28. Ithaca: Cornell University Press, 1999.

Guattari, Félix. *Chaosmosis: An Ethico-Aesthetic Paradigm*. Translated by Paul Bains and Julian Pefanis. Bloomington: Indiana University Press, 1995.

———. *Three Ecologies*. Translated by Ian Pindar and Paul Sutton. London: Continuum, 2008.

Hames, Raymond. "The Ecologically Noble Savage Debate." *Annual Review of Anthropology* 36 (January 2007): 177–90. https://doi.org/10.1146/annurev.anthro.35.0817.

Haraway, Donna. *Staying with the Trouble: Making Kin in the Chthulucene*. Durham: Duke University Press, 2016.

Hardt, Michael. "Foreword: What Affects are Good For." In *The Affective Turn: Theorizing the Social*, edited by Patricia Ticineto Clough and Jean Halley, ix–xiii. Durham: Duke University Press, 2007.

Hawking, Stephen. *A Brief History of Time*. New York: Bantam Books, 1988.

Hennessy, Elizabeth, and Amy L. McCleary, "Nature's Eden? The Production and Effects of 'Pristine' Nature in the Galápagos Islands." *Island Studies Journal* 6, no. 2 (November 2011): 131–56

Hesiod. *Theogony and Works and Days.* Translated by Catherine Schlegel and Henry Weinfeld. Ann Arbor: University of Michigan Press, 2006.

Holmes, Richard. *The Age of Wonder: How the Romantic Generation Discovered the Terror and Beauty of Science.* New York: Pantheon Books, 2009.

Kingsnorth, Paul, and Dougald Hine. "Uncivilization: The Dark Mountain Manifesto." *The Dark Mountain Project,* 2009. http://dark-mountain.net/about/manifesto/.

Iles, George. "Nature as Drama and Enginery." *Popular Science Monthly* 45 (August 1894). Wikisource. http://en.wikisource.org/wiki/Popular_Science_Monthly/Volume_45/August_1894/Nature_as_Drama_and_Enginery.

Jameson, Fredric. *Postmodernism: Or, the Cultural Logic of Late Capitalism.* Durham: Duke University Press, 1991.

Jameson, Frederic. "The End of Temporality." *Critical Inquiry* 29, no. 4 (Summer 2003): 695–718. https://www.jstor.org/stable/10.1086/377726.

Johansson, Gunnar. "Visual Perception of Biological Motion and a Model for its Analysis." *Perception & Psychophysics* 14, no. 2 (June 1973): 201–11. https://doi.org/10.3758/BF03212378.

Jonas, Hans. "Responsbility Today: The Ethics of an Endangered Future." *Social Research* 43, no. 1 (Spring 1976): 77–97. https://www.jstor.org/stable/40970214.

Joseph, Lawrence E. *Gaia: The Growth of an Idea.* New York: St. Martin's Press, 1990.

Joye, Yannick. "Architectural Lessons from Environmental Psychology: The Case of Biophilic Architecture." *Review of General Psychology* 11, no. 4 (December 2007): 305–28. https://doi.org/10.1037/1089-2680.11.4.305.

———— and Andreas de Block. "'Nature and I Are Two': A Critical Examination of the Biophilia Hypothesis." *Environmental Values* 20, no. 2 (May 2011): 189–215. https://doi.org/10.3197/096327111X12997574391724.

Kant, Immanuel. *Critique of Judgment.* Translated by James
    Creed Meredith. Oxford: Oxford University Press, 2007.
Keats, John. "Lamia." *Project Gutenberg,* http://www.gutenberg.
    org/files/2490/2490-h/2490-h.htm.
Kellert, Stephen, Judith Heerwagen, and Martin Mador, eds.
    *Biophilic Design: The Theory, Science, and Practice of Bring-
    ing Buildings to Life.* Hoboken: Wiley, 2008.
Kennedy Martin, Troy. *Edge of Darkness.* London: Faber and
    Faber, 1990.
Kirchner, James. "The Gaia Hypothesis: Fact, Theory, and
    Wishful Thinking." *Climatic Change* 52, no. 4 (2002):
    391–408. https://doi.org/10.1023/A:1014237331082.
Kolbert, Elizabeth. "The Big Kill: New Zealand's Crusade to
    Rid Itself of Mammals." *The New Yorker,* December 22, 2014.
    http://www.newyorker.com/magazine/2014/12/22/big-kill.
———. *The Sixth Extinction: An Unnatural History.* London:
    Bloomsbury, 2014.
Kosofsky Sedgwick, Eve. "Paranoid Reading and Reparative
    Reading; or, You're so Paranoid, You Probably Think This
    Introduction is About You." In *Novel Gazing: Queer Read-
    ings in Fiction,* edited by Eve Kosofsky Sedgwick, 1–37.
    Durham: Duke University Press, 1997.
Latour, Bruno. *Facing Gaia: Eight Lectures on the New Climatic
    Regime.* Translated by Catherine Porter. Cambridge: Polity
    Press, 2018.
———. *Politics of Nature: How to Bring the Sciences into
    Democracy.* Translated by Catherine Porter. Cambridge:
    Harvard University Press, 2004.
———. "The Puzzling Face of a Secular Gaia." Gifford Lec-
    tures: "Facing Gaia: A New Inquiry into Natural Religion."
    University of Edinburgh, February 21, 2013. http://www.
    ed.ac.uk/arts-humanities-soc-sci/news-events/lectures/
    gifford-lectures/archive/series-2012–2013/bruno-latour.
———. "Waiting for Gaia: Composing the Common World
    Through Arts and Politics." Lecture, French Institute,
    London, November 2011. http://www.bruno-latour.fr/sites/
    default/files/124-GAIA-LONDON-SPEAP_0.pdf.

———. *We Have Never Been Modern.* Translated by Catherine Porter. Cambridge: Harvard University Press, 1993.

———. "Why Has Critique Run Out of Steam? From Matters of Fact to Matters of Concern." *Critical Inquiry* 30, no. 2 (Winter 2004): 225–48. https://jstor.org/stable/10.1086/421123.

———, Chloé Latour, and Frédérique Ait-Touatti. "Cosmocolosse: A Radio Play." 2011. http://www.bruno-latour.fr/node/358.

Le Brun, Charles. "Le Brun's Lecture on Expression." Translated by Jennifer Montagu. In Jennifer Montagu, *The Expression of the Passions: The Origin and Influence of Charles Le Brun's "Conference sur l'expression generale et particulare,"* 125–40. New Haven: Yale University Press, 1994.

Lem, Stanisław. *Solaris, The Chain of Chance, A Perfect Vacuum.* Translated by Joanna Kilmartin and Steve Cox. Harmondsworth, Middlesex: Penguin, 1985.

Lessl, Thomas M. "The Priestly Voice." *Quarterly Journal of Speech* 5 (1989): 183–97. https://doi.org/10.1080/00335638909383871.

Lessl, Thomas M. "Science and the Sacred Cosmos: The Ideological Rhetoric of Carl Sagan." *Quarterly Journal of Speech* 71, no. 2 (1985): 175–87. https://doi.org/10.1080/00335638509383727.

Lilley, Sasha. "Introduction: The Apocalyptic Politics of Collapse and Rebirth." In *Catastrophism: The Apocalyptic Politics of Collapse and Rebirth,* edited by Sasha Lilley, David McNally, Eddie Yuen, and James Davis, 1–14. Oakland: PM Press, 2012.

Lockwood, Alex. "The Affective Legacy of Silent Spring." *Environmental Humanities* 1 (November 2012): 123–40. https://doi.org/10.1215/22011919-3610003.

Lovelock, James. *Gaia: A New Look at Life on Earth.* Oxford: Oxford University Press, 1979.

———. *Homage to Gaia: The Life of an Independent Scientist.* Oxford: Oxford University Press, 2000.

———. *The Ages of Gaia: A Biography of Our Living Earth.* Oxford: Oxford University Press, 1988.

———. "The Earth as a Living Organism." In *Biodiversity,* edited by E.O. Wilson and Frances M. Peter, 486–89. Washington, DC: National Academy Press, 1988.

———. *The Revenge of Gaia.* London: Penguin Books, 2007.

Margulis, Lynn, and Dorion Sagan, "God, Gaia, and Biophilia." In *The Biophilia Hypothesis,* edited by E.O. Wilson and Stephen Kellert, 345–64. Washington, DC: Island Press, 1993.

Margulis, Lynn, and Dorion Sagan. *What Is Life?* Berkeley and Los Angeles: University of California Press, 1995.

Margulis, Lynn, and J.E. Lovelock. "The Biological Modulation of the Earth's Atmosphere." *Icarus* 21, no. 4 (April 1974): 471–89. https://doi.org/10.1016/0019–1035(74)90150-X.

Martinez-Alier, Joan. "Distributional Obstacles to International Environmental Policy: The Failures at Rio and Prospects after Rio." *Environmental Values* 2, no. 2 (May 1993): 97–124. https://doi.org/10.3197/096327193776679936.

Massumi, Brian. *Parables for the Virtual: Movement, Affect, Sensation.* Durham: Duke University Press, 2002.

McIntosh, Alastair. "Foreward." In *Future Ethics: Climate Change and Apocalyptic Imagination,* edited by Stefan Skrimshire, vii–xi. London: Continuum, 2010.

McRae, Murdo William, ed. *The Literature of Science: Perspectives on Popular Scientific Writing.* Athens: The University of Georgia Press, 1993.

melodysheep [John Boswell]. "Carl Sagan – 'A Glorious Dawn' ft Stephen Hawking (Symphony of Science)." *YouTube,* September 17, 2009. https://www.youtube.com/watch?v=zSgiXGELjbc.

Mitchell, Robert. *Experimental Life: Vitalism in Romantic Science and Literature.* Baltimore: John Hopkins University Press, 2013.

Mortimer-Sandilands, Catriona, and Bruce Erickson, eds. *Queer Ecologies: Sex, Nature, Politics, Desire.* Bloomington: Indiana University Press, 2010.

Morton, Timothy. *Dark Ecology: For a Logic of Future Coexistence.* New York: Columbia University Press, 2016.

——. *Hyperobjects: Philosophy and Ecology after the End of the World.* Minneapolis: University of Minnesota Press, 2013.

——. *The Ecological Thought.* Cambridge: Harvard University Press, 2012.

de Mul, Jos. "Artificial by Nature: An Introduction to Plessner's Philosophical Anthropology." In *Plessner's Philosophical Anthropology: Perspectives and Prospects,* edited by Jos de Mul, 11–40. Amsterdam: Amsterdam University Press, 2014.

Naess, Arne. *Ecology, Community, and Lifestyle: Outline of an Ecosophy.* Translated by David Rothenberg. New York: Cambridge University Press, 1989.

——. "Spinoza and Ecology." In *Speculum Spinozanum 1677–1977,* edited by Siegfried Hessing, 45–54. London: Routledge & Kegan Paul, 1977.

NASA. "The Blue Marble from Apollo 17" (December 7, 1972). *Visible Earth Catalog.* http://visibleearth.nasa.gov/view.php?id=55418.

——. "Solar System Portrait: Earth as 'Pale Blue Dot'" (June 6, 1990). *Visible Earth Catalog.* http://visibleearth.nasa.gov/view.php?id=52392.

Nussbaum, Martha. *Upheavals of Thought: The Intelligence of Emotions.* Cambridge: Cambridge University Press, 2001.

Obama, Barack. "Second Inaugural Speech." *New York Times,* January 21, 2013. http://www.nytimes.com/2013/01/21/us/politics/obamas-second-inaugural-speech.html.

Otto, Rudolf. *The Idea of the Holy.* Translated by John W. Harvey. London: Oxford University Press, 1936.

Panagia, David. *The Political Life of Sensation.* Durham: Duke University Press, 2009.

Parsons, Howard L. "A Philosophy of Wonder." *Philosophy and Phenomenological Research* 30, no. 1 (1969): 84–101. https://doi.org/10.2307/2105923.

Perrault, Sarah. *Communicating Popular Science: From Deficit to Democracy.* New York: Palgrave Macmillan, 2013.

Raman, Varadaraja. "Vielfalt in der Mystik und Parallelen zur Naturwissenschaft." In *Biomystik,* edited by Christoph F.E. Holzhey, 61–79. Munich: Wilhelm Fink Verlag, 2007.

Rebovich, David Paul. "Sagan's Metaphysical Parable." *Society* 18, no. 5 (1981): 91–95. https://doi.org/10.1007/BF02701332.

Rosa, Harmut. *Social Acceleration: A New Theory of Modernity.* New York: Columbia University Press, 2013.

Rubenstein, Mary-Jane. *Strange Wonder: The Closure of Metaphysics and the Opening of Awe*. New York: Columbia University Press, 2008.

Sagan, Carl. *Contact*. New York: Pocket Books, 1985.

———. *Cosmos*. New York: Random House, 1980.

———. *Dragons of Eden*. London: Holder and Stoughton Limited, 1977.

———. *Pale Blue Dot*. New York: Ballantine Books, 1997.

———, F.D. Drake, Ann Druyan, Timothy Ferris, Jon Lomberg, and Linda Salzman Sagan. *Murmurs of the Earth: The Voyager Interstellar Record.* New York: Random House, 1978.

Seigworth, Gregory J. and Melissa Gregg. "An Inventory of Shimmers." In *The Affect Theory Reader,* 1–25. Durham: Duke University Press, 2010.

Serafin, Rafal. "Noosphere, Gaia and the Science of the Biosphere." In *The Biosphere and Noosphere Reader: Global Environment, Society, and Change,* edited by Paul Samson and David Pitt, 136–39. London: Routledge, 1999.

SETI Institute. "Carl Sagan Center." http://www.seti.org/carlsagancenter.

Seymour, Nicole. *Strange Natures: Futurity, Empathy, and the Queer Ecological Imagination.* Urbana: University of Illinois Press, 2013.

Shermer, Michael B. "Stephen Jay Gould as Historian of Science and Scientific Historian, Popular Scientist and Scientific Popularizer." *Social Studies of Science* 32, no. 4 (2002): 489–524. https://doi.org/10.1177/0306312702032004001.

Shin, Terry, and Richard Whitley, eds. *Expository Science: Forms and Functions of Popularization.* Dordecht: D. Reidel Publishing Company, 1985.

Steffen, Will, et al. "The Anthropocene: Conceptual and Historical Perspectives." *Philosophical Transactions of the Royal
Society A: Mathematical, Physical, and Engineering Sciences*
369, no. 1938 (2011): 842–67.

Suzuki, Severn. "At Rio+20, Severn Cullis-Suzuki Revisits
Historic '92 Speech, Fights for Next Generation's Survival."
Democracy Now, June 21, 2012. http://www.democracynow.
org/2012/6/21/at_rio_20_severn_cullis_suzuki.

Swimme, Brian. "The Cosmic Creation Story." In *The Reenchantment of Science,* edited by David Ray Griffin, 47–56.
Albany: State University of New York Press, 1988.

Thomas, Sue. *Technobiophilia.* New York: Bloomsbury, 2013.

Thrift, Nigel. "Still Life in Nearly Present Time: The Object
of Nature." In *Body and Society* 6, nos. 3–4 (2000): 34–57.
https://doi.org/10.1177/1357034X00006003003.

Tinker Perrault, Sarah. *Communicating Popular Science: From
Deficit to Democracy.* New York: Palgrave Macmillan, 2013.

Toulmin, Stephen. *The Return to Cosmology: Postmodern
Science and the Theology of Nature.* Berkeley: University of
California Press, 1982.

Trilford, Brittany. "Are You Here to Save Face—or Us?" *Democracy Now,* June 20, 2012. http://www.democracynow.
org/2012/6/21/are_you_here_to_save_face.

Turner, Fred. *From Counterculture to Cyberculture: Stewart
Brand, the Whole Earth Network, and the Rise of Digital
Utopianism.* Chicago: University of Chicago Press, 2006.

Uexküll, Jakob von. "A Stroll Through the Worlds of Animals
and Men: A Picture Book of Invisible Worlds." Translated by
Claire Schiller. *Semiotica* 89, no. 4 (1992): 319–91.

Ulrich, Roger S. "Visual Landscapes and Psychological Well-
Being." *Landscape Research* 4, no. 1 (March 1979): 17–23.
https://doi.org/10.1080/01426397908705892.

United Nations Conference on Sustainable Development. "The
Future We Want: Outcome Document." September 11, 2012.
*United Nations Sustainable Development Knowledge Plat-
form.* http://sustainabledevelopment.un.org/futurewewant.
html.

United Nations Framework Convention on Climate Change. "Kyoto Protocol to the United Nations Framework Convention on Climate Change." December 11, 1997. http://unfccc. int/essential_background/kyoto_protocol/items/1678.php.
———. "The Paris Agreement." November 4, 2016. http://unf-ccc.int/paris_agreement/items/9485.php.

Voluntary Human Extinction Movement. "About the Movement." http://www.vhemt.org/aboutvhemt.htm#vhemt.

van Wyck, Peter. *Primitives in the Wilderness: Deep Ecology and the Missing Human Subject.* Albany: State University of New York Press, 1997.

Vergano, Dan. "Voyager 1 Leaves Solar System, NASA Confirms." *National Geographic Online,* September 12, 2013. http://news.nationalgeographic.com/news/2013/13/130911-voyager-interstellar-solar-system-nasa-science-space/.

Volk, Tyler. *Gaia's Body: Toward a Physiology of Earth.* New York: Springer-Verlag, 1998.

Weber, Max. "Science as a Vocation." In *The Vocation Lectures, translated by Rodney Livingstone,* edited by David Owen and Tracy B. Strong, 1–31. Indianapolis: Hackett Publishing Company, 2004.

Wells, H.G. *The Time Machine.* Rockville: Phoenix Pick, 2009.

White, Jr., Lynn. "The Historical Roots of Our Ecologic Crisis." *Science* 155, no. 3767 (1967): 1203–7.

Whitley, Richard. "Knowledge Producers and Knowledge Acquirers: Popularisation as a Relation Between Scientific Fields and Their Publics." In *Expository Science: Forms and Functions of Popularization,* eds. Terry Shinn and Richard Whitley, 3–30. Boston: D. Reidel Publishing Company, 1985.

Wilson, E.O. *Biophilia.* Cambridge: Harvard University Press, 1984.
———. "Biophilia and the Conservation Ethic." In *The Biophilia Hypothesis,* edited by E.O. Wilson and Stephen Kellert, 31–41. Washington, DC: Island Press, 1993.
———. *Letters to a Young Scientist.* New York: Liveright Publishing Co., 2013.

———. *Sociobiology: The New Synthesis.* Cambridge: Harvard University Press, 1975.

———. *The Future of Life.* London: Little, Brown, 2002.

———. *The Social Conquest of Earth.* New York: Liveright Publishing Co., 2012.

——— and Frances M. Peter, eds. *Biodiversity.* Washington, DC: National Academy Press, 1988.

Wordsworth, William. "The Tables Turned." In *The Complete Poetical Works of William Wordsworth,* 361. London: Moxon, Son, & Co., 1869.

Zalesiewicz, Jan. *The Earth After Us: What Legacy Will Humans Leave in the Rocks?* Oxford: Oxford University Press, 2008.

Audiovisual

Barillé, Albert. *Il était une fois…la vie.* Canal+, 1987.

Björk. "Crystalline." *Biophilia,* CD. Polydor, 2011.

Druyan, Ann, and Steven Soter. *Cosmos: A Spacetime Odyssey.* DVD. 2014; Los Angeles: Twentieth Century Fox, 2014.

Edge of Darkness. DVD. Directed by Martin Campbell. 1985; BBC Worldwide, 2003.

Mitchell, Joni. "Woodstock." *Ladies of the Canyon,* CD. MCA, 1970.

Sagan, Carl, Ann Druyan, and Steven Soter. *Cosmos: A Personal Voyage.* DVD. 1980; Los Angeles: PBS, 2010.

Them! DVD. Directed by Gordon Douglas. 1954; Warner Brothers, 2013.